Nietzsche, Feminism and Political Theory

Edited by Paul Patton

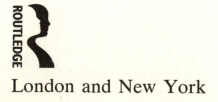

London and New York

First published 1993
by Routledge
11 New Fetter Lane, London EC4P 4EE

Simultaneously published in the USA and Canada
by Routledge Inc.
29 West 35th Street, New York, NY 10001

Phototypeset in 10 on 12 point Times by Intype, London

Printed in Great Britain by T.J. Press Ltd, Padstow

British Library Cataloguing in Publication Data

Nietzsche, Feminism and Political Theory
I. Patton, Paul
193

Library of Congress Cataloging in Publication Data

Nietzsche, feminism, and political theory/edited by Paul Patton.
    p.   cm.
Includes bibliographical references and index.
1. Nietzsche, Friedrich Wilhelm, 1844–1900—Contributions in political
science.   2. Nietzsche, Friedrich Wilhelm, 1844–1900—Contributions in
feminism.   I. Patton, Paul.
JC233.N52N55   1993   92–33978
320′.01—dc20

ISBN 0–415–08255–2   ISBN 0–415–08256–0

Contents

Notes on contributors

Keith Ansell-Pearson is currently Lecturer in Political Theory in the Department of Political Studies at Queen Mary and Westfield College, University of London, and from September 1993 will be Lecturer in Modern European Philosophy at the University of Warwick.

Howard Caygill is Lecturer in the School of Economic and Social Studies at the University of East Anglia, and is the author of *Art of Judgement* (1989).

Daniel W. Conway is Assistant Professor in the Department of Philosophy at Pennsylvania State University.

Penelope Deutscher is a Lecturer in Philosophy at The Australian National University, Canberra, where she teaches feminist theory and contemporary French philosophy. She has published in the *Newsletter of the Freudian Field* and *Australian Feminist Studies*.

Rosalyn Diprose is a Lecturer in Philosophy at The Flinders University of South Australia. She co-edited, with Robert Ferrell, *Cartographies: Poststructuralism and the Mapping of Bodies and Spaces* (Allen & Unwin, 1991), and is the author of *The Body of Woman: Ethics and Sexual Difference* (Routledge, forthcoming).

Elizabeth Grosz is Associate Professor in the Institute for Critical and Cultural Studies at Monash University. She has published *Sexual Subversions: Three French Feminists* (Allen & Unwin, 1989), *Jacques Lacan: A Feminist Introduction* (Routledge, 1990) and is currrently completing a book on the body and sexual difference.

Frances Oppel lectures in literary and cultural studies at Griffith University, Queensland. She is writing a book on 'woman' in Nietzsche's *Thus Spoke Zarathustra*.

Paul Patton lectures in philosophy at the University of Sydney. He has published numerous articles on contemporary European philosophy, and recently translated Gilles Deleuze's *Difference and Repetition* (1993).

Paul Redding is a Senior Lecturer in Philosophy at the University of Sydney. He teaches and writes in the areas of hermeneutic theory, epistemology and metaphysics and Hegelian philosophy. He is currently completing a book entitled *Hegel, Copernican Philosophy and Hermeneutics*.

Ted Sadler lectures on modern German philosophy at the University of Sydney. He is presently completing a book on Heidegger.

Marion Tapper lectures in philosophy at the University of Melbourne. She teaches and writes on modern European philosophy and feminism.

Cathryn Vasseleu is completing doctoral work in philosophy at the University of Sydney. She has published articles on animation, imaging technology and sexual difference.

Introduction

Nietzsche's views on women and politics have long been among the most problematic aspects of his thought. Philosophers prepared to find merit in his reflections on art, morals and truth have passed over his political doctrines in silence. In the aftermath of the Nazi appropriation of his texts, this silence has weighed heavily upon the political interpretation of Nietzsche. Until recently, it has prevented any serious consideration of his contribution to political theory. Nietzsche's relation to feminist theory has been no less troubled. His name is invariably linked with the infamous line from *Thus Spoke Zarathustra* – 'Are you visiting women? Do not forget your whip!' – while the other remarks on women scattered throughout his writings are often read as the more or less subtle expressions of an incurable personal misogyny. Even those concerned to defend his writings against the charge of anti-Semitism readily abandon his remarks on 'woman' as indefensible.

Against this background, it is perhaps one of the surprising effects of the explosion of interest in Nietzsche since the early 1970s that he has begun to be taken seriously by political theorists, including some whose primary orientation is feminist. The writings of Tracy B. Strong, Ofelia Schutte, Mark Warren, William Connolly and others have established Nietzsche as a thinker with much to offer those thinking through the dilemmas of political theory in the late twentieth century. The work of Sarah Kofman, Luce Irigaray and others has ensured that Nietzsche is now recognized as a valued interlocutor and resource for contemporary feminist theory. The present collection of essays displays some of the achievements and suggests some possible future gains, as well as risks, of this turn towards Nietzsche within social and political thought. While several of the essays interrogate Nietzsche's texts and thereby seek to advance the scholarly appreciation of their complexity, the principal focus of the collection lies somewhere between Nietzsche's texts and the questions thrown up by contemporary philosophical and political debates. Overall, these essays address the utility and effects of Nietzsche's philosophy not at their source but further downstream, with respect to present philosophical, moral and political concerns. They do not seek to present Nietzsche's philosophy as a new panacea for feminism or political theory, but neither do they rehearse the well-known difficulties posed by Nietzsche's remarks on women and politics.

The French philosopher Gilles Deleuze suggested that it was the aphoristic form of Nietzsche's writing which enabled it to establish immediate relations with the outside, in other words with forces and processes external to the text. However, Deleuze cites as an example a passage not from one of Nietzsche's early books of aphorisms but from *On the Genealogy of Morals*, a work usually regarded as approaching the style of a philosophical prose-essay. In effect, he is proposing a conception of the aphorism or of aphoristic writing which has less to do with the length of the paragraphs than with the discontinuous or pluralistic character of the thought expressed. Aphoristic writing deals with a multiplicity of objects without attempting to force these into the unity of a single object or totality. Similarly, the aphorism has no implicit subject, no authorial voice attached: it is an anonymous form of expression. Aphoristic writing therefore conveys a thought which is not tied to any field of interiority, whether defined in terms of the consciousness of its author or a supposed unitary object with which it deals. Such a thought entertains immediate relations with the outside, not mediated through any such interiority. Deleuze defines the aphorism as an amalgam or 'play of forces, the most recent of which – the latest, the newest and provisionally the final force – is always the most exterior' (Deleuze 1977: 145). On this basis, he suggests, the question of the politics of Nietzsche's writing is misconceived if it is posed in terms of interpretation. The point is not to try to show that fascist or misogynist readings are false, or distortions of the 'meaning' of Nietzsche's text, for the distinctive feature of aphoristic writing is precisely that it lays no claim to any such definitive meaning: an aphorism 'means nothing, signifies nothing, and is no more a signifier than a signified'. Rather, the point is to discover the new forces that come from without, to find the revolutionary or nomadic forces that are currently capable of occupying or making use of Nietzsche's text.

The essays collected here bear witness to a range of such intellectual and political forces which are 'active' in the present: these include the widespread desire of men and women to find ways of understanding and affirming sexual difference that do not imply social relations of domination and subordination; the interest of critical theorists in conceptions of power and practices of criticism which are not confined to the reactive perspective of slave morality; the interest of feminist and political theorists in ways of understanding self-hood that take adequate account of the embodied and historical nature of human existence; and the desire of many to find possible forms of relations to others, to knowledge and to self which might provide bases for less oppressive social relations. In order that such ethical and political forces be able to lay hold of Nietzsche's thought, a further condition is indispensable, namely the presence of those more sophisticated and *slow* readers who have learnt to read him well. Recent Nietzsche scholarship has made it possible to see through the masks of coarseness and apparent brutality which complicate his texts, and to discover within them more subtle features of his thought capable of making positive contributions to both feminist and political theory. In particular, *Thus Spoke Zarathustra* has begun to be taken seriously as a dramatic text in which it is not Nietzsche himself who speaks directly to readers but a variety of characters, and in which the principal character, Zarathustra, undergoes significant development in the course of the narrative. Any attempt to interpret the whip remark cited above must take account of the fact that it was uttered not by Zarathustra but by the Old Woman to whom he has spoken 'about woman'. She offers him in reply this 'little truth' which Zarathustra has earlier described as being 'unruly as a little child' (Nietzsche 1969: 91). Is it too much, one recent reader asks, 'to suggest that what is at issue here is the absence or presence of women, of genuine relations with "the other", which the whip serves to repress?' (Armstrong 1992: 5).

The whip is a complex symbol in Nietzsche's text, and its relationship to Zarathustra's masculinity is open to many interpretations besides those which see only a crude misogyny. Nowhere is this more apparent than in The Second Dance Song when the whip reappears at the end of Zarathustra's passionate but initially fruitless pursuit of his 'wanton companion', Life. In frustration or play, he reaches for his whip only to be admonished by the object of his desire, 'O Zarathustra! Do not crack your whip so terribly! You surely know: noise kills thought – and now such tender thoughts are coming to me' (Nietzsche 1969: 242). In this context, Aurelia Armstrong comments,

> neither consummation nor subordination, take place. The whip is ineffectual and clearly inappropriate in the context of a genuine meeting between two parties. Certainly there are power relations here, but they are not the fixed relations of domination instituted by violence, rather, they are relations of power at play: transformative relations which leave neither of the participants unmarked. At the end of the dance we find Zarathustra and Life together weeping and contemplating the dusk; changed in or between themselves and, thus, associating differently with the outside.
>
> (Armstrong 1992: 5)

Nietzsche's writings have always been a battlefield for conflicting interpretations. The present collection is no exception. Although several of the essays address Nietzsche's thought as this is refracted by 'post-structuralist' readings of his work, this approach itself does not go unchallenged. The current interest in Nietzsche among feminist and postmodern political theorists, as well as among theorists of the postmodern condition, is perhaps no more than a new campaign in an already old war of conflicting interpretations. After all, Nietzsche was admired by anarchists, socialists and feminists during the 1890s, long before he was championed by the Nazis (Hinton Thomas 1983). A century later, however, we find ourselves in a vastly different historical situation, one much closer to the epoch for which Nietzsche considered he wrote. He regarded the collapse of faith in the Christian God as an event of such magnitude that it would take centuries for the consequences to become apparent. Few can yet fathom, he wrote in *The Gay Science* 343, 'how much must collapse now that this faith has been undermined because it was built on this faith, propped up by it, grown into it, for example, the whole of European morality' (Nietzsche 1974: 279). The concerns of the present collection of essays illustrate Nietzsche's prescience with regard to the long-term effects of the crisis of modern cultural identity that he diagnosed under the name of nihilism. Traditional notions of self-hood, sexual difference, rationality and agency are among the presuppositions of modern social and political theory which have only recently been thrown into question. Renewed concern for the specific forms of social and corporeal existence has led some to question the modern ideals of justice and political equality. If we are able to confront these challenges as if before an open sea upon which 'at long last our ships may venture out again' (Nietzsche 1974: 280), it is in part because Nietzsche had already begun the exploration of these sea routes beyond modernity. To the extent that it charts directions which postmodern ethical and political thought might follow, Nietzsche's philosophy has perhaps at last become timely. ⸱

ACKNOWLEDGEMENTS

Several of the contributors to this volume have assisted with the conception and execution of the project at various stages. I am particularly grateful for the assistance of Cathryn Vasseleu, Rosalyn Diprose, Keith Ansell-Pearson and Paul Redding. I am also thankful to Lisa Trahair for her assistance with editing, and to Moira Gatens for her astute reader's comments and advice.

BIBLIOGRAPHY

Armstrong, A. (1992) ' "Woman" and the Whip', *Silenus Laughed* (4).

Connolly, W. E. (1988) *Political Theory and Modernity*, Oxford: Basil Blackwell.

Deleuze, G. (1977) 'Nomad thought', in D. B. Allison (ed.) *The New Nietzsche*, New York: Delta.

Hinton Thomas, R. (1983) *Nietzsche in German Politics and Society*, Manchester: Manchester University Press.

Nietzsche, F. (1969) *Thus Spoke Zarathustra*, trans. R. J. Hollingdale, Harmondsworth: Penguin.

—— (1974) *The Gay Science*, trans. W. Kaufmann, New York: Vintage.

1 Nietzsche and the pathos of distance

Rosalyn Diprose

Jeanette Winterson, in her novel *Sexing the Cherry*, describes the city of Jordan's dreams. A city

> whose inhabitants are so cunning that to escape the insistence of creditors they knock down their houses in a single night and rebuild them elsewhere. So the number of buildings in the city is always constant but they are never in the same place from one day to the next.
>
> For close families, and most people in the city are close families, this presents no problem, and it is more usual than not for the escapees to find their pursuers waiting for them on the new site of their choice.
>
> As a subterfuge, then, it has little to recommend it, but as a game it is a most fulfilling pastime and accounts for the extraordinary longevity of the men and women who live there. We were all nomads once, and crossed the deserts and the seas on tracks that could not be detected, but were clear to those who knew the way. Since settling down and rooting like trees, but without the ability to make use of the wind to scatter our seed, we have found only infection and discontent.
>
> In the city the inhabitants have reconciled two discordant desires: to remain in one place and to leave it behind forever.
>
> (Winterson 1989: 42–3)

This is a postmodern city. It is built on the recognition that one's place within a political and social space rests on unstable foundations. Places can change. This instability arises from the complex creditor–debtor relations which characterize subjectivity: the self gains a place in the world only by incurring a debt to the other, making self-present autonomy, freedom from this debt, impossible. The best one can hope for is a reconciliation of the desire for stability, for proximity to oneself (and hence to one's creditor) and the desire for change, for distance, for difference.

Winterson's city encapsulates Nietzsche's philosophy of self – a philosophy which sits uneasily between two streams of thought in Anglophone philosophy. On the one side there is mainstream social and political theory which, in the name of stability and sameness, assumes that society consists of relations of contract and exchange between free and equal, autonomous, self-present individuals. On the other side is the declaration that self-mastery and self-identity are dead along with the ideal of uniform social relations these notions of self-support. Rather than a society consisting of unified individuals governed by universal values, this alternative position variously posits a self dispersed into another, a multiplicity of differences, and finds universal values both invalid and oppressive.

This 'postmodernism' is often evoked in the name of feminism and sometimes in the name of Nietzsche. Craig Owens (1985), for example, defines postmodernism as the death of self-mastery, of the representation of woman as Other and of the repression of femininity that self-mastery entails. In the interests of opening up a multiplicity of sexual differences, he argues against the representation of 'positive' images of a revised femininity which may shore up a monolithic culture of centred masculinity (Owens 1985: 71). Similarly, Jean Graybeal (1990), in a sympathetic reading of Nietzsche and following Kristeva, concludes that rather than repressing the 'dividedness' within ourselves and projecting this 'otherness' on to women, we should take a leaf out of Nietzsche's book and 'delight' in our dispersed condition (Graybeal 1990: 160).

Nietzsche's aesthetics of self has more in common with these than it does with the self-presence underscoring conventional assessments of social relations. However, the reading of his philosophy which I offer below cautions against simple declarations of the death of self-presence which assume the ability to promote change and difference by distancing oneself from others. My aim is to explore Nietzsche's contributions to an understanding of both individual and sexual difference as the 'problematic of the constitution of place' in relation to others (Irigaray 1984: 13–14).

While he may delight in self-division, there are at least two aspects of Nietzsche's philosophy that I shall highlight which warn against the forms of postmodernism mentioned. The first is his analysis of the self as an embodied cultural artifact which suggests that any change in self involves a material production rather than a change of mind (or a simple declaration that the self is divided). Second, while Nietzsche's project for self-creation reads at times like an escape from others, there is much to suggest that even creative self-formation incurs a debt to the other. Both his philosophy of the body and his understanding of the self–other relation as a debtor–creditor relation rest on a certain concept of distance: distance as a division within the self and distance as difference between the self and others. And Nietzsche's understanding of the operation of distance has important consequences for re-thinking sexual difference within the context of a postmodern aesthetics of self.

THE BODY AND ONE'S PLACE

Central to Nietzsche's concept of self, and a point often overlooked by hyperreal postmodernism, is his recognition that the problematic of the constitution of place is a question of the social constitution of embodiment. In *Thus Spoke Zarathustra* he claims that 'body I am entirely, and nothing else; and soul is only a word for something about the body' (Nietzsche 1966: 34). In contrast to the assumptions that the self's identity can be reduced to consciousness and that the mind directs the body, Nietzsche claims that the body is what compares and creates and that thought and the ego are its instruments.

He is not suggesting that the body is an a-social fact in charge of operations. While 'in man *creature* and *creator*', matter and sculptor, are united (Nietzsche 1972: 136), it is not consciousness (transcendental or individual) which makes a man out of matter. Rather, the body like any 'thing' is the sum of its effects in so far as those effects are united by a concept (1967: 296). The 'body is only a social structure composed of many souls' (1972: 31) where 'soul' refers to a corporeal multiplicity or a 'social structure of the drives and emotions' (1972: 25). So, for Nietzsche, one's place in the world is determined by the concepts which govern the structure of the social world and which sculpture the body accordingly – a body which is a 'unity as an organisation' and is therefore a 'work of art' (1967: 419). ·

How the self is made as a social structure is first a question of how the body is unified through social concepts. Second, and related to this process of unification, is the question of how thought and the ego are instruments of the body. The body is the locus of pleasure and pain (which are already interpretations) and thought is a reflection on pleasure and pain. To quote Nietzsche:

The self says to the ego, 'Feel pain here!' Then the ego suffers and thinks how it might suffer no more – and that is why it is *made* to think.

The self says to the ego, 'Feel pleasure here!' Then the ego is pleased and thinks how it might often be pleased again – and that is why it is made to think.

(Nietzsche 1966: 35)

• Thought then is about the projection of bodily experience into the future: the conscious subject is an effect of temporalizing the body.

The target for much of Nietzsche's critical attention is the manner in which experience is unified and the body temporalized in the social relations of modernity. Here, the embodied self is constituted by social concepts which discourage difference, creativity and change. His account in the second essay of *On the Genealogy of Morals* begins with the idea that the unification of any body relies on the operation of memory and forgetting. 'Forgetting' is the incorporation of bodily affects before they become conscious and a making way for new sensations by allowing one to 'have done' with the old (1969: 58). But, while this not-remembering is necessary for the constitution of any self as present, the making of the modern moral subject, the individual who is responsible for his or her acts, requires a faculty which opposes forgetting – memory.

Nietzsche describes how the social and moral discourses of modernity constitute a particular kind of memory: a memory which unifies a selection of activities, events, experiences and effects such that they belong to one person (1969: 58). This memory makes the self constant and apparently unchanging through time by projecting the same body into the future. The operation of memory and forgetting unifies experience in another sense – it makes different experiences the same. What is remembered is not just an experience but a socially prescribed mode of interpreting that experience. As Nietzsche explains in *Twilight of the Idols* (1968: 50–3), effects and events are incorporated by interpretation using prevailing moral norms and the concept of cause. Unpleasant feelings are said to be caused by actions considered undesirable. Pleasant feelings are said to arise from good or successful actions (1968: 52). Hence, 'everything of which we become conscious is arranged, simplified, schematized, interpreted through and through – . . . pleasure and displeasure are subsequent and derivative phenomena' (1967: 263–4).[1] So even forgetting as having done with an event involves first, dividing effects into those which are written into the body and those which are not. Second, events which are incorporated and upon which we reflect are divided into a cause and an effect where the effect is pleasure or displeasure and the cause is interpreted according to social moral norms. Then, when encountering a new event or effect, the memory 'calls up earlier states of a similar kind and the causal interpretations which had grown out of them' (1968: 51). New experiences are subsumed under habitual interpretations making every experience a fabrication (1972: 97).

The individual is not the author of this dutiful memory: it is created through what Nietzsche calls the 'mnemotechnics of pain' (1969: 61), techniques of punishment which carry social norms and moral values. 'Body I am entirely' in so far as my conscience, sense of responsibility and uniformity are created by an ordering of sensations, and projection of the body into the future through a social disciplinary system. This ensures not only that an individual's experiences are consistent over time but, as we are subjected to the same moral values, we shall have 'our experience in common' (1972: 186). Forgetting in conjunction with a selective memory becomes a social instrument of repression against the dangers of inconsistency and variation. A society which favours consistency and conformity discourages us to leave our place behind.

Contrary to mainstream social and political theory, Nietzsche proposes that the individual is a cultural artifact whose existence is a product of the exclusion of other possibilities for one's embodied place in the world. But this account leaves Nietzsche with a problem shared also by those who find self-mastery and universal values oppressive: how can change be effected given that the self is the result of a socially informed material process of production? How can different possibilities for one's embodiment be opened, how can one leave one's place behind, without assuming the possibility of stepping outside either one's present body or one's social context? It is Nietzsche's concept of a distance within the self which addresses this apparent impasse.

DISTANCE AND LEAVING ONE'S PLACE BEHIND

The body which conforms to a uniform mode of subjection is one which acts out a social role imposed upon it.[2] In contrast to this actor, Nietzsche, in *The Gay Science*, privileges a process of self-fabrication with the artistic ability to stage, watch and overcome the self according to a self-given plan (1974: 132–3). He draws on two features of art and the artist to characterize creative self-fabrication

(1974: 163–4). The first is the suggestion that the self, like any artifact, is an interpretation, perspective or mask. Second, the relation between artists and their art illustrates the point that creating beyond the present self requires that we view ourselves from a distance in an image outside ourselves. Leaving behind the influence of social concepts which restrict our place in the world requires treating one's corporeality as a work of art.

The distinction that Nietzsche makes between the self as artist and the image or spectacle staged beyond the present body could imply a unique, extra-social invention. But, at a less ambitious and more realistic level, it suggests that you are never identical with yourself. Nietzsche sometimes refers to this difference within the self as the 'pathos of distance':

> that longing for an ever increasing widening of distance within the soul itself, the formation of ever higher, rarer, more remote, tenser, more comprehensive states, in short precisely the elevation of the type 'man', the continual 'self-overcoming of man', to take a moral formula in a supra-moral sense.
>
> (Nietzsche 1972: 173)

What Nietzsche is suggesting here is that the ability to move beyond oneself hinges on a relation within the soul (where the soul is something about the body). A distance or difference within the self, between the present self and an image of self towards which I aspire, is necessary for change to be incorporated in the constitution and enhancement of the bodily self. We should not confuse the artist and his work, says Nietzsche, 'as if [the artist] were what he is able to represent, conceive and express. The fact is that *if* he were it, he would not represent, conceive, and express it' (1969: 101). The self as a work of art is never the same as the self that creates it, not because the self as artist is the true or essential self in contrast to a false, unique, extra-social image projected. Rather, the image which the artistic self creates is a moment beyond the present self which creates it. The difference, or distance, between the two is a precondition to representation which for Nietzsche is always self-representation.

In *Thus Spoke Zarathustra*, Nietzsche accounts for this distance within the self in terms of a process of self-temporalization of the body which subverts the notion of linear time assumed in normalizing social structures. Unlike the 'last man', who views himself as the essential and unchangeable end point of his history (Nietzsche 1966: 202), the overman views himself as a moment. He risks his present self or, as Nietzsche puts it, 'goes under' (1966: 14–15). But, unlike the 'higher man', who, in a manner not unlike Owen's 'postmodern' self, affirms the future by negating the past and skipping over existence, thereby changing nothing (1966: 286–95), the overman risks himself by 'willing backwards': 'To redeem those who lived in the past and to recreate all "it was" into "thus I willed it" – that alone I should call redemption' (1966: 139). Creativity is not a matter of declaring oneself born again by simply reaching for a new part to play: it requires working on oneself. The overman then is the self that is a moment which temporalizes itself by recreating its past as a way of projecting itself into the future. This self-temporalization produces a distance or difference within the self.

The idea that the bodily self is reproduced differently as it is temporalized through the production of a distance within the self would seem to be at odds with Nietzsche's doctrine of eternal recurrence. Problems arise if we accept eternal recurrence as either a cosmological hypothesis, where the world repeats itself infinitely (1967: 521), or a psychological doctrine, where self-affirmation involves the desire for the self to recur eternally the same (1966: 322). However, as David Wood (1988) has demonstrated, interpreting the doctrine of eternal recurrence exclusively in either of these ways is ultimately untenable.[3]

Nietzsche's presentation of the doctrine in 'The vision and the riddle' (1966: 85–7) consists in a further revaluation of linear time which suggests that there is always difference in repetition. Here Zarathustra, on a 'bridge across becoming', recounts his vision of climbing a mountain while carrying on his back his 'archenemy, the spirit of gravity'. Zarathustra is attempting to climb toward the future, but the spirit of gravity, of which man suffers if he cannot go beyond himself, threatens to drag him back towards himself. 'You threw yourself up high', says gravity to Zarathustra, 'but every stone must fall . . . the stone will fall back on yourself' (Nietzsche 1966: 156). The spirit of gravity is suggesting a notion of return which is cyclic: you cannot escape what you are, you will always return to yourself the same.

While Zarathustra affirms this notion of repetition of self ('was that life? well then! once more'), he goes on to reinterpret it. He points to a gateway called 'the moment' claiming that from this moment a path leads backwards to eternity and another contradictory path leads forwards to eternity: the future contradicts the past and both the future and the past lead out from the present moment. Zarathustra then goes on to suggest that all that leads backwards from the moment, all that has been, has been before, as has this moment. And, because all things are knotted together then this moment draws after it all that is to come. Therefore, he asks, must not all of us have been at this moment before and must we not eternally return?

What Nietzsche seems to be suggesting is a return of self involving a relation to time where the self does not seek to escape the past (linear time) nor simply to repeat it (cyclic). By defining time as something which comes out of the moment, Nietzsche is suggesting, in keeping with his notion of self-overcoming, that one temporalizes oneself. The self *re-creates* the past (or what one has been) at every moment as it projects itself towards a future. The future is also created out of the present. The contingent future, governed by others, is made one's own through the present where the present is a re-constitution of the past. And, by making the present moment its own, the self also distances itself from a necessary past and future.

At the same time, according to Nietzsche, each moment eternally recurs and contains every other moment which constitutes the temporalized self. As Zarathustra suggests, there is no outside the moment that is the present self: 'how should there be an outside-myself? There is no outside' (Nietzsche 1966: 217). This is not to say that the self is transcendental or unchanging. On the contrary, to re-create the past, or one's 'it was', by making it 'thus I willed it' is to give birth to the self anew. But, while the self is different at every moment, these different moments are not self-contained. There is no outside the self in the sense that the moment, which is the present self, contains traces of its relation to a past and a future which are different. The structure of the moment is one where the self exceeds its present self rather than one where the self is self-present and self-identical. Man is 'an imperfect tense' (Nietzsche 1983: 61): his past is never complete in relation to his present.

The distancing effected by making the moment one's own is not a state of mind: it 'creates a higher body' (1966: 70) – the bodily self is reproduced differently. Reproduction as difference is also apparent in Nietzsche's use of the metaphor of pregnancy to characterize the artistic self.[4] The overman 'begets and bears' (1972: 113) a future self which is beyond and different from himself. The pathos of distance within the self, generated by making the moment one's own, allows one to remain in one place while leaving it behind forever. But this is not a simple rejection of one's embodied place. Nietzsche's formulation of a distance within the self re-opens what is denied by social discourses which, in assuming an unchanging subject over time, assume that 'what is does not *become*' (1968: 35). This assumption of sameness is an 'escape from sense-deception, from becoming, from history' (1968: 35). The history which conformity disavows is the process of incorporating new experiences and shedding the old, reconciling conflicting impulses, the ongoing process of corporeal self-fabrication according to concepts one had inherited and cultivated (1972: 96–104; 1974: 269–71).

DISTANCE AND THE CREDITOR–DEBTOR RELATION

While Nietzsche's understanding of creative self-fabrication allows a reconciliation of the discordant desires in Winterson's dream, it remains an uneasy formulation. Nietzsche often speaks as if the distance within the self effected by making the moment one's own is generated by the self alone: creative self-fabrication is often presented as an autonomous, self-contained project. Yet, in 'Schopenhauer as Educator', for example, Nietzsche suggests that, rather that finding ourselves within ourselves, we are more likely to find ourselves outside ourselves, that is in our effects, in 'everything [which] bears witness to what we are, our friendships and our enmities, our glance and the clasp of our hand, our memory and that which we do not remember, our books and our handwriting', in the objects we love (1983: 129). In other words, the self is not just divided between the remembered and the forgotten, the future and the past, but between the self and the other. There is something about our relation to others which determines the place we occupy within social relations. Hence, contrary to some postmodern formulations of a dispersed self who does not 'other' others, creative self-fabrication, changing places, must implicate others in some sense.

Nietzsche's genealogies of justice and punishment typically reveal the ways in which others are involved in the constitution of one's place in the world. The most fundamental social relation is, he claims, the creditor–debtor relation where 'one person first *measured himself* against another' (1969: 70). Inflicting pain on another was 'originally' a way of recovering a debt rather than creating the memory necessary for conformity. And this involved evaluating different parts of the body to ensure that the pain inflicted was equivalent to the debt owed (1969: 62–5). Under such a system, evaluation is of the body and operates by mutual agreement. Debts can be repaid through the body via a contractual arrangement between creditor and debtor.

But what is the nature of this debt which is supposedly repaid through corporeal measurement? As determining values, establishing and exchanging equivalences is the most fundamental social arrangement, it is not just a question of commerce in a literal sense. Evaluation of one's own body in relation to another is constitutive of one's place in the world. While Nietzsche sometimes speaks as if there is an original difference between debtor and creditor, the self becomes different, a distinct entity, only by distancing itself from others. And this distancing itself is a mode of production involving measurement.

The relation between self and other is governed by will to power: by language as an expression of power, by the use of concepts to measure, interpret, draw distinctions. According to Nietzsche, if we eliminate concepts which we impose, such as number, thing, activity and motion, then

> no things remain but only dynamic quanta, in relation of tension to all other dynamic quanta: their essence lies in their relation to all other quanta, in their 'effect' upon the same. The will to power not a being, not a becoming, but a *pathos* – the most elemental fact from which a becoming and effecting first emerge.
>
> (Nietzsche 1967: 339)

To say that will to power is pathos refers us to the distinction between ethos and pathos which Nietzsche evokes elsewhere (1974: 252). Ethos is usually understood as a way of life, one's habits and character, whereas pathos is how one is passively effected. While we think of our way of life as a given and an enduring ethos, our life, Nietzsche argues, is really pathos, a dynamic process of changing experience. The will to power is pathos: it is the movement by which experience is constituted and entities come into being such that they are in relation and can be affected and can effect.[5]

Will to power as interpretation operates within intersubjective relations where, as Nietzsche claims in reference to love, 'our pleasure in ourselves tries to maintain itself by again and again changing something new *into ourselves*' (1974: 88). Measuring the other is a way of enhancing our own form, capacities and effects. But again, neither the self nor the other (whether the other is another person or a 'thing') exists in essence apart from this relation, that is, apart from 'the effect it produces and that which it resists' (1967: 337). In other words, individuals, and the differences between them, are not given. They are an effect of creation and imposition of forms . . . [within] a ruling structure which *lives*, in which parts and functions are delimited and co-ordinated, in which nothing whatever finds a place that has not been first assigned a 'meaning' in relation to a whole.

(Nietzsche 1969: 86–7)

Will to power is this process of the constitution of place, of delimiting one from another, through the assignment of 'meaning' to effects and their interrelations. So any difference between parties to a contract is an effect of will to power as productive interpretation by which entities are constituted in relation. The distance/difference between self and other is predicated upon the proximity of measurement: the credit of difference incurs a debt to the other.

If the relation of measurement between creditor and debtor is one of mutual exchange, which Nietzsche suggests in his genealogy and which liberal political theory assumes, then it is a relation which already implies sameness. Nietzsche often notes that justice, as the fair settling of disputes (the possibility of mutual exchange without any loss of self), assumes the parties involved are already of 'approximately equal power' (1969: 70; 1984: 64). At one level 'equal power' means that both parties have the power to enforce their own evaluations. At a more fundamental level 'equal power' means a balance in the distribution of productive power. The possibility of justice, as mutual understanding, assumes that the selves involved are already constituted by the same mode of evaluation. That is justice assumes that will to power as interpretation operates uniformly to produce all bodies as the same. As Nietzsche puts it in *Beyond Good and Evil*:

> To refrain from mutual injury, mutual violence, mutual exploita-
> tion, to equate one's own will with that of another: this may in
> a certain rough sense become good manners between individuals
> if the conditions for it are present (namely if their strength and
> value standards are in fact similar and they both belong to *one*
> body).

(Nietzsche 1972: 174)

Belonging to one social body within which it is possible to settle one's debt to the other assumes a shared mode of evaluation by which the bodily self is constituted.

But the possibility of mutual understanding is at best limited on Nietzsche's model of self-fabrication. A social body may share a language, a mode of interpretation and evaluation, a mode of self-creation. But self-evaluation occurs in relation to another and there is always a disjunction between how one evaluates oneself and how one is evaluated by another. Interpretation of the other is a translation which is a 'form of conquest' (Nietzsche 1974: 137) and reduces the tempo of the other's style (1972: 41). The style projected becomes overlayed by other masks constituted through misunderstanding. The constitution of identity is dissimulation where one's absolute identity is deferred:

> Every profound spirit needs a mask: more, around every profound spirit a mask is continually growing thanks to the constantly false, that is to say *shallow* interpretation of every word he speaks, every step he takes, every sign of life he gives.
>
> (Nietzsche 1972: 51)[6]

Further, while one's identity is a self-fabrication of the body using concepts one inherits, there is always a disjunction between the social concepts we share and how each person applies them:

> Ultimately, the individual derives the value of his acts from himself; because he has to interpret in a quite individual way even the words he has inherited. His interpretation of a formula at least is personal, even if he does not create a formula: as an interpreter he is still creative.
>
> (Nietzsche 1967: 403)

What Nietzsche exposes in his genealogy of justice and the creditor –debtor relation is that the exchange of equivalences already assumes sameness. And second, in so far as the parties involved are only at best *approximately* the same then evaluation involves some subtraction from the other to the benefit of the self. Social exchange does not begin with a contract between independent individuals (1969: 86). It is always a matter of will to power as self-constitution and in so far as this exchange is 'successful' it assumes and promotes sameness. Yet, in assuming that the other is the same, one reduces the other to the self and 'deliberately and recklessly brush[es] the dust of the wings of the butterfly that is called moment' (1974: 137), that contradictory moment which is the site of self-creativity.

Despite indications that one's place can never be reduced to another's, the discourses of modernity assume sameness and encourage the desire to stay in one place. Law (which embodies notions of just and unjust) reflects a community's customs in the sense of a mode of evaluation and interpretation (Nietzsche 1969: 71–6;

1984: 219). While some law may be necessary to preserve a certain life against difference and transgression, Nietzsche objects to laws (moral or secular) which universalize notions of just and unjust and therefore impose absolute values equally upon all. In this the notion of justice changes from one which explicitly assumes sameness to one which attempts to achieve sameness of outcome. Yet, what is good for one another is 'a question of who *he* is and who the *other* is' (a question of identity as measurement) and, as this question cannot be answered (identity is dissimulation), then 'what is right for one *cannot* by any means be right for another' (1972: 132, 139). The change in the meaning of justice to equal rights for all is, therefore, the beginning of injustice. ' "Equal rights" could all too easily change into equality of wrongdoing' because it legislates against anything rare, the ability to be different and the need for independence (1972: 125). 'Equality' legislates against the possibility of changing places.

Nietzsche equates this fetishization of value (of the meaning of just and unjust) with the rise of the democratic state, the secularization of morality in the form of utilitarianism and the change in the meaning of punishment from debt to guilt. All these changes involve taking the responsibility for self-evaluation, and therefore for one's existence, away from the individual. (Although, it should be noted that, as evaluation, according to Nietzsche, always involves at least two parties or sets of effects and a social context of customs, the responsibility for evaluation never ultimately resides with the · self – itself a product of evaluation and therefore never identical with itself.)

With the rise of liberal democracy the state, according to Nietzsche, functions as the 'new Idol' (1966: 48–51). The state takes over the responsibility for one's existence and 'captures' the individual through what Nietzsche calls a division of labour (1967: 382–3), a division between creature and creator, the spectacle and the artist. One's place is conditioned through the family and the penal, economic and class systems. The state is the artist: it creates the individual as a function of itself through discipline and education, maintaining itself as an end in itself. The individual is mere creature: docile and passive operating under the doctrine of selflessness and the virtues of obedience, duty and patriotism.

According to Nietzsche, ' "Equality", a certain actual rendering similar of which the theory of "equal rights" is only an expression, belongs essentially to decline' (1968: 91). 'Equality' belongs to 'decline' because the liberal democratic state achieves equality of outcome only in so far as it captures individuals, normalizes them and makes them useful. What this operation of will to power creates, by enhancing certain capacities and effects at the expense of others, is what Nietzsche calls 'inverse cripples': individuals who are fragments, having 'too little of everything and too much of one thing' (1966: 138). To function at all such partial individuals must be part of a larger system: equality of rights does not bring the freedom it promises but produces dependence through normalization.

Relating Nietzsche's notion of will to power, as the productive measurement involved in self-constitution, to his claim that equality is possible only if equality is already actual, suggests that democratic institutions do not even achieve equality of outcome. He says as much when claiming that the democratic, 'selfless' individual constitutes its place in the world by negating the value of the other's difference:

> Slave morality says No to what is 'outside', what is 'different', what is 'not itself'; and *this* No is its creative deed. This inversion of the value positing eye – this *need* to direct one's view outward instead of back to oneself – is the essence of *ressentiment*; in order to exist, slave morality always needs a hostile external world; it needs, physiologically speaking, external stimuli in order to act at all – its action is fundamentally reaction.
>
> (Nietzsche 1969: 36–7)

The democratic, consistent self is produced and maintained through the operation of will to power as evaluation, by exploitation, appropriation, through the imposition of a particular form and through the exclusion of others.

But, ironically, even the social body of equal and harmonious forces, which Nietzsche evokes as a sign of true justice, exists as such by marking itself off from an 'outside' to which it is hostile:

> Even that body within which, as it was previously assumed, individuals treat one another as equals – this happens in every healthy aristocracy – must, if it is a living and not a decaying body, itself do all that to other bodies which the individuals within it refrain from doing to one another: it will have to be will to power incarnate, it will want to grow, expand, draw to itself, gain ascendancy – not out of any morality or immorality, but because it *lives*, and because life *is* will to power.
>
> (Nietzsche 1972: 175)

Some commentators (e.g. Warren 1985: 202–5) point to such statements as evidence of Nietzsche's tendency to illegitimately apply
his ontological doctrine of will to power to justify the necessity of
political domination. However, the reading of will to power I have
provided suggests another interpretation: even within the pretence
of equality, whether within a 'healthy' aristocracy or a nihilistic
democracy, the self, or the complex of selves rendered equal, maintains itself by marginalizing others deemed inappropriate to the
system. Nietzsche is not necessarily justifying political domination.
He is exposing the fact that even a political system which claims
not to exercise domination, and which claims equality of outcome,
is merely a disguised and nihilisitic mode of domination. ·

If there is a difference between a 'healthy' and 'unhealthy'
relation to the other it is that creative self-fabrication, rather than
negating the other's difference by reducing the other to the self,
constitutes a distance, as difference, between self and other. But,
significantly, there is no escaping a debt to the other when making
the moment one's own: the pathos of distance *within* the self,
necessary for a creative re-constitution of self, is, as with democratic
normalization, predicated upon a certain relation to the other.
According to Nietzsche, in the same passage defining the pathos of
distance within the self, referred to above.

> Without the *pathos of distance* such as develops from the incar-
> nate differences in classes, from the ruling caste's constant look-
> ing out and looking down on subjects and instruments and from
> its equally constant exercise of obedience and command, its hold-
> ing down and holding at a distance, that other, more mysterious
> pathos could not have developed either, that longing for an ever
> increasing widening of distance within the soul itself.
>
> (Nietzsche 1972: 173)

This distancing between creditor and debtor, necessary to leave
one's designated place behind, has its productive effects and applies
not only to relations between classes but also to relations between
the sexes. It is to the operation of distance between the sexes, its
effects on women and the possibility of women's artistry that I shall
now turn.

WOMAN AND ACTION AT A DISTANCE

Just as measurement is involved in the constitution of any self
separate from another, Nietzsche suggests that men create an image

of woman in order to shore up something about themselves (1974: 126). In particular, the democratic man who conforms to an unchanging image of himself requires a certain construction of the other to affirm and maintain the appearance of self-consistency and autonomy. This reactive approach to the other does not have to be explicitly denigrating. A man can maintain himself by constructing an ideal and essential image of woman which is simply complementary to himself, yet designed for his consumption. This image still serves to affirm the self as unchanging: it silences the noise of other possibilities, the 'noise' of the 'forgotten'. As Nietzsche puts it in *The Gay Science*:

> When a man stands in the midst of his own noise, in the midst of his own surf of plans and projects, then he is apt also to see quiet, magical beings gliding past him and to long for their happiness and seclusion: *women*. He almost thinks that his better self dwells there among the women.
>
> (Nietzsche 1974: 124)

The truth of woman, the eternal feminine, promises to affirm an unchanging self. But, as identity is constituted in relation, the self which posits itself as autonomous and transcendental is not complete without incorporation or negation of what is other: man's desire is to possess this image of woman which he has constituted in relation to himself.[7]

To those who seek possession, Nietzsche issues a warning:

> [man thinks] that in these quiet regions even the loudest surf turns into deathly quiet, and life itself into a dream about life. Yet! Yet! Noble enthusiast, even on the most beautiful sailboat there is a lot of noise, and unfortunately much small and petty noise. The most magic and the powerful effect of woman is, in philosophical language, action at a distance, *actio in distans*; but this requires first of all and above all – *distance*.
>
> (Nietzsche 1974: 124)

Possessing the image of woman as other to the self does not bring the omnipotence or self-completion promised. If woman was the complementary image man constructs, possessing this image would bring a kind of death to the self. It would efface the distance within the self necessary for the incorporation of experience in self-overcoming. While conformity relies on constituting and possessing an image of woman, under the pretence of autonomy, creative self-fabrication relies on maintaining a distance from this image. Leaving one's place behind requires sexual difference: a 'noble' mode of valuation, a spontaneous mode of self-affirmation which 'seeks its opposite only so as to affirm itself more gratefully and triumphantly' (Nietzsche 1969: 37).

But in distancing himself from woman, the creative man still incurs a debt to her. In the definition of active self-evaluation just given, Nietzsche implies an original distance between self and other. Yet, as I have suggested, he also acknowledges that even in creative self-fabrication the 'pathos of distance' involved is located at 'the origin of language itself as an expression of power' where the 'noble' spirit names itself, gives itself identity and value 'in contra-distinction to all the low, low-minded, common and plebian' (1969: 26). The distancing/differencing effected by will to power in self-overcoming materially constitutes woman as other to the aesthetic self. While the key to creativity lies in maintaining this action at a distance, something remains to be said about its effect on women.

Nietzsche not only claims that the creative man must distance himself from the image of woman he necessarily constitutes, but also claims that 'woman forms herself according to this image' (1974: 126). This suggests that women are artistic only in so far as they are actors of a role imposed upon them. For women to be artistic in the proper sense would require the ability to incorporate experience according to one's own plan. This requires distance within the self between the present self and the concept or image towards which one aspires which, in turn, is predicated upon a distance between self and other.

In the extract given above from *The Gay Science*, there are two modes of self-constitution apparently open to women in relation to men: proximity, resulting from possession by a man, and action at a distance. The first, from a woman's perspective, requires her conditional submission to the concept of unfathomable depth man has of her. In obeying man in this way, women think, according to Nietzsche, that they will find 'depth for their surface' (1966: 67). But, in submitting to men's needs, women reduce the distance between themselves and the other and hence the distance within themselves necessary for the creative incorporation of experience. Nor do they find depth for their surface. Like the actor they reflect forms not their own, merely repeating themselves according to an image provided by others.

Submission results in the constitution of woman's bodily self as a calcified image of shame. Calcified because submission collapses the difference between her appearance (surface) and the concept of unfathomable depth man has of her (1974: 125). Such a woman *is* the concept, the truth of woman, fetishized. Submission brings shame in two senses. It involves being sexually possessed by a man and, connected to this, is the shame involved in the revelation through submission that woman is not the profound, unfathomable depth, the mysterious eternally feminine, which man's desire seeks. In submitting to man's desire, in giving up everything that she could be, woman's shame is constituted in revealing herself as surface. The shame deals a double blow when man loses interest. Again, to quote Nietzsche:

> There are noble women who are afflicted with a certain poverty of spirit, and they know no better way to *express* their deepest devotion than to offer their virtue and shame. They own nothing higher. Often this present is accepted without establishing as profound an obligation as the donors had assumed. A very melancholy story!
>
> (Nietzsche 1974: 125)

The second mode of self-constitution Nietzsche attributes to women is action at a distance. From a woman's point of view this involves maintaining one's virtue where virtue means both distance from man's desire as well as maintaining one's difference. This woman maintains the appearance of being unfathomable and changing, over the shame of being surface. Or, as Nietzsche puts it:

> old women are more skeptical in their most secret heart of hearts than any man: they consider the superficiality of existence its essence, and all virtue and profundity is to them merely a veil over this 'truth', a very welcome veil of a pudendum – in other words, a matter of decency and shame, and no more than that.
>
> (Nietzsche 1974: 125)

Action at a distance means maintaining the concept of unfathomable changeability – this is woman's virtue. But there is a catch: man's desire, whether he is artistic or democratic, is maintained. Also, the sexual 'difference' so constituted is in accordance with a concept given by man. It is in man's interest, rather than woman's, that this distance, as antithetical 'difference', is maintained.

For a start action at a distance, in 'philosophical language' (as Nietzsche stresses) does not bring autonomy. Action at a distance is defined philosophically (in the language of Newtonian physics) as the idea that one body can affect another without any intervening mechanical link between them. The bodies are separated by empty space yet when one moves so does the other. Woman is still moved my man's desire: a kind of mimicry is implied where woman is changeable only to the extent that man's interpretations move her. This 'action at a distance' does not distance woman from the other, nor does it allow the distance within herself necessary for her self-overcoming. In fact the mimicry implied in woman's virtue of unfathomable changeability is similar to Dionysian experience described by Nietzsche in the *Twilight of the Idols*. Here

> the entire emotional system is alerted and intensified: so that it discharges all its powers of representation, imitation, transfigur-ation, transmutation, every kind of mimicry and play-acting, con-jointly. The essential thing remains the facility of metamorphosis, the incapacity *not* to react (– in a similar way to certain types of hysteric, who also assume any role at the slightest instigation). . . . [The Dionysian individual] enters into every skin, into every emotion; he is continually transforming himself.
> (Nietzsche 1968: 73)

This kind of changeability is creative and Nietzsche explicitly ties it to a feminine disposition of dissatisfaction (1974: 98–9) and histri-onics (1974: 317). But it is only a precondition to change. To be productive the immediacy of mimicry must be offset by the distanc-ing within the self necessary to stage and overcome the self. This distancing is the effect of the Apollonian world of images and language, that is the will to power as interpretation, where the self is constituted as separate from another. But, as I have argued, what woman becomes through this action at a distance is in accordance with a concept provided by man. So, neither in submission to the democratic man nor at a distance from the artist do women embody the kind of aesthetics of self enjoyed by Nietzsche's 'overman'. Contrary to the assumptions of some postmodern aesthetics, it would seem that man's desire to create himself anew is satisfied only if woman remains in one place.

Nietzsche is not insensitive to the difficulties faced by woman as the object of man's desire. The imperative placed on women by men is to hold together a contradictory image of both virtue and shame, distance and submission, changeability and calcification. He claims that the comedy of love (1974: 125–6) and the impossibility of harmonious relations between the sexes (1969: 267) are based on the contradictory nature of man's self-constitution: the require-ment of both distance and proximity in relation to the other. He also suggests that woman's scepticism, about her role in relation to man, and in the assumption of an essential self, is founded on the impossibility of being the contradictory double image of virtue and shame which man requires. On the effect on women of this require-ment Nietzsche observes:

> Thus a psychic knot has been tied that may have no equal. Even the compassionate curiosity of the wisest student of humanity is inadequate for guessing how this or that woman manages to accommodate herself to this solution of the riddle, and to the riddle of a solution, and what dreadful, far-reaching suspicions must stir in her poor unhinged soul – and how the ultimate philosophy and skepsis of woman casts anchor at this point!
>
> Afterward, the same deep silence as before. Often a silence directed at herself, too. She closes her eyes to herself.
>
> (Nietzsche 1974: 128)

ANOTHER PLACE FOR WOMEN

Woman's solution to the riddle of a femininity constructed by man is to 'close her eyes to herself'. This closing is an opening in its suggestion of other possibilities for self-formation aside from conforming to an impossible image of the feminine posited by men. Man's dependence upon women conforming to an image of the feminine, as well as other possibilities for women, is suggested by Nietzsche in the following passage:

> Would a woman be able to hold us (or, as they say, 'enthral' us) if we did not consider it quite possible that under certain circumstances she would wield a dagger (any kind of dagger) *against* us? Or against herself – which in certain cases would be a crueler revenge.
>
> (Nietzsche 1974: 126)

As man's self-image depends upon woman conforming (whether in submission or at a distance) to an image that man has constituted for himself then, if woman does not conform to this image, she effectively wields a dagger against his notion of self. That women can wield the dagger suggests the possibility of non-conformity, the possibility of artistry.

There are several modes of revenge open to women, several ways of distancing themselves from the concept 'woman' and re-creating the self differently. One possibility that Nietzsche mentions, in the context of woman closing her eyes to herself, is that she can find 'atonement' for her honour through bearing children (1966: 66; 1969: 267; 1974: 128–9). However, as Alison Ainley (1988) suggests, Nietzsche tends to place a lower value on pregnancy in women than he does on the 'spiritual' pregnancy of the overman. A second mode of revenge is feminism of equality. But as my discussion has indicated, Nietzsche does not approve of this option: 'equality' amounts to turning women into men and is therefore not a distancing at all.[8]

The possibility of woman's creativity comes uneasily from Nietzsche's uncertainty about distance. In submission or at a distance, woman is not what she promises to be or what man thinks she is ('even on the most beautiful sailboat there is a noise'). The metaphor of noise suggests that women exceed the concept 'woman' which man posits. That women may change places rests on what Nietzsche means by noise and this calls for a further reassessment of the notion of 'distance' in his philosophy.

Jacques Derrida (1979: 49) suggests, in his reading of Nietzsche, that perhaps woman is distance itself. Perhaps, but this needs qualification. Woman, operating at a distance, is the complementary image or the difference man posits in constituting himself at present. But the 'empty space' between them is effected by will to power as interpretation by which borders are established and bodies constituted. Distancing, will to power as the measurement of woman, is the difference which preceeds, exceeds and constitutes the distance within the self and between man and his 'other' woman. Given the necessity of this other distancing, woman cannot be possessed – she exceeds the difference or distance over which man reaches for her or, more exactly, for himself. In proximity, or when possessed, woman will be noisy – there will be excess information. A woman is more than the concept man has of her. Her truth or identity, and therefore his, is deferred and sexual difference, as distancing, is always already maintained.

If the truth of woman is to work for man he must turn away from her – he can't live with this concept but he can't live without it. But, not only does the creative man turn away from the truth of woman he has constituted, so does the creative woman ('she closes her eyes to herself'). Nietzsche says of truth as a woman: 'certainly she has not let herself be won' (1972: 13). Women do not become this essential image, even in submission. As Nietzsche puts it:

Reflect on the whole history of women: do they not *have* to be
first of all and above all else actresses? Listen to the physicians
who have hypnotized women; finally, love them – let yourself
be 'hypnotized by them'! What is always the end result? That
they 'put on something' even when they take off everything.
 Woman is so artistic.

(Nietzsche 1974: 317)

Even when forming herself by submitting to the concept of 'woman'
which man projects, woman is acting as something other to both
this concept and to herself.[9]

So woman's artistry lies in her power of dissimulation and her
power of dissimulation is based on the fact that, as absolute identity
is always deferred, the uncovering of the veil which is the surface
of woman reveals, not the truth of woman, nor therefore man's
self-presence, but further dissimulation. This 'putting on something'
even when they take off everything is not necessarily a deliberate
resistance to subjection. It is a feature of intersubjective evaluation:
'around every profound spirit a mask is continually growing thanks
to the constantly false . . . interpretations' (1972: 51). Man's
evaluation of woman, whether active or reactive, creates the mask
that is woman's socially inscribed difference *in relation to him*. But
the distancing involved in the constitution of woman's difference in
relation to man ensures that the distance between them cannot be
effaced – something will always be 'put on' which maintains a
distance or difference. Men may assume they can capture the
dangerous plaything they need to discover the child in themselves
(to create themselves anew). But the Old Woman's advice to these
men is: 'You are going to women? Do not forget the whip' (1966: 67).

It is one thing to conclude that 'woman' is distance (or distancing)
and, therefore, that women do not coincide with either the surface
as fetish or with the truth of woman beneath. It is another to
suggest that the concept of woman which man forms for himself
has no effect on women. Derrida, for example, following Nietzsche,
appears to risk this conclusion:

That which will not be pinned down by truth is, in truth –
feminine. This should not however, be mistaken for a woman's
femini*ty*, for female sexual*ty*, or for any other essentializing
fetishes which might tantalize the dogmatic philosopher, the
impotent artist or the inexperienced seducer who has not yet
escaped his foolish hopes for capture.

(Derrida 1979: 55)

And

> Because a 'woman' takes so little interest in truth, because in
> fact she barely even believes in it, the truth as regards her, does
> not concern her in the least. It rather is the 'man' who has
> decided to believe that this discourse on woman or truth might
> possibly be of any *concern* to her.

(Derrida 1979: 63)

It is necessary to qualify Derrida's distinction between the 'feminine' and an 'essentializing fetish'. Women may not coincide with
either, but the distance/difference between female sexuality (the
surface that is a woman is at any particular moment) and the
feminine (the undecidable concept of woman) is what constitutes
women – at least in so far as women are artistic. Even in 'overcoming' themselves women rely on concepts they have inherited
whether or not they may interpret these differently from men or
differently from each other. Women are not outside nor completely
inside the feminine as the truth of woman. But the truth of woman,
as elusive and as changeable as it is, is a name. And, as the
discussion above on the relation between social concepts and
embodiment suggests, 'what things *are called* . . . gradually grows
to be part of a thing and turns into its very body' (Nietzsche 1974:
121–2). Even if what things 'are' can never be decided, concepts
of 'woman' have their material effects in the constitution of the
bodily self that is a woman. Woman may not believe in man's
discourse on her but, given the constitutive effects of this discourse
on woman's difference, to imply, however carefully, that it doesn't
concern her at all is a little hasty.

Nietzsche's understanding of the 'pathos of distance' exposes not
only that normative discourses assume a male subject, but also that
they rely on constructing woman in a certain way. Man creates an
image of woman as other in order to secure his corporeal identity.
At a distance woman's 'difference' is complementary and promises
to affirm man's self-presence; in proximity her 'sameness' heralds
the death of the self. There is no exchange between man and his
creditor, woman. Rather, woman's 'gift' to man is his (impossible)
self-certainty; the 'return' for her investment is a contradictory
corporeality – suspended between virtue and shame. In so far as
women fulfil this impossible role as man's other they uneasily
embody these contradictory concepts without a place of their own.
But, as I have argued, the operation of will to power is such that
women's bodies also remain open to possibilities aside from those

which position them under man. The embodied meaning of 'woman' is dispersed beyond virtue and shame, beyond the riddle of femininity Nietzsche tends to uphold.

If there is a limitation in Nietzsche's approach to the problematic of the constitution of place, it is in the suggestion, apparent at times in his work, that an aesthetics of self can avoid incurring a debt to the other. This assumption is amplified in some postmodern claims that we can avoid projecting otherness outward or that we can simply declare an end to self-identity and its attendant objectification of others. To deny that an aesthetics of self modifies or objectifies the other is merely a *disavowal* of the differential relations operating in the constitution of one's embodied place in the world. As I have argued, Nietzsche's concepts of will to power and the 'pathos of distance' suggest the impossibility of such an uncontaminating space. And, that action at a distance, in its simplest formulation, still relies on keeping woman in her place is testimony to the dangers lurking in any claims to the possibility of leaving one's place behind forever.

NOTES

1 Nietzsche makes a similar comment about the derivative nature of pleasure and pain in *Beyond Good and Evil* (1972: 135–6).

2 For a discussion of the problem of the actor in Nietzsche's philosophy see Patton (1991b).

3 Besides the cosmological and psychological doctrines of eternal recurrence, Wood (1988) discusses a third possible interpretation, the 'ontological', which I have found useful.

4 For discussions of Nietzsche's use of the metaphor of pregnancy see Ainley (1988) and Patton (1991a: 49–52).

5 Nietzsche makes a further connection between interpretation and will to power as a form-giving force in *On the Genealogy of Morals* (1969: 79).

6 Nietzsche makes similar observations on the disjunction between self-interpretation and interpretation by another elsewhere in *Beyond Good and Evil* (1972: 97, 142).

7 For Nietzsche's understanding of the different ways that a man can possess a woman and what these say about the man's self-image see *Beyond Good and Evil* (1972: 98–9).

8 I discuss Nietzsche's opposition to feminism of equality in more detail elsewhere (Diprose 1989).

9 Nietzsche's claim that women put on something when they take off everything has often been interpreted as faking orgasm – woman's constitution of her own self-presence when appearing to guarantee man's. Or, as Gayatri Spivak suggests: 'Women, "acting out" their pleasure in the orgasmic moment, can cite themselves in their very self-presence' (1984:

22). I take issue with Spivak only in her claim that it is self-presence (rather than undecidable difference) which is being cited in woman's dissimulation.

BIBLIOGRAPHY

Ainley, A. (1988) ' "Ideal selfishness": Nietzsche's metaphor of maternity', in D. F. Krell and D. Wood (eds) *Exceedingly Nietzsche: Aspects of Contemporary Nietzsche – Interpretation*, London: Routledge.

Derrida, J. (1979) *Spurs: Nietzsche's Styles*, trans. B. Harlow, Chicago, Ill.: University of Chicago Press.

Diprose, R. (1989) 'Nietzsche, ethics and sexual difference', *Radical Philosophy* 52: 27–33.

Graybeal, J. (1990) *Language and the Feminine in Nietzsche and Heidegger*, Bloomington, Ind.: Indiana University Press.

Irigaray, L. (1984) *Ethique de la Différence Sexuelle*, Paris: Les Editions de Minuit (draft translation by C. Sheaffer-Jones with the assistance of E. Grosz and M. Sheaffer).

Nietzsche, F. (1966) *Thus Spoke Zarathustra: A Book for All and None*, trans. W. Kaufmann, Harmondsworth: Penguin.

—— (1967) *The Will to Power*, ed. W. Kaufmann, trans. W. Kaufmann and R. J. Hollingdale, New York: Random House.

—— (1968) *Twilight of the Idols and The Anti-Christ*, trans. R. J. Hollingdale, Harmondsworth: Penguin.

—— (1969) *On the Genealogy of Morals and Ecce Homo*, trans. W. Kaufmann, New York: Random House.

—— (1972) *Beyond Good and Evil*, trans. R. J. Hollingdale, Harmondsworth: Penguin.

—— (1974) *The Gay Science*, trans. W. Kaufmann, New York: Random House.

—— (1983) *Untimely Meditations*, trans. R. J. Hollingdale, Cambridge: Cambridge University Press.

—— (1984) *Human, All Too Human: A Book for Free Spirits*, trans. M. Faber with S. Lehmann, Lincoln, Nebr.: University of Nebraska Press.

Owens, C. (1985) 'The discourse of others: feminists and postmodernism', in H. Foster (ed.) *Postmodern Culture*, London: Pluto Press (originally published in 1983 as *The Anti-Aesthetic*, Port Townsend, Calif.: Bay Press).

Patton, P. (1991a) 'Nietzsche and the body of the philosopher', in R. Diprose and R. Ferrell (eds) *Cartographies: Poststructuralism and the Mapping of Bodies and Spaces*, Sydney: Allen & Unwin.

—— (1991b) 'Postmodern subjectivity: the problem of the actor (Zarathustra and the Butler)', in A. Yeatman (ed.) *Postmodern Critical Theorising*, special issue of *Social Analysis* 30 (December).

Spivak, G. C. (1984) 'Love me, love my ombre, elle', *Diacritics* 14(4): 19–36.

Warren, M. (1985) 'Nietzsche and political philosophy', *Political Theory* 13(2).

Winterson, J. (1989) *Sexing the Cherry*, London: Vintage.

Wood, D. (1988) 'Nietzsche's transvaluation of time', in D. F. Krell and D. Wood (eds) *Exceedingly Nietzsche: Aspects of Contemporary Nietzsche – Interpretation*, London: Routledge.

2 Nietzsche, woman and political theory

Keith Ansell-Pearson

To go wrong on the fundamental problem of 'man' and 'woman', to deny the most abysmal antagonism between them and the necessity of an eternally hostile tension, to dream perhaps of equal rights . . . – that is a *typical* sign of shallowness.

(Nietzsche, *Beyond Good and Evil*, 1966: section 238)

He is the thinker of pregnancy which, for him, is no less praiseworthy in a man than it is in a woman.

(Derrida, *Spurs*, 1979: 65)

The basic error and the most elementary human blindness is not a refusal to acknowledge death, but a refusal to remember birth, that one was born.

(Sloterdijk, 'Eurotaoism', 1988: 113)

We cannot afford to allow the vibrations of death to continue to drown out the vibrations of life. . . . Our culture cannot carry on the eternal war between men, between men and nature, failing to make a public and cultural alliance between the world of women and that of men.

(Irigaray, in Mortley 1991: 78)

as my father I have already died, as my mother I still live and grow old.

(Nietzsche, *Ecce Homo*, 1979: 38)

INTRODUCTION

In an essay on 'Nietzsche's Revolution', the American philosopher Stanley Rosen reflected on the curious fact that Nietzsche is currently the most widely read and debated philosopher in the western, non-Marxist world (Rosen 1989: 189). This present volume is itself evidence of this fact and testimony to the growing influence of Nietzsche's ideas in areas which, for a long time,. have been hostile to them. However, to those who do not find Nietzsche a source of inspiration (indeed, many continue to regard his influence – on the young, in the academy, at the 'high table' – as a pernicious one) (Canovan 1988; Foot 1991), the nature and extent of his influence is a puzzle and a mystery. Rosen himself argues that Nietzsche's rise to intellectual dominance ought to be regarded as a 'political fact of the highest importance', since it is remarkable that someone who espoused an aristocratic, anti-egalitarian political ethos, who spoke with snobbish disdain about the 'rabble', who demanded a new order of rank in society, and who frequently spoke of women as the inferior sex because of their 'inherent' emotional and physiological weaknesses, should today be deemed to be one of the highest authorities for progressive liberals, politically correct professors, left-wing critics of bourgeois society, and certain strands of current feminist thought (Rosen 1989: 190). In a similar vein, Wilfried van der Will spoke with alarm, at a conference convened in 1991 on the fate of the 'new Nietzsche', on the strange manner in which the deconstructionist and poststructuralist 'Nietzsche' blots out 'the more violent, militantly elitist and plainly anti-democratic strands' of his thought (van der Will 1991: 2).

In debates, however, on Nietzsche's status as a political thinker, and on the relationship between Nietzsche and political thought, it has been recognized for some time now that his thought is characterized by both positive, emancipatory tendencies, and by deeply negative, debilitating ones. In her study of 1984, for example, which attempted to read Nietzsche without the masks that other readers (not exclusively male) had brought to an interpretation of his work in order to conceal its dark and troublesome aspects (namely, the politics), Ofelia Schutte spoke of Nietzsche as a double thinker, as a Jekyll and Hyde philosopher who, on the one hand, celebrated 'life' as recurring Dionysian flux and energy, and who, on the other, argued in favour of the necessity of an Apollonian polity of masters and slaves, resting on fixed hierarchies and laws of nature. Whereas the former conception of life can be seen to be positively liberatory, in that it affirms a force which overturns all fixed boundaries and natural laws ('self-overcoming' as the only affirmatory law of life), the latter represents an authoritarian conception which culminates in a highly reactionary politics (Schutte 1984: ch. 8; see also the study by Warren 1988).

How are these tensions in Nietzsche's work, and in our reception of it, reflected in feminism's engagement with Nietzsche? The consensus which seems to be emerging at the present moment in time is that the most fertile aspect of his writings for the formulation of a radical philosophy lies, not in their overt pronouncements (on women, for example), but rather in their 'style'(s), in their attempt to communicate a philosophy of the body, in their disclosure of the metaphoricity of philosophical discourse, and in the exemplary way in which they are seen to deconstruct the logocentric bias of western thought and reason (Winders 1991: 120–3). Debra Bergoffen has argued that there is no good reason why Nietzsche's radical critique of western culture – of its rationalism, scientism and positivism – cannot be extended to a critique of western *patriarchal* culture (Bergoffen 1989: 77).[1] Furthermore, it might be no coincidence that the 'discovery' of Nietzsche – *the* philosopher of difference, according to Gilles Deleuze (1983) – by feminist writers is taking place at the same time that radical political theorists, including feminists, are seeking to articulate a philosophy of otherness and difference. A number of feminists have argued that it is necessary to go beyond the impasse of equality (a form of limited political emancipation perhaps?), and suggested that what is required is a new mode of thought, which is able to affirm difference and celebrate otherness without positing a totalitarian politics based on a spurious universalism (total *human* emancipation?). It is this search for a new ethics and politics which makes the reception of Nietzsche potentially fertile and productive within feminism at the present juncture. But a number of questions need to be asked about this appropriation of Nietzsche: how useful is Nietzsche's thought for a feminist politics of difference given his commitment to an aristocratic polity and his affirmation of a masculine, Napoleonic virility? Is it sufficient for feminism, and radical political thought in general, simply to engage with Nietzsche solely in terms of the question of style (in the manner of Derrida, for example)? Or must they not also engage with the substance of his saying?

In this chapter I intend to look at the topic from a number of angles. The aim is to be neither systematic nor exhaustive, but rather to give the reader a sense of the main debates and of the key issues which are at stake in posing the question of the relationship between Nietzsche, feminism and political theory.

NIETZSCHE CONTRA EUROPEAN FEMINISM

In his own time Nietzsche wrote as a critic of European feminism, speaking out against what he saw as the emasculation of social life and the rise of a sentimental politics based on altruistic values. He attacked the idea that women would be emancipated once they had secured equal rights. Certain passages in his work show quite unequivocally that he regarded the whole issue of women's emancipation as a misguided one. The great danger of the women's movement in attempting to enlighten women about womanhood is that it teaches women to unlearn their fear of man. When this happens, he argues, woman – 'the weaker sex' – abandons her most womanly instincts (Nietzsche 1966: 167). Why, Nietzsche asks, should women wish to become like men when woman's 'prudence and art' consist in grace, play and lightness? Why should they want to pursue the 'truth' about woman when her great art is the lie and her highest concern 'appearance and beauty' (Nietzsche 1966: 163)? In opposition to 'modern ideas' on man and woman, Nietzsche argues that real instruction on the relationship of the sexes is to be found in Oriental cultures. He suggests that a man of depth, 'including that depth of benevolence which is capable of severity and hardness', needs to think of woman 'as a possession (*Besitz*), as property (*Eigenthum*) that can be locked, as something predestined for service and achieving her perfection in that' (Nietzsche 1966: 167). Nietzsche detects a 'masculine stupidity' in the women's movement, one which can lead only to a degeneration of 'woman'. No 'social contract' can put right the inequality of men and women, and the necessary injustice in their relationship (Nietzsche 1974: 319). The problem, he suggests, like problems associated with other 'modern ideas', goes back to the French Revolution and its ideals of equality. In order to combat this process of degeneration, the sexes must learn that what men respect in woman is her '*nature* . . . the tiger's claw under the glove, the naiveté of her egoism, her uneducability and her inner wildness' (1966: 169). He idealizes Napoleon as the figure who triumphed over the plebeian ideals of the Revolution and once again established 'man' as 'master over the businessman, the philistine', and over ' "woman" who has been pampered by Christianity and the enthusiastic spirit of the eighteenth century, and even more by "modern ideas" ' (1974: 318).

Nietzsche's aristocratism rests on a critique of notions of the subject and of self-hood (of the single subject, of free will, etc.) which inform both Christian-moral culture and modern secular ideologies, such as liberalism and socialism. Here the self is conceived in terms of a metaphysical substrate which underlies all action in the world. In the *Genealogy of Morals* Nietzsche traces the origins of the emergence of a belief in the 'soul' to a slave revolt in morality. It is the weak and the oppressed who devise a notion of a 'neutral, independent "subject" ' as a form of 'sublime self-deception' in which they seek to convince themselves, and others, that they are 'free' to be weak and humble; at the same time such a notion makes it possible for them to attribute blame and responsibility to the strong and powerful for their strength and feeling of superiority (Nietzsche 1969: 44–6). For Nietzsche, however, the doer and the deed are one; the self must become what it is by conceiving itself as a piece of fate. Individuals prove themselves, and establish their worth, not through some belief in an innate inner self, but through displaying their role-related talents and attributes (courage, prowess, wisdom, etc.) in the *agon* (contest). Nietzsche's thought is 'sexist' in that, like most traditional aristocratic thinking (Plato being the obvious exception), it excludes woman from engaging in the public *agon*, and restricts her role to the private or domestic sphere. Woman's primary role for Nietzsche is one of adornment. While I would concur with the view that feminism must certainly attack Nietzsche's views on women, I would not suggest that it necessarily follows that it must reject his commitment to aristocratic values. For what Nietzsche's essentialism (whether biological or cultural) ignores is that women – as the history of the women's movement amply testifies – have their own depth, their own courage, wisdom and severity. Nietzsche's critique of Christian and liberal notions of the self can certainly be of use to a noble and courageous feminist politics of difference.

It is difficult to believe that a philosopher who stated that a real friend of women is someone who tells them that 'woman should be silent about woman' (Derrida's advice too?) (Nietzsche 1966: 164), and who, moreover, spoke disparagingly of 'emancipated women' as 'abortive females' (Nietzsche 1979: 75–6), could be of any use to feminism. Recent readings of Nietzsche by a number of women philosophers and political theorists, however, have advanced positive and powerful ways in which his ideas and texts can be opened up and moved in the direction of a feminist textual and political practice. Rosalyn Diprose, for example, has argued that Nietzsche's critique of the self, of the idea that lying behind all action there is to be found a constant, stable, fixed ego, describes a 'positive mode of resistance to social domination and normalization' (Diprose 1989: 31). Nietzsche's thinking contains an emphasis on ambiguity, on plural identity, on the affirmation of the constructed self in terms of an artistic task in which one freely gives 'style' to one's character, all of which can be useful for articulating a kind of feminist mode of thought which seeks to subvert an essentializing of human identity, whether female or male, and which would simplify and efface 'difference'(s). The mythical subject that needs to be attacked and deconstructed in this fashion is the male subject of bourgeois society and bourgeois history. Diprose's own view on how a progressive or feminist reading should approach the problem of Nietzsche's aristocratism is worth citing:

> For Nietzsche, the 'other' placed most at risk, by an ethics of equality is not woman but the sometimes cruel, sometimes enigmatic, always exceptional Noble spirit. The way Nietzsche appears to single out a sole aristocratic victim is somewhat surprising to a contemporary reader and has drawn criticism from some commentators. However, that Nietzsche appears to seek to save an elite and somewhat frightening figure from the workings of the democratic state is, in part, a product of historic necessity. It was the noble man, embellished by a memory of Greek nobility, who, more than any other, symbolized what was thrown into relief by the rise of the liberal individual in the nineteenth century. But this is no longer the case: a century of 'equality' has created its own hierarchy of value and hence, its own order of differences to be marginalized and effaced. All the same, on the question of Nietzsche's explicit exclusion of women from the possibility of self-creation, the excuses run out.
>
> (Diprose 1989: 31)

A great deal of the 'reactive' nature of Nietzsche's aristocratic radicalism can be seen to stem from the *ressentiment* of the noble man who feels that his privileges are under threat, and the value he places on difference and distance about to be rendered extinct. Diprose suggests that Nietzsche's anti-feminism 'is not so much inconsistent but symptomatic of his own *ressentiment*' (1989: 32). As Diprose acknowledges, there is an important aspect to Nietzsche's critique of nineteenth-century egalitarianism from which feminism can learn; indeed, his point has become a matter of increasing concern to feminists themselves with the maturity of the feminist movement. In the attempt to seek and establish equality – primarily, that of equality before the law – oppressed groups often make the mistake of clothing themselves in the attire of their oppressors or masters. Of course, what they seek is, quite understandably, a portion of the power which the masters have and which they wield. But, in the satisfaction of this very human desire, these groups fail to realize that 'the law' which will make them equal is the law as defined and legislated by those in power: for women living under patriarchy, for example, the law is the law of man.

Although she perhaps underestimates the extent of Nietzsche's commitment to noble values, Diprose construes the problem of

Nietzsche's aristocratism in a novel and instructive way. Neverthe-less, we still need to ask whether Nietzsche's thinking is irredeem-ably phallocentric, or whether it contains contradictory aspects to it which can push it in another direction. Elizabeth Grosz offers a useful definition of phallocentrism and its reduction of all things feminine and womanly to masculine norms:

> Phallocentrism functions to reduce or categorise femininity so that it is conceived as a simulacrum, mirror-image or imperfect double of masculinity. *Our received images of femininity have been masculine – inverted, projected images of male ideals and fantasies, images of the male 'other' rather than a female subject*. . . . It proceeds by two processes: one, a levelling pro-cess, whereby all differences are reduced to variations of same-ness; and the other, a hierarchising process, requiring judgement of the two sexes by the same criteria.
>
> (Grosz 1986: 68, my emphasis)

It is with this definition in mind that I shall now look at the question of woman in Nietzsche as it has been posed by Jacques Derrida, Sarah Kofman and Luce Irigaray.

DERRIDA ON NIETZSCHE, STYLE AND WOMAN

One of the principal tasks that deconstruction sets itself is to under-mine the hierarchical oppositions on which the tradition of western metaphysics has been built – oppositions such as reason/passion, logos/pathos, intelligible/sensible, etc. – so as to open up philo-sophic discourse to a free play of signs in which new, more complex and hybrid identities can be formed and created. In his celebrated and contentious essay, *Spurs* (a highly disingenuous work, I would contend), Derrida suggests that Nietzsche's radicalness lies in the way in which his thinking is characterized by a plurality of styles, and by a practice of writing which eschews adopting stable identities or positing fixed essences. When, in the preface to *Beyond Good and Evil*, Nietzsche claims that all (male) philosophers have been dogmatic in their assumptions about truth, and compares this to their inexpertise with women, he is saying that just as there is no single, unitary 'Truth' about life or reality to be discovered, so there is no such 'truth' about woman to be found, for, like 'truth', she does not exist. The provocative suggestion contained in Derrida's reading is that Nietzsche's objections to classical feminism can be seen to contain the 'post-feminist' message that women's attempts to define 'woman as such' commit the same essentialist fallacies as the masculinist tradition of western philosophy. He writes: 'Feminism is nothing but the operation of a woman who aspires to be like a man. . . . It wants a castrated woman. Gone the style' (Derrida 1979: 65). In the next section I shall argue that it is not feminism which castrates woman, but Derrida.

Perhaps the most important contention in *Spurs* is the claim that what cannot be defined in philosophy's attempt to master reality is 'truth' understood as a 'feminine' operation, and, moreover, that the 'feminine' is not to be mistaken for woman's 'femininity' or for female sexuality, that is, for any 'of those essentializing fetishes which might still tantalize the dogmatic philosopher, the impotent artist or the inexperienced seducer who has not yet escaped his foolish hopes of capture' (Derrida 1979: 55). Derrida contends that we can locate three figures of woman in Nietzsche. The triadic schema which governs Nietzsche's writing is as follows:

> He was, He dreaded this castrated woman.
> He was, He dreaded this castrating woman.
> He was, he loved this affirming woman.
>
> (Derrida 1979: 101)

Kelly Oliver has usefully defined this typology of woman in Nietzsche as corresponding to three types of will, namely the will to truth, the will to illusion, and the will to power. The castrated woman refers to 'the feminist who negates woman in order to affirm herself as man' (Oliver 1984: 187). Instead of creating truth and a plural identity, the castrated woman claims to discover truth, to discover woman as she is 'in and for herself'. In striving for 'objective truth' about woman, she denies the freedom which resides in affirming the ambiguity and multiplicity of meaning. As such, the type of feminism which pursues objectivity is hostile to the flux of life, to life as will to power (Oliver 1984: 188). The 'castrating woman' is the artist who plays with truth in order to disguise herself and resist the metaphysician's attempt to pin her down and fix her meaning. However, this kind of woman can be easily seduced by her own illusion when she clings fanatically to her ideals and forgets that she herself created them: 'She is the actor as the hysterical little woman. She mistakes the means, her illusion, for an end. The castrating woman becomes another version of the castrated woman' (Oliver 1984: 193). The 'affirming woman' signifies the self-overcoming of the will to truth and the will to illusion; she is the Dionysian force which abandons all foundations and certainties, 'the original mother, the unexhausted procreative will of life which is the will to power' (Oliver 1984: 195). Moreover:

> She is hollow like a womb. She is the space, the womb, from which everything originates. This space is distance: the affirming woman is not an object in the distance: rather she is distance. Her power is distance. As distance, as space – pure womb – she does not exist. Just as there is no woman, there is no truth.
> (Oliver 1984: 196; see Nietzsche 1974: 123–4, 'Women and their action at a distance')[2]

What Derrida is doing in *Spurs* is enlisting Nietzsche's attempt to write with style(s) (conceived as a feminine operation) in the cause of deconstruction and its critique of the metaphysics of presence, where being is always 'present' to itself. The question of style becomes a question of *strategy* in which the possibility of a 'radically deferred, indeterminate style of writing' is explored 'in order to avoid all essentialisms and stable categories' (Winders 1991: 121). As Derrida puts it himself:

> Reading is freed from the horizon of the meaning or truth of being, liberated from the values of the product's production or the present's presence. Whereupon the question of style is immediately unloosed as a question of writing.
> (Derrida 1979: 107)

CONTRA DERRIDA

In spite of its suggestive brilliance, Derrida's reading of Nietzsche is a troubling one. The way in which he freely quotes Nietzsche's remarks on woman, including some of the passages in which Nietzsche *derides* women and their struggle for independence (though he always manages to do it in a way which removes their sting), without any sense of alarm, is disquieting. It is important that the question of woman is not reduced to being a mere figure or metaphor, possessing only the status of a rhetorical trope. To overlook, or to disregard in so confident a manner as Derrida does, Nietzsche's sexist remarks is not simply naive, but politically dangerous. To claim, as he does, that Nietzsche writes with the hand of woman or that his philosophy speaks of the 'feminine', is to run the risk of adding insult to injury by adding further to philosophy's insidious silencing of women. For if male philosophers such as Nietzsche or Derrida can write with the hand of woman, what is the role and purpose of female philosophers (Oliver 1988: 25–9)? As Rosi Braidotti has written: 'Isn't it strange that it is precisely at the time in history when women have made their voices heard socially, politically, and theoretically that philosophical discourse – a male domain *par excellence* – takes over "the feminine" for itself?' (Braidotti 1986: 2). It is Derrida who castrates woman by reducing the issue of woman's emancipation from a question of *politics* (of power) to one of style. Not once in *Spurs* does he engage with either the history or the theoretical and practical struggles of feminism. Moreover, the 'feminine' Derrida writes about is totally neutered, desexed. The intentions behind his reading may not have been misogynistic, but that is certainly its result.[3]

Not only does Derrida's posing of the question of style castrate women, but also it castrates Nietzsche. He simply refuses to take seriously that Nietzsche meant what he said and that he believed that women should have neither political power nor social influence. Does Derrida think that these questions are unimportant? What we need to know from him is how the question of 'woman' as a question of *style* relates to the political question of women's emancipation from centuries of patriarchal oppression. As one commentator has pointed out, Derrida's exploration of the question of woman in Nietzsche as a question of style 'removes the social issue of woman from the cultural context' (del Caro 1990: 145). It is a strategy which results in an idealized man and an idealized woman, as well as an idealized notion of style. While readers of Nietzsche know what they are getting and are able to take up a critical stance against it, if they so wish, readers of Derrida are denied any accessibility to the issue of gender either in Nietzsche or in the tradition of western philosophy as a whole. Derrida's position is characterized by its sheer vagueness and remoteness (del Caro 1990: 156). The danger of adopting Derrida's 'playful' approach is that it runs the risk of turning gender – indeed, the very question of woman it raises – into a non-issue, or an issue of only dubious interest to dogmatic philosophers who have no real knowledge or familiarity with the charms and graces of women. It is time we admitted to ourselves a certain truth, namely that 'all the deconstructions in the world still cannot escape what is disturbing about Nietzsche's own sexual politics, however complicated and contradictory they may have been' (Winders 1991: 142). How can we account for this truth regarding such a 'radical' philosopher? Does Derrida help us to answer this question?

The fact that Derrida never expresses any real concern over this last point, that he never *agonizes* over it – indeed, he makes it all sound so easy, turning the question of woman's emancipation into a non-issue, trivial at best – makes it difficult to take seriously the claims he makes on behalf of Nietzsche's style of writing. Derrida's reading does justice neither to Nietzsche nor to feminism. One final, curious point can perhaps be made: Derrida's celebration of the freedom one attains by learning how to 'dance with the pen', results in a highly intellectualist and idealist conception of freedom without any real connection to the corporality of experience – one is almost tempted to say that the 'question of style' is but the latest expression of the ascetic ideal.

NIETZSCHE AND THE FEMININE: KOFMAN AND IRIGARAY

In this section I want to show that the question of style *may* be an important question to explore in Nietzsche, but only if we give some substance – some 'femininity' and sexuality, as well as a notion of *experience* – to his flirtations with the 'feminine'.

Nietzsche's critique of metaphysics is a critique of its dualistic nature. For example, he challenges the way in which it has established reason as superior to, and over, emotion or passion. As such, it can be seen to offer a form, or a style, of critique which seeks to reinstate the 'feminine' in philosophy, and to do so in a way which ultimately challenges any hierarchical opposition of 'masculine' and 'feminine'. If we read Nietzsche's texts carefully we discover, not simply that they are littered with misogynistic remarks, but that they also deconstruct their own phallocentric pretensions, largely through a celebration of woman as a metaphor representing the creative forces of life (life and woman conceived as the force of difference). Nietzsche's critique of the tradition of philosophy from Plato to Kant and Hegel rests on the insight that it has misunderstood the body. From Plato onwards, philosophers have castrated their reflections on life from the body of experience which underlies them. Their fundamental world-views rest on a metaphysics of resentment: resentment towards sensual life, towards desire, towards the body; in short, towards woman. For Nietzsche, philosophy is maternal in that it rests on the unity of body and soul. The task is not, as it is in Plato, to liberate the soul from the prison house of the body, but to recognize that the 'soul is only a word for something in the body' (Nietzsche 1961: 61–3, 'Of the despisers of the body'). The true philosopher is one who recognizes that her thoughts are born out of the pain of experience which, like the experience of childbirth, should be endowed with 'blood, heart, fire, pleasure, passion, and agony, conscience, fate, and catastrophe' (Nietzsche 1974: 35–6). It is only the experience of great pain which affords us the deepest insights into the human lot. Nietzsche makes the important point that the experience of such pain does not make us 'better' human beings, but only more 'profound' ones. The aim of such 'dangerous exercises in self-mastery' should not be 'self-forgetting', but rather to emerge from them a 'changed' and 'different' person. We are still capable of loving life, he says, but the kind of love we have for it can be compared to that of our love for someone (in his case a woman) who now causes *doubt* in us (Nietzsche 1974: 37).

What is important about Nietzsche's style of philosophizing is its attempt to communicate the singular experience – the experience of what he calls 'the new, the unique, the incomparable' (Nietzsche 1974: 266). Of course, such a task is ultimately paradoxical, impossible even, for as soon as this experience is uttered it becomes subjected to comparison and susceptible to equalization. This is one of the reasons why his work is notable for its dazzling array of forms, of aphorisms, treatises, essays, poems, parables, polemics, and so on. Through a proliferation of styles and masks, Nietzsche attempts to give voices to the many facets of his personality in order to bear faithful witness to the rich tapestry and mystery of human existence. It is not without significance that he commences his inquiry into the genealogy of morality with the claim that the reason why we moderns are so unfamiliar to ourselves is precisely because we no longer know how to communicate the experience of life: not only do we no longer give our hearts to it, we no longer lend our ears to it as well.

> We are necessarily strangers to ourselves, we do not comprehend ourselves, we *have* to misunderstand ourselves, for us the law 'Each is furthest from himself' applies to all eternity – we are not 'knowers' with respect to ourselves.
>
> (Nietzsche 1969: 15)

What Nietzsche seeks, in calling for a self-overcoming of morality, is new 'postmodern' readers (postmodern in the sense that they are 'over' [*über*] *moderner Mensch* as if 'over' a sickness) who have learned what he calls the 'art of interpretation' (*Auslegung*); that is they know how to read themselves and their experiences not in metaphysical terms of truth and falsity, of good and evil, but in terms of representations of ascending (active) or descending (reactive) modes of life (Nietzsche 1969: 20–3).

Sarah Kofman has warned against rushing headlong into pronouncing Nietzsche to be a straightforward misogynistic philosopher. She argues that it is highly significant that Nietzsche should, in the preface to the second edition of *The Gay Science* (1887), use the Greek female demon Baubô as a symbol for 'truth'. What is necessary, Nietzsche writes in the section where he speaks of this demon, is to stop courageously at the surface, at the fold, the skin, to adore appearance, and in this way one achieves superficiality 'out of profundity'. The true philosopher, Kofman suggests, is as Nietzsche describes, namely the one who wills illusion as illusion, for whom 'truth' is beyond good and evil, recognizing that neither an essence of 'truth' nor of 'woman' exist, and that both have good reasons to hide their existence behind veils and masks. By identifying the wisdom of life with Baubô, Nietzsche is identifying 'truth' not simply with woman, but in particular with the female reproductive organs which symbolize the eternal fecundity and creativity of life, its cycle of creation and decay, the circle that is a will to power, a will to dance, a will to innocence, and a will to reproduction through the 'abysmal antagonism of the sexes' (Nietzsche 1967: 33–41). As Kofman notes, 'in the Eleusian mysteries, the female sexual organ is exalted as the symbol of fertility and a guarantee of regeneration and eternal return of all things' (Kofman 1988: 197). As the female double of Dionysus, what Baubô promises is the possibility of inaugurating a mode of reflection that has gone beyond (*über*) the metaphysical distinction of 'male' and 'female', a distinction which the tradition of philosophy has always conceived in terms of a natural hierarchy in which all that is male and masculine is affirmed, and all that is female and feminine is excluded and denigrated.

Among contemporary French theorists, it is Luce Irigarary who, however problematic a task it might be, has arguably done the most to articulate the 'feminine' in philosophy. Although often accused of subscribing to a self-defeating biological essentialism, it can be argued, in defence, that Irigaray's much misunderstood work attempts to articulate a complex, non-hierarchical experience of the world in which the female voice that has been excluded from the discourse of philosophy is uttered and received for the first time. Irigaray herself instructively locates the source of her own difficulties, and of any attempt to speak the voice of the other, in the following terms:

Woman has no gaze, no discourse for her specific specularization that would allow her to identify with herself (as same) – to return into the self – or break free of the natural specular process that now holds her – to get out of the self. Hence, woman does not take an active part in the development of history, for she is never anything but the still undifferentiated opaqueness of sensible matter, the store (of) substance for the sublation of self, or being as what is, or what he is (or was), here and now.

(Irigaray 1985: 224)

Irigaray's attempt to 'write the body' by evoking the female genitals to describe a libidinal economy centred on touch, feeling, flow and perpetual play (see Winders 1991: 137–41), challenges the phallo-centric prejudices and assumptions of male reason and rationality which persist in governing the discourse of philosophy as well as the institutions of our political life.

In her own amorous engagement with Nietzsche, Irigaray interrogates Nietzsche's pretensions as a philosopher of maternity and of the body. Her reading serves as a challenge to those put forward by Kofman and myself. She questions his fears, his anxieties, and his dreams and nightmares about woman, and locates in his thinking a fundamental *ressentiment*:

A man who really loves does not spare the one he loves, you claim. And that just shows how little you feel when you refuse to fight with – your woman. Keeping for the night your envy and your hate.

But I want to interpret your midnight dreams, and unmask that phenomenon: your night. And make you admit that I will dwell in it as your most fearsome adversity. So that you can finally realize what your greatest *ressentiment* is. And so that with you I can fight to make the earth my own, and stop allowing myself to be a slave to your nature. And so that you finally stop wanting to be the only god.

(Irigaray 1991: 25)

Nietzsche affirms woman as the source of life only by denying to woman her own independent reality and experience of the world. Her mediation of the world through a man always assumes the form of an inferior position, one of natural servitude and obligation. And so his affirmation of woman contains a negation of her autonomous being: he will not let woman be, will not let her speak for herself. On Nietzsche's exclusion of woman, Irigaray writes:

If from her you want confirmation for your being, why don't you let her explore its labyrinths? Why don't you give her leave to speak? From the place where she sings the end of your becoming, let her be able to tell you: no.

(Irigaray 1991: 23)

Zarathustra's/Nietzsche's greatest affliction is that he suffers from an envy of the womb. In his desire to achieve the impossible, namely *to give birth to himself*, Nietzsche expresses a fundamental resentment towards that which he feels ardour for and most esteems – maternal creativity. This resentment on his part towards the creative powers of woman is comparable to the resentment he detects in the will's desire to will backwards, that is to will the past and what has been. As Irigaray writes on this complex and crucial point:

> To overcome the impossible of your desire – that is surely your last hour's desire. Giving birth to such and such a production, or such and such a child is a summary of your history. But to give birth to your desire itself, that is your final thought. To be incapable of doing it, that is your highest *ressentiment*. For you either make works that fit your desire, or you make desire itself into your work. But how will you find the material to produce such a child?

With extraordinary insight Irigaray examines the nature of Nietzsche's masculine resentment towards life and towards woman:

> And, going back to the source of all your children, you want to bring yourself back into the world. As a father? Or a child? And isn't being two at a time the point where you come unstuck? Because, to be a father, you have to produce, procreate, your seed has to escape and fall from you. You have to engender suns, dawns, and twilights other than your own.
>
> But in fact isn't it your will, in the here and now, to pull everything back inside you and to be and to have only one sun? And to fasten up time, for you alone? And suspend the ascending and descending movement of genealogy? And to join up in one perfect place, one perfect circle, the origin and end of all things?

(Irigaray 1991: 34)

In other words, Nietzsche, Irigaray contends, because of his desire to create, and care only for, himself, is wrapped up in his own solipsistic universe. Nietzsche wants to attain the impossible and to will backwards so as to be able to give birth *to himself*. To achieve this he must devalue woman by construing her existence as dependent on man for its fulfilment (when, in reality, every male that exists is dependent on a woman for their coming into the world, for their gift of life). Nietzsche's resentment of the creative independence of women is surely evident in his description of the emancipated woman as an abortive female. But note, there is nothing particularly unique about Nietzsche's resentment: it is typical of patriarchy.

Irigaray's reading of Nietzsche/*Zarathustra* is provocative and contentious. A proper engagement with it would require a detailed reading of *Zarathustra*, and would have to take into account interpretations of the kind developed by Gary Shapiro, who has argued that the central teaching of the book, the doctrine of eternal return, entails a 'radical dissolution of selfhood' (Shapiro 1989: 86). According to Shapiro's reading, the significance of the doctrine of return is that it surrenders the search for a foundation which would secure a ground on which to base a notion of the human self as coherent and integrated, as fully present to itself (Shapiro 1989: 92). In contrast to Irigaray's reading, he is suggesting that what Nietzsche is putting forward in *Zarathustra* is not a notion of the self as hegemonic and imperial, but rather one which exceeds the boundaries of a narrowly defined identity and is overfull in its openness to otherness and the world. Equally important to consider in this context, however, is Peter Sloterdijk's (1988) challenging reading of Nietzsche, which argues that the conception of autonomy, of self-creation through self-birth (the autogenesis of the subject), to be found in Nietzsche's work (notably the opening of the second essay of the *Genealogy of Morals*), is a 'masculine' one. It is masculine, Sloterdijk argues, in the sense that the subject posited is one which must stand its own ground, independent, beautiful and proud, and suppress what it regards as the horror and ugliness of its own birth: a birth in which it was in a relationship of dependency. Nietzsche speaks of the necessity of ridding oneself of the nauseous view presented to us by the miscarried, the stunted and the poisoned (Sloterdijk 1988: 110–11). Sloterdijk raises the crucial question, I think, when he asks: is not 'this self-birthing . . . only the exertion of the original evasion of an unbearable origin?' (Sloterdijk 1988: 110). Nietzsche's evasion of his – and our – human, all too human origin, results in a hatred of the mediocre, the handicapped, the feminine and the natural (see Sloterdijk 1988: 109).

In *Zarathustra* Nietzsche construes male–female relationships in accordance with his aristocratic prejudices. For example, in the discourse on 'Of Old and Young Women', man is conceived in terms of 'depth' and woman in terms of 'surface'. A strict apartheid is to govern their relationship: whereas the man is simply a means for the woman (the end is the child: 'everything about woman has one solution: it is called pregnancy'), for the man the woman is both danger and play: 'Man should be trained for war and woman for the recreation of the warrior: all else is folly'. Moreover, 'The man's happiness is: I will. The woman's happiness is: He will' (Nietzsche 1961: 91–2). Nietzsche's presumptions here are sexist because he conceives of woman's 'shallowness' not, as Derrida claims, because she is a 'mystery' and an 'ambiguity', but because she is a 'lack': woman needs a man to give her depth.

This fact alone explains why feminists can take such serious offence at what Nietzsche says. The insensitivity of Derrida on this point is incredible. Instead of recognizing the problematic nature of Nietzsche's description of woman as 'artistic', Derrida blindly and stupidly affirms it. What is disturbing about Derrida's affirmation of Nietzsche, and corresponding negation of feminism, is that it seems to rest on the presumption that it requires a male philosopher to instruct woman on the depths (the profundity!) of her superficiality and shallowness.

WOMAN AND POLITICAL THEORY

Nietzsche, I would argue, can become important for radical thought today only when the question of style is transformed into a question of politics. To begin with, the question of the 'feminine' has to be linked up with the history of women's oppression and of patriarchy. These are not two separate issues: the exclusion of the feminine from philosophy corresponds to the exclusion of women from public life and the supremacy of 'masculine' values over 'feminine' ones in political life. Even when a western philosopher, such as Plato for example, seems to go against the grain and to grant equality to women, this is only in so far as women subdue their female qualities (emotion, passion, intuition, etc.), and acquire male characteristics. As Diana Coole notes, 'Emancipated women are consequently those who approximate the male norm: they are rational, repressed, self-disciplined, autonomous, competitive, and so on' (Coole 1988: 3). Even when Nietzsche celebrates the body, *whose* body is it that is being affirmed?

The discourse of political theory has been established on the basis of a series of oppositions (male/female, reason/desire, public/private), which presuppose the validity of the historical construction of the self as a juridical subject. This self is not neutral but 'male', replete with 'masculine' virtues and values. As feminists repeatedly emphasize, what we are is not 'nature' but 'history'. William Connolly (1988) has argued that Nietzsche is an important theorist to draw on for a radical politics in that, although he himself ends up espousing a dubious aristocratic conservatism, his genealogy of the moral subject undermines such a position by showing that the subject is a material construction which depends for its identity on the negation and exclusion of forms of otherness (judged in terms of deviancy, irrationality, perversity, etc.) that are deemed to be socially inferior and which are politically marginalized (Connolly 1988: 156–7). As Rosalyn Diprose (1989) has argued, this notion of the subject as a social and historical construction poses an important challenge to the notion of the subject to be found in liberal political thought, where its existence is simply taken for granted and its rationality and autonomy assumed. It is clear that our identities as political and legal subjects have been constructed on the basis of a negation of 'woman' and the 'feminine' as forms of otherness. Thus, a postmodern (as in 'post-man') politics must place at the top of its agenda the issue of sexual difference. Nancy Fraser and Linda Nicholson provide a useful definition of a 'postmodern feminism' in terms of a non-universalism which would replace unitary notions of 'woman' and 'feminine gender identity' with conceptions of social identity in which gender is treated as one relevant strand of the human being, along with class, race, ethnicity and sexual orientation, and which would allow political space for the construction of plural, heterogeneous, complex identities (Fraser and Nicholson 1988).

Hélène Cixous (1986), who like Irigaray has had to face the charge of biological essentialism in her effort to articulate a 'feminine writing', has responded with instruction on a number of difficulties surrounding such a radical project. One of the difficulties stems from the fact that otherness has never been tolerated in history, but has been perpetually subjected to reappropriation and assimilation. Equally important, Cixous urges us to speak with caution on the question of sexual difference, suggesting that the oppositions of 'man/masculine' and 'woman/feminine' should be used with qualification in order to recognize that not all men repress their femininity, while some women inscribe only their masculinity.

Thus, 'Difference is not distributed . . . on the basis of socially determined "sexes" ' (Cixous 1986: 81). She argues this precisely to warn against the dangers of lapsing into an essentialist interpretation. Instead she speaks positively and constructively of a possible future beyond metaphysics in which it would be possible to write a non-phallocentric history:

> There is 'destiny' no more than there is 'nature' or 'essence' as such. Rather, there are living structures that are caught and sometimes rigidly set within historicocultural limits so mixed up with the scene of History that for a long time it has been impossible (and it is still very difficult) to think or even imagine an 'elsewhere' . . .
>
> It is impossible to predict what will become of sexual difference – in another time (in two or three hundred years?) But we must make no mistake: men and women are caught up in a web of age-old cultural determinations that are almost unanalyzable in their complexity. One can no more speak of 'woman' than of 'man' without being trapped within an ideological theater where the proliferation of representations, images, reflections, myths, identifications, transform, deform, constantly change everyone's Imaginary and invalidate in advance any conceptualization.
>
> (Cixous 1986: 83)

What is to be imagined? Cixous invites us to conceive of a radical transformation of behaviour, roles, mentalities, and of politics, the effects of which are unthinkable from the narrow horizon of present perspectives. She singles out three things needed for radical reform: first, a general change in the structures of training and education (effecting the production and reproduction of meaning, myth and representation); second, a liberation of sexuality aimed at transforming each person's relationship to his or her body in the direction of an affirmation of bisexuality, so as to approximate 'the vast, material, organic, sensuous, universe that we are'; and third and final, political transformations of social institutions and structures, as there can be no change in libidinal economy without a change in political economy. The result of all this, as she points out, would be that what we interpret as 'masculine' and 'feminine' today would no longer remain, and neither would the common logic of difference be contained within the dominant opposition of a phallocentric mode of reasoning and a masculine form of politics (Cixous 1986). What is required to realize this task is the coming into being, the birth, of what Nietzsche named the over-human, that is new human beings who have gone beyond man the sick animal and constituted themselves as the over-human (*übermensch*). 'We', Nietzsche taught, 'must *become* those that we *are*'; in the words of Cixous: men and women who are 'complex, mobile, open' (1986: 84). In becoming those that they 'are', the overhuman ones will become men and women whose identities surpass anything even Nietzsche could have imagined in his wildest dreams.

Ultimately it is necessary to recognize and locate a real ambiguity at the heart of Nietzsche's thinking; namely that it is caught in a tension between two quite different libidinal economies. On the one hand, it manifests an 'economy of the proper' (of property, possession and appropriation), and on the other hand it expresses an 'economy of the gift' (of squandering – see the 'gift-giving virtue' in *Zarathustra*). Thus, the will to power in Nietzsche is posited *both* in terms of a will to mastery and in terms of a will to let go and let be (*Gelassenheit*). It is not hard to see where the resources reside in his work for current postmodern (post *man*) thinking on the feminine.

ACKNOWLEDGEMENTS

Some of the ideas developed in this chapter were first explored in essays published in *Political Studies* and *Journal of the History of Ideas*. I am grateful to the editors of both journals for allowing me to draw on this material.

NOTES

1 I am grateful to Margaret Whitford for drawing this article to my attention.
2 Nietzsche (1974: 60): 'The magic and the most powerful effect of women is, in philosophical language, action at a distance, *actio in distans*: but this requires first of all and above all – *distance*'. This idea of 'action at a distance', which Nietzsche uses to describe the effect of woman's presence (as received by the male philosopher), refers to an aspect of Newton's theory of gravity: namely, that which describes the instantaneous action between two gigantic bodies (such as the Sun and the Moon), even though they have no direct contact.
3 Margaret Whitford hits the nail on the head concerning the problematic status of Derrida's engagement with feminism, I feel, when she accuses his thought of 'utopian phantasy'. Her charge is that, instead of 'rearticulating' the question of sexual difference ('as it appears from the side of women'), Derrida's thinking *elides* it. She writes: 'If multiplicity is to be celebrated, it has to be *after* sexual difference and not, as at present, by simply bypassing it'. In other words, the danger of the kind of 'precipitate

celebration of sexual multiplicity' which marks Derrida's writing, is that it serves to confirm 'the sexual indifference of our culture, in which women's difference is not represented in the symbolic' (Whitford 1991: 83, 84).

BIBLIOGRAPHY

Ansell-Pearson, K. (1991) 'Nietzsche on autonomy and morality: the challenge to political theory', *Political Studies* 39(2): 270–86.

—— (1992) 'Who is the *übermensch*: time, truth, and woman in Nietzsche', *Journal of the History of Ideas* 53(2): 309–33.

Bergoffen, D. (1989) 'On the advantage and disadvantage of Nietzsche for women', in A. B. Dallery and C. E. Scott (eds) *The Question of the Other: Essays in Contemporary Continental Philosophy*, Albany, NY: State University of New York Press.

Braidotti, R. (1986) 'The ethics of sexual difference: the case of Foucault and Irigaray', *Australian Feminist Studies* 3: 1–13.

Canovan, M. (1988) 'On being economical with the truth: some liberal reflections', *Political Studies* 38(1): 5–20.

Cixous, H. (1986) 'Sorties', in H. Cixous and C. Clément, *The Newly Born Woman*, trans. B. Wing, Minneapolis, Minn.: University of Minnesota Press.

Connolly, W. E. (1988) *Political Theory and Modernity*, Oxford: Basil Blackwell.

Coole, D. (1988) *Woman and Political Theory*, Brighton, Sussex: Harvester Press.

Del Caro, A. (1990) 'The pseudoman in Nietzsche, or the threat of the neuter', *New German Critique* 50 (Spring/Summer): 133–56.

Deleuze, G. (1983) *Nietzsche and Philosophy*, trans. H. Tomlinson, London: Athlone Press.

Derrida, J. (1979) *Spurs: Nietzsche's Styles*, trans. B. Harlow, Chicago, Ill.: University of Chicago Press.

Diprose, R. (1989) 'Nietzsche, ethics, and sexual difference', *Radical Philosophy* 52 (Summer): 27–33.

Foot, P. (1991) 'Nietzsche's immoralism', *New York Review of Books*, 13 June: 18–22.

Fraser, N. and Nicholson, L. (1988) 'Social criticism without philosophy: between feminism and postmodernism', *Theory, Culture, and Society* 5 (June): 373–94.

Grosz, E. (1986) 'Irigaray and sexual difference', *Australian Feminist Studies* 2: 63–77.

Irigaray, I. (1985) *Speculum of the Other Woman* (orig. Paris 1974), trans. G. C. Gill, Ithaca, NY: Cornell University Press.

—— (1991) *Marine Lover of Friedrich Nietzsche*, trans. G. C. Gill, New York: Columbia University Press.

Kofman, S. (1988) 'Baubô: theological perversion and fetishism', trans. T. B. Strong, in M. A. Gillespie and T. B. Strong (eds) *Nietzsche's New Seas*, Chicago, Ill.: University of Chicago Press.

Mortley, R. (1991) *French Philosophers in Conversation*, London: Routledge.

Nietzsche, F. (1961) *Thus Spoke Zarathustra*, trans. R. J. Hollingdale, Harmondsworth: Penguin.

—— (1966) *Beyond Good and Evil*, trans. W. Kaufmann, New York: Random House.

—— (1967) *The Birth of Tragedy*, trans. W. Kaufmann, New York: Random House.

—— (1969) *On the Genealogy of Morals*, trans. R. J. Hollingdale and W. Kaufmann, New York: Random House.

—— (1974) *The Gay Science*, trans. W. Kaufmann, New York: Random House.

—— (1979) *Ecce Homo*, trans. R. J. Hollingdale, Harmondsworth: Penguin.

Oliver, K. (1984) 'Woman as truth in Nietzsche's writing', *Social Theory and Practice* 10(2): 185–99.

—— (1988) 'Nietzsche's woman: the poststructuralist attempt to do away with women', *Radical Philosophy* 48 (Spring): 25–9.

Rosen, S. (1989) 'Nietzsche's revolution', in S. Rosen, *The Ancients and the Moderns: Re-thinking Modernity*, New Haven, Conn.: Yale University Press.

Schutte, O. (1984) *Beyond Nihilism: Nietzsche without Masks*, Chicago, Ill.: University of Chicago Press.

Shapiro, G. (1989) *Nietzschean Narratives*, Bloomington, Ind.: Indiana University Press.

Sloterdijk, P. (1988) 'Eurotaoism', in T. Darby *et al.* (eds) *Nietzsche and the Rhetoric of Nihilism*, Ottawa, Ontario: Carleton University Press.

van der Will, W. (1991) 'Nietzsche and postmodernism', paper delivered at the annual Conference of the 'Friedrich Nietzsche Society', April 1991, University of Warwick, England.

Warren, M. (1988) *Nietzsche and Political Thought*, Cambridge, Mass.: MIT Press.

Whitford, M. (1991) *Luce Irigaray: Philosophy in the Feminine*, London: Routledge.

Winders, J. A. (1991) *Gender, Theory, and the Canon*, Madison, Wis.: University of Wisconsin Press.

3 Nietzsche and the stomach for knowledge

Elizabeth Grosz

If, as a kind of intellectual wager or experiment, we think of subjectivity as a flat surface, a surface of at least two dimensions, then the mind or psyche can be seen, as it were, as the inside plane of this surface, and the body as its outside, social plane. In keeping with this thought experiment, psychoanalysis and phenomenology can be regarded as knowledges concerned with the psychical inscription and coding of bodies, pleasures, sensations and experiences, a mode of psychical (re)tracing or writing that marks the 'inside' of this flat surface. What marks its 'outside' surface is more law, right, requirement, social imperative and custom, corporeal habits. If the psychical writing of bodies retraces the paths of biological processes using libido and desire as its marker-pen, then the inscription of the social surface of the body is the tracing of pedagogical, juridical, medical and economic imperatives, laws and practices on to the flesh to carve out a social subject as such, a subject capable of labour, of production and of manipulation, a subject both capable of acting as a subject, and, at the same time, capable of being deciphered, interpreted, understood; an 'appropriate' subject who functions socially and collectively as well as psychically and individually. Michel de Certeau (1979) argues that juridical inscriptions constitute the body as part of social or collective order, structuring the broad category of subjectivity which is required in particular epochs, while medical inscription constitutes the body as individualized, particularized:

This machinery transforms individual bodies into a social body. It brings to bear in these bodies the text of a law. Another machinery doubles itself, parallel to the first, but of medical or surgical, and no longer of the juridical type. It uses an individual and no longer collective therapeutics. The body that it treats is distinguished from the group. Only after having been a 'member' – arm, leg or hand of the social unit, or a meeting place of forces or cosmic 'spirits' – it gradually stood out as a totality with its diseases, its stabilities, its deviations and its *own* abnormalities. A long history has been necessary, from the fifteenth to the eighteenth centuries, for this individual body to be 'isolated', in the way in which one 'isolates' a body, in chemistry or in microphysics; for it to become the basic unit of a society in which it appeared as a miniaturization of the political and celestial order – a 'microcosm'.

(De Certeau 1979: 4–5)

Flesh, a raw, formless, bodily materiality, the mythical 'primary material', is constituted, through corporeal inscriptions (juridical, medical, punitive, disciplinary), as a distinctive body capable of acting in distinctive ways, performing specific tasks in socially concrete ways. Bodies are fictionalized, that is positioned by various cultural (religious, familial, secular, educational, etc.) narratives and discourses, which are themselves embodiments of canons, norms and representational forms; they are culturally established as living narratives, narratives not always or even usually transparent to themselves. Bodies become emblems, heralds, badges, theatres, tableaux, of social laws and rights, illustrations and exemplifications of law, in-forming and rendering the pliable flesh into determinate bodies, producing the flesh as a point of departure and a locus of incision, a point of 'reality' or 'nature' understood (always fictionally) as prior to, and the raw material of, social practices. De Certeau conceives of this intextuation of bodies as meeting limits imposed from two directions. On the one hand, there must be a certain resistance of the flesh, a residue of its materiality left untouched by the body's textualization; on the other hand, there is a limit imposed by the inability of particular texts or particular languages to say or articulate everything:

> This discursive image must inform an unknown 'real', formerly designated as 'flesh'. From the fiction to the *unknown* that will embody it, the relay is effected by instruments multiplying and diversifying the unforeseeable resistances of the body to (con)formation. Between the tool and the flesh, there is . . . a play which is translated on the one hand by a change in the fiction . . . and on the other, by a cry, an inarticulate, unthought suffering of corporeal difference.

(De Certeau 1979: 8)

The subject is thus marked as a series of (potential) messages or inscriptions from/of the social (Other). Its flesh is transformed into a *body* organized and hierarchized according to the requirements of a particular social and familial nexus. The body becomes a 'text', is fictionalized and positioned within myths and belief-systems that form a culture's social narratives and self-representations. In some cultural myths, this means that the body can be read as an agent, a contractual, exchanging being, a subject of social contracts; while in others, it becomes a body-shell capable of being overtaken by the other's messages (for example, in shamanism or epilepsy). Social narratives create their characters and plots through the textualiz-ation of the body's contours and organic outlines by the tools of body-writing. Writing instruments confine and constitute corporeal capacities, both stimulating and stifling social conformity (the acting out of these narratives as 'live theatre' and a corporeal resistance to the processes of social inscription). The consequences of this are twofold: the 'intextuation of bodies', which transforms the discur-sive apparatus of regimes of social fiction/knowledge, 'correcting' or updating them, rendering them more 'truthful' and ensuring their increasingly microscopic focus on the details of psychical and corporeal life; and the *incarnation* of social laws in the movements, actions, behaviours and desires of bodies.

Where models of the subject as psychical interior introduce the dimension of social relations and the external world through notions of 'bringing in', that is introjection and incorporation, implying that the social 'enters' the subject through the mediation and internaliz-ation of social values and mores (usually by means of some kind of identification with social representatives such as the parents), the model of social inscription I shall elaborate here, by contrast, implies that social values and requirements are not so much incul-cated into the subject through a kind of ideological absorption or interpellation (this is how psychoanalysis has been used by feminists to explain the functioning of patriarchal ideology) as etched upon the subject's body. This may explain why the problematic of sociali-zation – which provides the model for understanding the trans-mission and reproduction of social values – is replaced, in models of social inscription, with the problematic of *punishment*; that is why law and constraint replace the model of desire and lack. Desire, through its constitutive lack, induces the subject from within to accept the mediation of social regulations in its attempts to gain gratification (Freud's distinction between the pleasure principle and the reality principle), in other words, there is something already inside the subject (need, desire) that impels it towards others, and through others, to the social. On the inscriptive model, on the contrary, it is the social exterior, or at least its particular modes of inscription, that commands or induces certain kinds of behaviour and practices. Punishment is the 'externalized' counterpart of social-ization; both are forms of codification of the social on to the cor-poreal, though from two different directions.[1]

The notion of corporeal inscription of the body-as-surface, as it is primarily developed in a number of scattered writings of Nietzsche, rejects the phenomenological framework of intentionality and the psychoanalytic postulate of psychical depth; the body is not a mode of expression of a psychical interior, nor a mode of communication or mediation of what is essentially private and incommunicable. Rather, it can be understood as a series of surfaces or energies and forces, a mode of linkage, a discontinuous series of processes, organs, flows and matter. The body does not hide or reveal an otherwise unrepresented latency or depth, but is a set of operational linkages and connections with other things, other bodies. It is a series of powers and capacities, micro-wills, forces, impulses, trajectories. The body is not simply a sign to be read, a symptom to be deciphered, but a force to be reckoned with.

If on the psychical view the body is the external expression of an interior, on this other view it is seen as a pure surface represent-ing nothing. In the first case, metaphors of latency, depth, interior-ity, inside are crucial; while the image of the flat surface, a pure externality, is central to the second. For the first, the body needs to be interpreted, read, in order to grasp its underlying meaning; for the second, the body is a surface to be inscribed, written on, which can be segmented, dissolved into flows or seen as a part (or parts) of a larger ensemble or machine, when it is connected to other organs, flows and intensities.

It is my task in this chapter to explore the various fragments, paragraphs and occasional references that Nietzsche makes regard-ing the ways in which subjectivity itself may be reconsidered, not in terms of a body clothing or housing a psychical interior or soul, but in terms of the body as writing surface for the inscription, the production, of interiority. In my reading, I shall not so much try to link these fragments and provide a more systematic or coherent account than Nietzsche's – a sure-fire way of taming and muting the power of his insights; rather I shall attempt to refract through his fragments, the insights of a number of theorists who have fol-lowed in his wake – particularly Foucault, Deleuze and Guattari,

Lyotard and Lingis – themselves all theorists of a 'flat' subjectivity, a subjectivity composed of planes, surfaces, matter rather than emotions, attitudes, beliefs: all theorists, that is, of what might be called an asubjective subjectivity.

NIETZSCHE, KNOWLEDGE AND THE WILL TO POWER

Nietzsche does not have a coherent theory of the body as such. However, there are abundant references in most of his writings to the body, and from them it may be possible to extract an account (even if not a coherent theory) of his understanding of the body. Here I propose to explore the body's role on the one hand, in the production of knowledge and truth, and on the other, its relations to the will to power. Nietzsche's conception of the body, it should be noted, is considerably more positive and productive than Foucault's: for Foucault, the body is penetrated by networks and regimes of power-knowledge that actively mark and produce it as such: the body seems to be the passive raw data manipulated and utilized by various systems of social and self-constitution, an object more or less at the mercy of non-intentional or self-directed, conscious production; in Nietzsche, by contrast, it is the body, both at an intra-organic or cellular level, and as a total, integrated organism, an animal, that is active, the source and site for the will to power and the movement of active (as well as reactive) forces.[2] Knowledge and power are, for Nietzsche, the results of the body's activity, its self-expansion and self-overcoming. The will to power involves a struggle to survive, to grow, to overcome itself on the level of cells, tissues, organs, where the lower order bodily functions are subordinated to and harnessed by higher order bodily processes and activities (the brain being considered the highest (Nietzsche 1968: 348–9)). These forces and energies comprising the body are not in any sense reducible to atoms, elementary particles, objects or organs (Nietzsche strongly opposes both empiricism and one of its extreme forms, atomism) but is made up of forces, micro-wills which struggle amongst themselves – Nietzsche likens them to aristocratic nobles, social equals – for supremacy:

> The assumption of a single subject is perhaps unnecessary: perhaps it is just as permissible to assume a multiplicity of subjects whose interaction and struggle is the basis of our thought and our consciousness in general? A kind of aristocracy of cells in

which dominion resides? To be sure, an aristocracy of equals, used to ruling jointly and understanding how to command?

My hypothesis: The subject as multiplicity.

(Nietzsche 1968: 270)

Here Nietzsche suggests a kind of parallelism between the organic and the subjective: for just as the subject is a multiplicity of forces, so too, the organism is not singular and unified. It too is a series of interacting and conflicting energies which struggle among themselves, which gain dominion or become subordinated through the dominance of others. The unity (of either subject or body), if it is possible at all, is the result of the suppression or subordination of the multiple conflicting forces, the result of a fundamental *cruelty*. For Nietzsche, these organs, bodily processes, muscles and cells do not, indeed cannot, as the empiricist presumes, yield knowledge or even error; rather, the body necessarily generates and presumes interpretations, perspectives, partial and incomplete acquaintance which serves its needs in the world, and which may enhance its capacity and hunger for life. They enable the organism to function pragmatically in the world but do not yield truth or knowledge. The will to power is the drive towards self-expansion, the movement of becoming, for it increases the body's quantity and quality of forces and energies, a drive towards 'vigorous, free, joyful activity' (Nietzsche 1969: 33).

Instead of seeing the body in terms of the mind/body distinction, or regarding it as a substance to which various attributes, like consciousness, can be added, Nietzsche sees it more in terms of a political/social organization, but one in which there is a kind of chaos of whirling forces, defined in terms of their quantities and intensities more than in terms of distinct characteristics. These forces or energies (at both the levels of organic and inorganic matter) are divided into dominant or active, and subordinated or reactive forces:

A quantum of power is designated by the effects it produces and that which it resists. The adiaphorous state is missing. . . . It is a question of struggle between two elements of unequal power: a new arrangement of forces is achieved according to the measure of power in each of them.

(Nietzsche 1968: 633–4)

Active forces 'care' for, concern themselves with, only their own well-being and expansion; reactive forces, by contrast, give primary concern to active forces, finding their principle of action outside themselves. As Deleuze stresses in his reading of Nietzsche:

> even by getting together reactive forces do not form a greater force, one that would be active. They proceed in an entirely different way – they decompose; they *separate active force from what it can do*; they take away a part or almost all of its power. In this way reactive forces do not become active, but, on the contrary, they make active forces join them and become reactive in a new sense . . . when reactive forces separate it from what it can do.
>
> (Deleuze 1983: 57)

The active forces, within and outside the body, are noble, aristo-cratic, for they govern, they expand. Reactive forces are not weaker than active ones (on the contrary, they tend to overpower active forces and convert them into reactive forces); they are slavish in so far as they are adapted towards the active forces, reacting to their initiative and impetus:

> reactive force is:
> 1) utilitarian force of adaptation and partial limitation;
> 2) force which separates active force from what it can do, which denies active force . . . ;
> 3) force separated from what it can do, which denies or turns against itself . . .
>
> And, analogously, active force is:
> 1) plastic, dominant and subjugating force;
> 2) force which goes to the limit of what it can do;
> 3) force which affirms its difference, which makes its difference an object of enjoyment and affirmation. Forces are only con-cretely and completely determined if these three pairs of characteristics are taken into account simultaneously.
>
> (Deleuze 1983: 61)

Given the plasticity and mobility of active forces, and given that these forces are not governed by or directed towards pre-ordained objects, the body itself must be seen as a pliable and potentially infinitely diverse set of energies, whose capacities and advances can never be predicted. For Nietzsche, the body's capacity for becoming cannot be known in advance, cannot be charted, its limits cannot be definitely listed. The body itself, in its micro-forces, is always in a position of self-overcoming, the expansion of its capacities.

Out of the chaos of active and reactive forces comes a dominating force that commands, imposes perspective, or perspectives (for there is no implication of singularity here). Consciousness can be regarded as the direct product or effect of reactive forces in the governance of the body. Consciousness is, for Nietzsche, a belief, an illusion, on the one hand useful for life, a convenient fiction; on the other hand, an effect of the inwardly inflected, thwarted will to power or force that, instead of subduing other bodies and other forces, has sought to subdue itself.[3] The subject's psychical interior or 'soul' can be seen as nothing but the self-inversion of the body's forces, the displacement of the will to power's continual self-transformation back on to the body itself. In this sense, there is and has always only ever been body: consciousness, soul or subjectivity are nothing but the play of the body's forces that, with the help of metaphysics, have been congealed into a unity and endowed as an origin. The body's forces, instincts, are not simply part of nature or essence (both nature and essence are metaphysical descriptions of the play of forces in the will to power), they are entirely plastic, fluid, capable of taking on any direction and attempting any kind of becoming:

> All instincts that do not discharge themselves outwardly *turn inward* – this is what I call the *internalization* of man: thus it was that man first developed what was later called his 'soul'. The entire inner world, originally as thin as if it were stretched between two membranes, expanded and extended itself, acquired depth, breadth and height, in the same measure as outward discharge was *inhibited*.
>
> (Nietzsche 1969: 84–5)

Consciousness or psyche is an effect or consequence of the modulations and impulses of the body. It is for this reason Nietzsche suggests that looking inward, as is ordained by introspection or psychology, self-consciousness or self-reflection, is both illusory and misleading. Illusory, because the psychical interior is in fact a 'category', project or product of the body that, for various reasons (grammatical, cultural, habitual), has been mistaken for mind; and misleading, in so far as self-reflection, the goals of self-knowledge, mistakes an effect for a cause, mistakes an instrument or tool with its producer:

> We psychologists of the future – we have little patience with introspection. We almost take it for a sign of degeneration when an instrument tried 'to know itself': we are instruments of knowl-

edge and would like to possess all the naivete and precision of an instrument – consequently we must not analyze ourselves, 'know' ourselves. First mark of the great psychologist: he never seeks himself, he has no eyes for himself, no interest or curiosity in himself.

(Nietzsche 1968: 230)

As that activity supposedly concerned with the activities of reason, knowledge, mind, philosophy is the discipline most implicated in a will to ignorance. It has resolutely ignored the body, leaving physiology to the medical disciplines. If it is true that 'Belief in the body is more fundamental than belief in the soul: the latter arose from unscientific reflection [on the agonies] of body' (Nietzsche 1968: 271), then philosophy is based on a disavowal of its corporeal origins and its status as corporeal product. The body is the intimate and internal condition of all knowledges, especially pertinently, of · that knowledge that sees itself as a knowledge of knowledges themselves – philosophy. But in order to see themselves as objective, true, valid for all, independent of formulation and context, outside of history, immutable, knowledges must disavow or deny that they are the consequence not only of particular bodies, but, even more narrowly, of particular, dominant forces or passions of the body. A genealogy of various epistemological attitudes and ontological commitments could be devised such that their origin in bodily states, carnal motives and physiological processes may be discerned. Just as all moral virtues are, at base, the misrecognized effects of corporeal processes,

> All virtues are physiological *conditions*: particularly the principal organic functions considered as necessary, as good. All virtues are really refined *passions* and enhanced states.
>
> Pity and love of mankind as development of the sexual drive. Justice as the development of the drive to revenge. Virtue as pleasure in resistance, will to power. Honor as recognition of the similar and equals-in-power.
>
> (Nietzsche 1968: 148)

so too are philosophical principles, procedures, concepts and systems. In this sense, philosophy can be seen as reactive force, a *ressentiment*, a certain fleeing before life and the world in which we live, a fear of and reaction to the body's activity, its constitutive role in the production of language, values, morals, truths or knowledges:

Why philosophers are slanderers – The treacherous and blind
hostility of philosophers towards the senses – how much of mob
and middle class there is in this hatred!
    . . . if one wants a proof of how profoundly and thoroughly
the actually barbarous needs of man seek satisfaction, even when
he is tamed and 'civilized'. One should take a look here at the
'leitmotifs' of the entire evolution of philosophy – a sort of
revenge on reality, a malicious destruction of the valuations by
which men live, an unsatisfied soul that feels the tamed state as
a torture and finds a voluptuous pleasure in a morbid unraveling
of all the bonds that tie it to such a state.
    The history of philosophy is a secret raging against the precon-
ditions of life, against the value feelings of life, against partisanship in favor of life. Philosophers have never hesitated to affirm
a world provided it contradicted this world.

(Nietzsche 1968: 253)

Just as all moral values are in fact bodily passions and energies
which are misrepresented as the products of mind or reason, so
too, knowledges, including the sciences, are functions or effects of
the knower's corporeality:

Through the long succession of millennia, man has not known
himself physiologically: he does not know himself even today.
To know, for example, that one has a nervous system (– but
no 'soul' –) is still the privilege of the best informed. . . .
One must be very humane to say 'I don't know that', to afford
ignorance.

(Nietzsche 1968: 229)

Philosophy, and knowledge more generally, are not only dependent
for their conceptual origins on the body and its forces. Philosophy,
and its privileged object, truth, are ultimately dependent on language. Truth is, for Nietzsche, nothing but a set of congealed or
frozen metaphors whose metaphorical status has been mistaken for
the literal: 'What is truth but a mobile army of metaphors . . . ?'
And language itself, he suggests, is at base, corporeal. Words are
doubly metaphorical: as he claims in *On Truth and Lies in an Extra-
Moral Sense*, they are transcriptions or transpositions of images,
which are themselves transpositions of bodily states:

This creator only designates the relations of things to men, and
for expressing these relations he lays hold of the boldest metaphors. To begin with, a nerve stimulus is transferred into an

image: first metaphor. The image, in turn, is imitated in a sound: second metaphor.

(Nietzsche 1979: 82)

Philosophy is not, in spite of its self-representation, a rational, intellectual system of inquiry and knowledge acquisition, based purely on truth considerations and the requirements of conceptual coherence. It is a practice, a strategy, and thus part of a struggle, a battle. Philosophy is not a reflection on things or concepts from a transcendent position; it is a practice that *does things*, legitimizing and challenging other practices, enabling things to happen or preventing them from occurring. For Nietzsche, knowledges in general, and philosophy in particular, are drives for mastery – consequences of the will to power. Far from being contemplative reflection, philosophy is a consequence of the drive to live, to conquer, a will to power that is primarily corporeal. Philosophy is a product of the body's impulses that have mistaken themselves for psyche or mind. Bodies construct systems of belief, knowledge, as a consequence of the impulses of their organs and processes. Among the belief systems that are the most pervasive, long-lived and useful are those grand metaphysical categories – truth, subject, morality, logic – which can all be read as bodily strategies, or rather, resources, which contribute to the will to power. For example, to posit a 'doer' beyond the 'deed' is a useful or enabling fiction, a fantasy that helps to expand the body's drive to life, to joy, to power.

If knowledge is or has been unable to acknowledge its own history, origin or genealogy in the history and functioning of the body, none the less, it can be judged and assessed, not in terms of its truth, its internal consistency, its parsimony or its use of minimal ontological commitments – that is what it is in its own self-representations – but rather, in terms of its effects, what it does, what it enables bodies, powers, to do. If its 'origin' and history are the consequences of reactive forces, then nevertheless, it can be actively affirmed, positively retrieved and used for self-expansion, if its limits, its corporeal status and its ends are more clearly, powerfully, understood: 'Truth is the kind of error without which a certain species of life could not live. The value for life is ultimately decisive' (Nietzsche 1968: 272).

Beliefs are adjuncts to the senses, modes of augmentation of their powers and capacities; and, like the senses, they yield interpretations, perspectives, and not truths, perspectives which may be life-enhancing, which may favour movement, growth, vigour, expansion. Knowledge has survival value rather than truth value. These perspectives are not a partial view of an abiding, inert unchanging object; they are the modes of differential production of the 'object'. They are all that there is. The appearance discerned, constituted through perspective, is a generative, differential power or force.[4] Where knowledge exists, it is not a transparent reflection, a meditative proposition, pure ideality, but an ability or resource. It is for this reason that the body can be said to have a 'great intelligence', that muscles, tissues, cells, have knowledge, memory:

> I wish to speak to the despisers of the body. Let them not learn differently nor teach differently, but only bid farewell to their own bodies – and so become dumb . . .
>   . . . the awakened, the enlightened man says; I am body entirely, and nothing beside; and soul is only a word for something in the body.
>   The body is a great intelligence, a multiplicity with one sense, a war and a peace, a herd and a herdsman.
>   Your little intelligence, my brother, which you call 'spirit', is also an instrument of your body, a little instrument and toy of your great intelligence.
>   You say 'I' and you are proud of this word. But greater than this – although you will not believe in it – is your body and its great intelligence, which does not say 'I' but performs 'I'.
>
> (Nietzsche 1961: 61–2)

The will to power animates, moves, energizes and strives to proliferate. This may explain why Nietzsche insisted on a new type of philosophy or knowledge, one which, instead of remaining sedentary, ponderous, stolid, was allied with the arts of movement: theatre, dance and music. Philosophy itself was to be written walking – or preferably, dancing. This is because philosophy itself is a bodily activity, and is capable, if wrenched from the hands of the most reactive forces (ascetics, priests of various kinds), of dynamizing and enhancing life, producing great joy, flight. Philosophy, truth, are capable of affirming active power when they, in their turn, return power and force to the body from which they derive. In so far as philosophy is capable of providing resources for the lifting of the body higher, the elevation of its forces and perspectives, it is capable of reversing its reactive status:

> In the main, I agree more with the artists than with any philosopher hitherto: they have not lost the scent of life, they have

loved the things of 'this world' – they have loved their senses. To strive for 'desensualization': that seems to me a misunderstanding or an illness or a cure, where it is not merely hypocrisy or self-deception. I desire for myself and for all who live, *may* live, without being tormented by a puritanical conscience, an ever-greater spiritualization and multiplication of the senses: indeed, we should be grateful to the senses for their subtlety, plenitude, and power and offer them in return the best we have in the way of spirit. What are priestly and metaphysical calumnies against the senses to us!

(Nietzsche 1968: 434)

Where philosophy, or what counts as truth, enhances the body's capacities, enlarges its powers of becoming, intensifies the body's sensations, makes it able to do other things in the world, such a philosophy is affirmative and productive of the overcoming of man, the production of new, hitherto unimagined possibilities, the transformation of man into the higher man:

Put briefly: perhaps the entire evolution of the spirit is a question of the body; it is the history of the development of a higher body that emerges into our sensibility. The organic is rising to yet higher levels. Our lust for knowledge of nature is a means through which the body desires to perfect itself or rather: hundreds of thousands of experiments are made to change the nourishment, the mode of living and of dwelling of the body: consciousness and evaluations in the body, all kinds of pleasure and displeasure, are signs of these changes and experiments. It is not a question of man at all: he is to be overcome.

(Nietzsche 1968: 358)

A knowledge that could acknowledge its genealogy in corporeality would also necessarily acknowledge its perspectivism, its incapacity to grasp *all*, or anything in its totality. Perspectives cannot simply be identified with appearance, underlying which there is an abiding and stable reality. Rather, there are *only* perspectives, *only* appearances, *only* interpretations. There is nothing beyond the multiplicity of perspectives, positions, bodily forces, no anchor in the real. The body itself is a multiplicity of competing and conflicting forces, which, through the domination of one, comes to have a perspective and position, one among a number of competing, or complementary, perspectives vying for ascendancy.

NIETZSCHEAN BODY-WRITING

Although Nietzsche defines and understands the body with reference to a concept of instincts that may at first appear ahistorical or
naturalistic, it is clear that he has a complex notion of nature that
precludes associating instincts with their usual biologistic and non-
historical connotations. Nature is not the origin, source or designer
of instincts; nature itself is a destination, product or effect. In man,
there is nothing natural, if by nature is understood what is inert,
transhistorical, governed by law, conquerable:

> How man has become more natural in the nineteenth century
> (the eighteenth century is that of elegance, refinement, and *senti-
> ments*) – Not 'return to nature' – for there has never yet been
> a natural humanity. The scholasticism of the un- and the anti-
> natural value is the rule, is the beginning; man reaches nature
> only after a long struggle – he never 'returns' – Nature: that is,
> daring to be immoral like nature.
>
> (Nietzsche 1968: 73)

In *On the Genealogy of Morals* Nietzsche outlines the rudiments of
an account of body-inscription as the cultural condition for establishing social order and obedience. This account is not disconnected
from his epistemological researches, his notion of the will to power
and his understanding of active and reactive forces. Active and
reactive forces are personified in *The Genealogy* through the figures
of the aristocratic noble and the base slave respectively. It should
be noted here that Nietzsche is not advocating feudal relations of
power and domination in any straightforward way: he is not simply
identifying these two types or categories of individual with pre-
existing class-based models. On the contrary, there are aristocratic
and base impulses within all individuals; and those individuals who
may belong to one class or another (by accident of birth or environment) may exhibit base and/or noble impulses. The values characterizing the noble assume a will to 'powerful physicality, a flourish-
ing, abundant, even overflowing health, together with that which
serves to preserve it: war, adventure, hunting, dancing, war games,
and in general all that involves vigorous, free, joyful activity' (Nietzsche
1968: 33). These values are self-directed and self-affirming
(not to mention virile!): the noble impulse is concerned with its
self-production and expansion independent of the other. It affirms
its own capacities as well as whatever contingencies may affect it.
It looks, not to the past but only to the future (the past tends to

tie and limit it to what has been, what grounds and contains it, while the future is open, limitless, capable of being infinitely characterized). It affirms its own possibilities of becoming joyously and without fear; it aspires to height, to power, to intoxication, revelling in its corporeality. Because the past is of little concern, the noble impulse is forgetful, retaining no memory, no nostalgia, no resentment; this leaves it always open to the intensities of the present, unclouded by previous impressions and impulses; it is dionysiac, dynamic, playful, celebratory. By contrast, the slavish impulse is always reactive. Its position is always dictated by *ressentiment* of the other, a desire for revenge, a mortal and self-converting hatred of the other, against which all its activities are measured. It functions surreptitiously, thwarted in acts, and thus enticed by imaginative wishes and fantasies. Slavish impulses are fundamentally negative; they always say no to 'what is "outside", what is "different", what is "not itself"'; and this No is its creative deed' (Nietzsche 1969: 36). It is thus always bitter, embittered by the world, by the activity of others and by its own frustrations. This resentment and spirit of hostility means that reactive or slavish forces are devious, deceptive, indirect, clever: 'His soul *squints*; his spirit loves hiding places, secret paths, and back doors, everything covert entices him' (Nietzsche 1969: 38). The slavish impulse never forgets; it is bound up with the past, and thus is incapable of openness to the present and future; all past incidents and events are recorded, stored, brooded over, and well up into an unsatisfied hostility. Where the noble soul has no memory, has cultivated forgetfulness, the soul of *ressentiment* cannot erase, cannot overcome.

If the aristocratic impulse can be illustrated with three privileged figures from Nietzsche's writings, they would be the artist, the noble and the sovereign individual, for they actively affirm the pleasures of life and the body, the power to forget and the power of will in making promises, respectively.[5] Each figure affirms 'his' power to intensify corporeal experiences, dreams, the past and the future. Counterposed to these figures of affirmation are the exemplars of *ressentiment*, the priest, the nihilist and the philosopher. The priest, the object of Nietzsche's most scathing condemnation, is the figure of hatred, hatred of this world and its replacement by another, more perfect; passive in the face of the world, the priest devises all manner of rationalizations to justify inertia, passivity and acceptance; like the nihilist and the philosopher, the priest turns away from the world, is disappointed with it and yearns for something other. They despise the body, the other and themselves.

Nietzsche focuses on the question of what kind of force is necessary to constrain and train reactive forces before culture can reach its pinnacle, the active 'man', the sovereign individual of the second essay of *The Genealogy*. What must culture resort to if it is always a struggle between the forces of action and those of reaction? How is the active, affirmative force capable of subduing the forces of reaction so that they can be acted out, converted into action, reversed in their very reversal of action into reaction, so that they can (re)turn to activity? Nietzsche's genealogy of morals is an attempt to read morality from the point of view of the confrontation of active and reactive forces, indeed, to explain their genesis in terms of corporeality:

> every table of values, every 'thou shalt' known to history or ethnology, requires first a *physiological* investigation and inter-pretation, rather than a psychological one; and every one of them needs a critique on the part of medical science.
>
> (Nietzsche 1969: 55)

Nietzsche wants to locate the primordial or mythical origins of culture in the ability to make promises, the ability to keep one's word, to propel into the future an avowal made in the past or present. This ability to make promises is dependent on the consti-tution of an interiority, a moral sense, a will. The will to remember, which Nietzsche characterized in this case as an active desire, a desire not to rid oneself, a desire for the continuance of something desired once, a *real memory of the will* (Nietzsche 1969: 58), is counterposed with and in opposition to the active will to forget, that mode of forgetfulness, necessary for 'robust health' which enables subjects not only to ingest and incorporate experience but also to digest and expel it (the alimentary metaphor is Nietzsche's), ready and open for new stimulation. The ability to make promises involves renouncing forgetfulness, at least in part, and, in spite of inter-vening events, being able to put intention or commitment into action. A counter-forgetfulness needs to be instituted.

Nietzsche's insight is that pain is the key term in instituting memory. Civilization instils its basic requirements only by branding the law on bodies through a *mnemonics of pain*, a memory fashioned out of the suffering and pain of the body:

> One can well believe that the answers and methods of solving

this primeval problem [the problem of how to instil a memory in the subject] were not precisely gentle; perhaps indeed there was nothing more fearful and uncanny in the whole prehistory of man than his *mnemotechnics*. 'If something is to stay in the memory it must be burned in: only that which never ceases to hurt stays in the memory' – this is a main clause of the oldest (unhappily also the most enduring) psychology on earth. One might even say that wherever on earth solemnity, seriousness, mystery and gloomy coloring still distinguish the life of man and a people, something of the terror that formerly attended all promises, pledges and vows on earth is *still effective*. . . . Man could never do without blood, torture, and sacrifices when he felt the need to create a memory for himself; the most dreadful sacrifices and pledges (sacrifices of the first-born among them), the cruelest rites of all the religious cults and all religions are at the deepest level systems of cruelties – all this has its origin in the instinct that realized that pain is the most powerful aid to mnemonics.

(Nietzsche 1969: 61)

The degree of pain inflicted, Nietzsche suggests, is an index of poverty of memory: the worse memory is, the more cruel are the techniques for branding the body. It is almost as if the skin itself served as a notebook, a reminder of what was not allowed to be forgotten. Where this procedure is internalized to form what is known as conscience, the less pain or sacrifice is required. The 'unforgettable' is etched on the body itself:

The worse man's memory has been, the more fearful has been the appearance of his customs; the severity of the penal code provides an especially significant measure of the degree of effort needed to overcome forgetfulness and to impose a few primitive demands of social existence as *present realities* upon the slaves of momentary affect and desire.

(Nietzsche 1969: 61)

The establishment of a memory is the key condition for the creation of social organization; it is also a cornerstone in the creation and maintenance of economic and contractual relations and systems of justice. For example, economic and social relations function only if the relation that bonds debtors to creditors is founded on some sort of contractual *guarantee* which ensures that debts, in some way or other, will always be paid. The presumption founding economic, social and judicial relations is that every debt and obligation has an equivalence, in the last instance, an equivalence between the debt owed and the pain the creditor can extract from the debtor. Pain becomes, in Deleuze's words 'a medium of exchange, a currency, an equivalent' (Deleuze 1983: 130). The cost or price of an unkept promise, an unpaid debt, an act of forgetfulness is the debtor's pain. This system of equivalences, which is very often carefully codified in terms of the precise values of body organs and intensities of pain, is the foundation of systems of justice; and the means justice uses to achieve such an equivalence is punishment. This equivalence ensures that, even in the case of economic bankruptcy, the debt is still retrievable from the body of the debtor, that in some sense at least, the debt can always be repaid. Nietzsche cites a number of examples from Roman law where

> the creditor could inflict every kind of indignity and torture upon the body of the debtor; for example, cut from it as much as seemed commensurate with the size of the debt and everywhere and from early times one had exact evaluations, all evaluations, of the individual limbs and parts of the body from this point of view, some of them going into horrible and minute detail. I consider it an advance, as evidence of a freer, more generous, more *Roman* conception of law when the Twelve Tables of Rome decreed it a matter of indifference how much or how little the creditor cut off in such cases.
>
> (Nietzsche 1969: 64)

Damages are not measured by equivalent, that is substitutable, values, as occurs in economic exchange, but by the extraction of organs, parts, forces and energies from the debtor's body. This is clearly a system of recompense through socially and juridically sanctioned cruelty. Contractual relations thus found justice – contrary to legal idealizations which based contractual connections on a prior system of justice – and both of these are themselves founded on blood, suffering and sacrifice. The equivalence of the pain caused to the debtor and the amount owed on the debt is the formula of the social contract. Any contract is thus ultimately founded on a kind of bodily collateral. The social order is not, contrary to Lévi-Strauss, founded on exchange, but on credit: on the rule that, at bottom, the body can be made to pay, to guarantee. The injury caused by the failure to keep promises, by the failure to pay off debts, by the failure to remember to what one is committed, is rendered commensurate with the degree of pain extracted from the body. This equivalence is rendered possible by, is itself founded on, the prior equivalence of the degree of suffering (of the debtor) with the degree of pleasure in causing suffering (for the creditor) – a kind of primitive, aristocratic urge to sadism:

> Let us be clear as to the logic of this form of compensation: it is strange enough. An equivalent is provided by the creditor's receiving, in place of a literal compensation for an injury (thus in place of money, land, possessions of any kind), a recompense in the form of a kind of *pleasure* – the pleasure of being allowed to vent his power freely upon one who is powerless, the voluptu- ·
> ous pleasure '*de faire le mal pour le plaisir de la faire*', the enjoyment of violation.
>
> This enjoyment will be the greater the lower the creditor stands in the social order, and can easily appear to him as a most delicious morsel, indeed as a creditor participates in a *right of the masters*: at last he, too, may experience for once the excited sensation of being allowed to despise and mistreat someone as 'beneath him'. . . . The compensation, then, consists in a warrant for and title to cruelty.
>
> (Nietzsche 1969: 64–5)

Significantly, a compensatory recourse not only to the debt owed, but also to class and social (though clearly not sexual) privilege is implied for the creditor here – a pleasure in the exercise of will alone, a pleasure sanctioned and approved, in which the debtor is now forced to participate in and to share the memory of the credi- tor. As far as Nietzsche is concerned, this debtor–creditor relation and its lust for cruelty is the basis of all other social relations, · moral values and cultural production. Morality and justice share a common genealogy in barter and cruelty: memory, social history, cultural cohesion are branded on to the flesh:

> it was in this sphere, the sphere of legal obligations, that the · moral conceptual world of 'guilt', 'conscience', 'duty', 'sacredness of duty' had its origin: its beginnings were, like the beginnings of everything great on earth, soaked in blood thoroughly and for a long time. And might one not add that, fundamentally, this world has never since lost a certain odor of blood and torture? (Not even in good old Kant: the categorical imperative smells of cruelty.) . . . To . . . what extent can suffering balance debts and guilt? To the extent that to make suffer was in the highest degree pleasurable, to the extent that the injured party

exchanged for the loss he had sustained, including the displeasure caused by the loss, an extraordinary counterbalancing pleasure: that of *making* suffer – a genuine *festival*.

Without cruelty, there is no festival: thus the longest and most ancient part of human history teaches – and in punishment there is so much that is *festive*.

(Nietzsche 1969: 66–7)

Although this socially validated system of cruelty and coercion stands at the (mythical) origins of civilization, as the system which institutes trust, faith and a common bond between individuals who share a culture, the advances of civilization are themselves no less cruel or corporeal: there has been a kind of social sublimation, a desensualization and a series of refinements to these processes of social engraving of the law on bodies but it remains more or less a requirement of the social taming of the will to power. The law today is no less corporeal, no more cerebral, just or fair than it has ever been; nor is it necessarily any kinder or more humane (a point Foucault stresses throughout his analysis of the history of punishment: there is no discernible enlightenment in the various historical transformations punishment has undergone):

Perhaps the possibility may even be allowed that this joy in cruelty does not really have to have died out; if pain hurts more today, it simply requires a certain sublimation and subtilization, that is to say, it has to appear translated into the imaginative and psychical and adorned with such innocent names that even the tenderest and most hypocritical conscience is not suspicious of them.

(Nietzsche 1969: 68)

The possibility of theorizing a 'cruelty principle' in place of Freud's pleasure principle remains an enticing even if a rather remote possibility. It would involve replacing the conception of the subject as an internalizing, absorbing interiority, regulated by its secret desires and pleasure, its own internal impetus, with a conception of the subject as a set of forces, materialities, energies, micro-wills, which face the world, and through this engagement, produce themselves, produce interiors, latencies, depths. It would involve rethinking the relations between the social and the subjective so they are no longer seen as polar opposites; rethinking all the productions of 'mind' – theory, knowledge, art, cultural practices – in terms of their corporeal formations; and rethinking notions of agency and political action in terms of micro-processes, thousands of sub-struggles and proliferating the field of politics and struggle so that it encompasses the entire social field. Force is the operative term in all psychical, subjective, social, political and aesthetic relations; but understanding these complexes or assemblages as force involves reconceptualizing how we understand each of these terms. The task remains ahead.

NOTES

This is a modified and shortened version of a chapter of my forthcoming, and as yet untitled, book on the body and sexual difference, to be published by Indiana University Press.

1 It is significant that the history of the concept of desire is itself a chart of the history and vicissitudes undergone by notions of corporeality. Although the correlation is not exact, there are, broadly speaking, two conceptions of desire – negative and positive – as there are (at least) two broad understandings of the body. The negative notion of desire, like the subordination of body to mind can be dated to the work of Plato. In *The Symposium*, for example, Socrates claims, in a speech to Agathon, that 'one desires what one lacks' (199e). Hegel, along with Freud and Lacan, continues this long tradition in so far as each sees desire as a yearning for what is lost, absent or impossible. Desire is posited in an economy of *scarcity*, where reality itself is missing something (the object whose attainment would yield completion), and linked to death (the struggle for mutual recognition) and annihilation (which the object of desire threatens). In opposition to this broad Platonic tradition is a second, less pervasive and privileged notion of desire, which may be located in Spinoza, in which desire is seen as a positivity or mode of fullness which produces, transforms and engages directly with reality. Instead of seeing desire as a lack, Spinoza, in *The Ethics*, lll, ix, sees it as a form of production, including self-production, a process of making or becoming. Nietzsche, Foucault, and particularly Deleuze and Guattari are contemporary examples of this second tradition:

> If desire produces, its product is real. If desire is productive, it can only be so in reality and of reality.
>
> (Deleuze and Guattari 1983: 26)

Where desire is construed as negative, a lack or incompletion it is a function and effect of the mind, psyche or idea: it is experiential; its phenomenal form dictates its key characteristics. Where desire is understood as positive production it is viewed 'behaviorally', in terms of its manifest connections and allegiances, its artifice, its bodily impetus.

2 See Lash (1984: 3–5).

3 'Consciousness is present only to the extent that consciousness is useful. It cannot be doubted that all sense perceptions are permeated with value judgements' (Nietzsche 1968: 274).

4 See Lingis (1985: 42–3).
5 'The artist is the first figure of powerful life. What is powerful in the artist is the compulsion to dream and the compulsion to orgiastic state. The noble is the second figure of powerful life. What is powerful in the noble is the power to forget. The third figure of powerful life is the sovereign individual. What is powerful in the sovereign individual is the memory of his will, his power to keep his word' (Lingis 1985: 58).

BIBLIOGRAPHY

De Certeau, M. (1979) 'Des outils pour écrire le corps', *Traverses* 14/15.

Deleuze, G. (1983) *Nietzsche and Philosophy*, trans. H. Tomlinson, London: Athlone Press.

Deleuze, G. and Guattari, F. (1983) *Anti-Oedipus: Capitalism and Schizophrenia*, trans. R. Hurley, M. Seem and H. R. Lane, Minneapolis, Minn.: University of Minnesota Press.

Foucault, M. (1977) *Discipline and Punish: The Birth of the Prison*, trans. A. Sheridan, London: Allen Lane.

Lash, S. (1984) 'Genealogy of the body: Foucault/Deleuze/Nietzsche', *Theory, Culture and Society* 2(2).

Lingis, A. (1985) 'The will to power', in D. B. Allison (ed.) *The New Nietzsche*, Boston, Mass.: MIT Press.

Nietzsche, F. (1961) *Thus Spoke Zarathustra*, trans. R. J. Hollingdale, Harmondsworth: Penguin.

—— (1968) *The Will to Power*, trans. W. Kaufmann, New York: Vintage.

—— (1969) *On the Genealogy of Morals and Ecce Homo*, trans. W. Kaufmann and R. J. Hollingdale, New York: Vintage.

—— (1979) *Philosophy and Truth*: *Selections from Nietzsche's Notebooks of the early 1870's*, ed. and trans. D. Breazeale, Atlantic Highlands, NJ: Humanities Press.

4 Not drowning, sailing

Women and the artist's craft in Nietzsche

Cathryn Vasseleu

With his incorporation of aesthetic values into western narratives of subjectivity, Nietzsche announces himself as a philosopher who is willingly seduced by art. Art is nothing less than the will to power, and it is in terms of being an artist that man (specifically)[1] achieves his unique powers of self-creation. If for other philosophers the corporeal self is something to be overcome by reason, for Nietzsche, the body is the desired effect of the will to power. · Corporeality is itself a work of art. But while the self is an aesthetic phenomenon, it is also the effect of an ethical disjunction between a present disposition, and an other being yet to be embraced.

There is an ambivalence towards this other which plays throughout Nietzsche's ethics of self-creation, expressed perhaps most strikingly in the breaks and convergences in Nietzsche's attitude towards women and towards the sea. This ambivalence creates a tension in Nietzsche's claims about the relationship between self and other in creative interpretation, and is symptomatic of a determination of the other which disrupts the artist's self-creating style.

On the one hand, Nietzsche conceives of interpretation as a productive violence, through which all values and all 'things' come into being. There is nothing but interpretation; the other is the creation of an exploitative and dominating will to power. Alternatively, life is drawn as that which exceeds and resists all measure. According to Nietzsche, its alterity renders the search for origin and essence a fanciful illusion – a quest whose trail ends in the interpretative action of the will. Its unknowability is celebrated by Nietzsche as a meaninglessness which glistens with possibility, and a horizon whose infinity bears no questioning.

This tension can be traced through Nietzsche's use of metaphors related to the sea.[2] The elemental conceptual significance of the sea in philosophical thought is evoked, for example, in Hume's comment:

"tis impossible to take possession of it, or form any such distinct relation with it' (1888: 511 note). For Irigaray (1991), the marine element evokes the amniotic fluid, or the asymmetry and irreversibility of an intra-uterine origin to which Nietzsche can never return. My aim is to critically explore the shifts and complexities which these metaphors set in motion, and to draw attention to woman's figuration within this movement. Although less intimate in its intention than Irigaray's marine lover, my approach is a responsive one. It is informed by and takes up Nietzsche's own ideas on the nature and role of metaphor in self-affirmation.

In the following aphorism, Nietzsche describes the powerful attraction and awe-inspiring danger of the sea to the lonely seafarer:

> *In the horizon of the infinite*: We have left the land and have embarked. We have burned our bridges behind us – indeed, we have gone farther and destroyed the land behind us. Now little ship, look out! Beside you is the ocean: to be sure it does not always roar, and at times it lies spread out like silk and gold and reveries of graciousness. But hours will come when you will realize that it is infinite and that there is nothing more awesome than infinity. Oh, the poor bird that felt free and now strikes the walls of this cage! Woe, when you feel homesick for the land as if it had offered more *freedom* – and there is no longer any 'land'.

> (Nietzsche 1974: 180)

The scene is Nietzsche's portrayal of the human condition once God has been pronounced dead. The metaphysical firmament which guaranteed values, authorized morality and inspired belief in ultimate truth has been dissolved, and Nietzsche's modernist subject has cast himself, like Columbus setting out from Genoa, to chart his own course on the amorphous infinity of life's possibilities. In order to become such a mariner, the nihilism which haunts the subject who would live without the assurance of ultimate truth must be embraced as a positively willed existence.

Oppositional values, upon which metaphysical authority is built, form the interpretative structure which Nietzsche (1969) seeks to expose in his genealogy of the fundamental conceptual oppositions generated by metaphysics. Nietzsche's hypothesis of the origin of 'bad conscience', or the reactive qualities which lead to resentment and inhibition of life affirming forces is described metaphorically as a consequence of life's emergence from the water and its shift to the land:

> I regard the bad conscience as the serious illness that man was bound to contract under the stress of the most fundamental change he ever experienced – that change which occurred when he found himself finally enclosed within the walls of society and of peace. The situation that faced sea animals when they were compelled to become land animals or perish was the same as that which faced these semi-animals, well adapted to the wilderness, to war, to prowling, to adventure: suddenly all their instincts were disvalued and 'suspended'. From now on they had to walk on their feet and 'bear themselves' whereas hitherto they had been borne by the water: a dreadful heaviness lay upon them.
>
> (Nietzsche 1969: 84)

The 'land' animals, or men of *ressentiment* came into being only through their opposition to an earlier noble, wild and freedom loving master race, in whom guilt, responsibility and consideration of others are entirely unknown in their creation of their own values:

> Their work is an instinctive creation and imposition of forms; they are the most involuntary, unconscious artists there are – wherever they appear something new soon arises, a ruling structure that *lives*, in which parts and functions are delimited and co-ordinated, in which nothing whatever finds a place that has not first been assigned a 'meaning' in relation to the whole.
>
> (Nietzsche 1969: 86–7)

Unlike these noble self-affirming masters, for whom life's changeable fluidity was made into apparent objects, bodies and things by the imposition of their own needs upon it, men of bad conscience were forced to vent their creative will on the manufacture of negative values. They turned to imposing form not on life but upon oneself as an ideal in opposition to life.

In contrast to oppositional values, Nietzsche describes another mode of interpretation which Derrida (1978: 292) has characterized as an affirmation which 'plays without security'.[3] Life, in its changeable ebb and flow, is a cause for celebration and pleasure, and art shows us that 'life is at the bottom of things, despite all the changes of appearances, indestructibly powerful and pleasurable' (Nietzsche 1967: 59). The apparent world is the world as it appears selectively to the beings who arrange it according to their own particular needs. Reality is the consequence of such arrangements (Nehamas 1985: 45–6).

The apparent incoherence of life is thus simply a misunderstanding of the nature of interpretation. Coherence is structurally imposed upon life, which has no intrinsic features of its own. The lack of any 'thing-in-itself' or origin of meaning allows for a fluidity of interpretation when form and meaning are recognized as nothing more than self-imposed values. This position does not lead to nihilism when its lack of fixity is taken up as one's life's potential for infinite changeability. Life cannot be construed as lacking in relation to any absent ideal, where all ideals, objects and categories are constituted solely through interpretation. Life has no ontological structure. Every different interpretation of the world manifests the will to power of those who engage in arranging it into a definite form of any kind (Nehamas 1985: 96–7).

For Nietzsche, the drive towards the formation of metaphors is the most fundamental human drive. A subjective relation to things is structured by metaphor. Nietzsche describes this progress as follows:

> To begin with, a nerve stimulus is transferred into an image: first metaphor. The image, in turn, is imitated in a sound: second metaphor. And each time there is a complete overleaping of one sphere, right into the middle of an entirely new and different one.
>
> (Nietzsche 1978a: 82)

Aesthetics is applied physiology (Nietzsche 1970: 664), but not in the scientific sense of physiology. Science denies that the will can be the cause of sensations, but is concerned instead with explaining them (Nietzsche 1968a: 352). According to Nietzsche, concepts are no more than rigidified metaphors, while myth and art are avenues for their free play. Only by forgetting the spacing of the primal world of metaphor can faith in any concept or object be sustained as *this* thing or truth. All truths are illusions which have forgotten that their origin is no more than illusion.

The metaphysical firmament from which the mariner has stepped, was a bondage to an other which shielded man from the painful task of discovering his own solitary creative powers. He has burnt his bridges and been delivered from the spirit of reactive being, for whom bridges are, until they fall, a means of avoiding the abyss, the flux; an assurance of the 'firmness' of concepts: 'all "good" and "evil" – all that is *firm*' (Nietzsche 1978b: 201). Elsewhere, we hear that this embarkation takes place from the shore of 'the blessed isles' (Nietzsche 1978b: 152, 155).[4] It is from these isles that Zarathustra first describes the sea in all its attraction, not as the infinity of an other (God) but as an infinity of one's own:

> Behold what fullness there is about us! And out of such overflow it is beautiful to look out upon distant seas. Once one said God when one looked upon distant seas; but now I have taught you to say: overman.
>
> (Nietzsche 1978b: 85)

To discover that God is a conjecture is a step towards self-affirmation, but to believe that man could create himself as the god of his own conjecture is the act which impels him towards the sea.

The attraction is not without apprehension and anticipated distress. Civilized man must take the painful and lonely journey back through his sickness of *ressentiment* and accumulated civilization in order to discover again the creative beast – the 'sea-animal' who must learn a new way to bear himself (Nietzsche 1969: 84). Self-creation requires first of all an endless forgetting of the distinction between self and other: 'For me – how should there be any outside –myself? . . . There is no outside' (Nietzsche 1978b: 217). Standing high on the ridge of the blessed isles, Zarathustra is confronted by the significance of his choice to take to the sea:

> Now my ultimate loneliness has begun.
>
> Alas, this black sorrowful sea below me! Alas, this pregnant nocturnal dismay! Alas, destiny and sea! To you I must now go *down*! Before my highest mountain I stand and before my longest wandering; to that end I must first go down deeper than ever I descended – deeper into pain than I ever descended down into its blackest flood. Thus my destiny wants it. Well, I am ready. . . . It is out of the deepest depth that the highest must come to its height.
>
> (Nietzsche 1978b: 154)

However, this moment of reflection describes the anticipation of a different experience of the sea to that anticipated by a seafarer. Zarathustra is describing a going *under*, becoming fluid, becoming the sea which absorbs and dissipates all reactive values before he can achieve the height of his powers:

> One must be a sea to be able to receive a polluted stream

without becoming unclean. Behold I teach you the overman: he is this sea; in him your great contempt [for man] can go under.
(Nietzsche 1978b: 13)

Zarathustra celebrates the capacity to become a fluid outpouring. He is a lake, and then a river which rushes to join the sea:

Let the river of my love plunge where there is no way! How could a river fail to find its way to the sea? Indeed, a lake is within me, solitary and self-sufficient; but the river of my love carries it along, down to the sea.
(Nietzsche 1978b: 84)

Here we read of Zarathustra's outpourings merging with the sea. In the next breath he yearns to be sailing across it:

Like a cry and a shout of joy I want to sweep over wide seas, till I find the blessed isles where my friends are dwelling.
(Nietzsche 1978b: 84)

Becoming the sea and being borne by water – Nietzsche oscillates between these two states. The figure, which appears in the latter and distinguishes it from the former, is the boat which carries the mariner over the flood he both feels himself as being and resists becoming. The mariner feels the sea beneath him but remains divided from it because of his craft.

This (surface) tension has its parallel in the *Apollonian* and *Dionysian* duality which Nietzsche discerns in artistic creativity. Apollo is the god of sculpture, of dreams and beautiful illusions, of calm and measured restraint that brings forth life as perfect forms and images in contrast to the confusion of daily existence. These images are not valued for their truth, but for their power to make visible what would otherwise remain invisible (Lingis 1985: 46). Nietzsche likens Apollo to Schopenhauer's description of the man wrapped in the veil of illusion, which he quotes:

'Just as in a stormy sea that, unbounded in all directions, raises and drops mountainous waves, howling, a sailor sits in a boat and trusts in his frail bark: so in the midst of a world of torments the individual human being sits quietly, supported by and trusting in the *principium individuationis*.' In fact, we might say of Apollo that in him the unshaken faith in this *principium* and the calm repose of the man wrapped up in it receive their most sublime expression; and we might call Apollo himself the glorious divine image of the *principium individuationis*, through whose gestures and eyes all the joy and wisdom of 'illusion', together with its beauty, speak to us.

(Nietzsche 1967: 35–6)

Dionysus, on the other hand, is the god of intoxication, demented flowering, of dance, music, of reaffirmation of the union between man and nature, beyond speech, beyond cognition. Dionysian dissolution of the ego is not the outcome of alienation, but rather, a voluptuous compulsion; art functioning organically as sexual excitation (Nietzsche 1968a: 426). As Nietzsche writes in *The Birth of Tragedy*:

> Either under the influence of the narcotic draught, of which the songs of all primitive men and peoples speak, or with the potent coming of spring that penetrates all nature with joy, the Dionysian emotions awake, and as they grow in intensity everything subjective vanishes into complete self-forgetfulness.
>
> (Nietzsche 1967: 36)

These two principles – Dionysian and Apollonian – are both contradictory and interdependent aspects of artistic genius, following and augmenting one another (Nietzsche 1967: 49). The multiplicity and exuberance of Dionysian emotion must employ Apollo's veil to bring itself forth, that is to stage itself as a work of art. Dionysian genius without the images of the god Apollo would remain nothing but primordial emptiness. The world of images and symbols grows out of this void. Apollo, likewise, reveals the language of Dionysus when he obscures the play of multiplicity and ambiguity disguised in every moment of appearance. The artist can live happily in the insubstantiability of images, while maintaining his individuation or distance: 'by this mirror of illusion, he is protected against becoming one and fused with his figures' (Nietzsche 1967: 50) However, Apollo's beautiful clear images are the 'mere appearance of mere appearance' (Nietzsche 1967: 45) – the metaphor of Dionysian metaphor, which is forgotten in the superficial moment of artistic illusion (Blondel 1988: 173).

Art is conceived by Nietzsche as 'the *good* will to appearance', the heroic foolishness which allows us to *float* above all seriousness and fixity of truth (Nietzsche 1974: 163). The principles of Apollo and Dionysus, which come together in Greek tragedy, represent a celebration of surface appearance, of the superficial image:

> Oh, those Greeks! They knew how to live. What is required for that is to stop courageously at the surface, the fold, the skin, to

adore appearance, to believe in forms, tones, words, in the whole Olympus of appearance. Those Greeks were superficial – *out of profundity*.

(Nietzsche 1974: 38)

In *Thus Spoke Zarathustra* and subsequent works, Nietzsche subsumes the two principles under the one phenomenon – the will to power. Apollo's use of Dionysus becomes the 'self-overcoming' of man's undisciplined animality, while Dionysus becomes synonymous with the *overman*, the man in whom the will to power has been sublimated into a purely creative force (Nietzsche 1968b: 198, Appendix H). The way of Dionysian creativity is to adore the surface, to celebrate life in its blind, changeable ebb and flow, to become one with the images and forms by which higher man expresses himself.

On his journey towards the overman, Zarathustra discovers that the sea is no more profound than its surface. There is nothing to be gained by delving into its mysteriousness. There is no mystery – only one's failure to grasp that this 'mystery' is one's own projection:

> Into your eyes I looked recently, O life! And into the unfathomable I then seemed to be sinking. But you pulled me out with a golden fishing rod; and you laughed mockingly when I called you unfathomable.
>
> 'Thus runs the speech of all fish,' you said; 'what *they* do not fathom is unfathomable. But I am merely changeable and wild and a woman in every way, and not virtuous – even if you men call me profound, faithful, eternal, and mysterious. But you men always present us with your own virtues, O you virtuous men!'
>
> (Nietzsche 1978b: 108)

In attempting to name life, Zarathustra is endowing it with his own value. The other is presented as nothing more than what he makes of it. To fathom it is to find only his own will in whatever image appears.

The relationship between self and other is an aesthetic relationship, entirely without causality. It is established by treating the self as the measure of all things and forgetting that perceptions themselves are metaphors and not things (Nietzsche 1978a: 79–91). Man builds his world with conceptual material which is first manufactured through interpretation:

> one may certainly admire man as a mighty genius of construction,

who succeeds in piling up an infinitely complicated dome of concepts upon an unstable foundation, his construction must be like one constructed of spiders' webs: delicate enough to be carried along by the waves, strong enough not to be blown apart by every wind.

(Nietzsche 1978a: 85)

An image is emerging of the boat in which Nietzsche's mariner has cast out to sea, to float, to travel the surface of the infinite ocean. The boat is made of his own metaphors, a gossamer fine enough to be forgotten, but strong enough to resist and cleave a way through the flood.

Nietzsche's seafarer navigates the ocean with *style*. The self is something that one constructs, or becomes through one's own actions, thoughts, desires. Style consists in the ability to hold together, in a coherent and harmonized fashion, the multiple powerful and conflicting drives which are the will to power.

> To 'give style' to one's character – a great and rare art! It is practiced by those who survey all the strengths and weaknesses of their nature and then fit them into an artistic plan until every one of them appears as art and reason and even weaknesses delight the eye. . . . In the end when the work is finished, it becomes evident how the constraint of a single taste governed and formed everything large and small.

(Nietzsche 1974: 232)

'Facility in self-direction' is what is meant by style and the freedom which it brings (Nietzsche 1968a: 375). What is essential to the creation of style is the ability to control and recognize every part of oneself as one's own – and this means being inspired and sustained by one's own interpretative powers.

Style has another dimension, described by Derrida as a *spur*. Style advances by force through that which presents itself, like a prow: 'the projection of the ship which surges ahead to meet the sea's attack and cleave its hostile surface' (1979: 39). Style protects its own being in its simultaneous appropriation and resistance of the other, whose alterity wavers in the distinction. Nietzsche maintains on the one hand that interpretation must be recognized as one's own – that the other is one's own metaphor. On the other hand, style is portrayed as thrusting aside the other which cannot be grasped except as metaphor. Meaning is no more than the trace, or the wake of the metaphor's displacement of the other and the appropriation of that mark as the thing itself; its content; its meaning.

Nietzsche appears to be making two conflicting claims about the other. First, there is no more to the other than one's own interpretation. Zarathustra claims that he *is* the sea. He also claims that he loves this sea both for its surface – upon which he floats, and its depths – which 'sparkle with swimming riddles and laughters' (Nietzsche 1978b: 116). However, although he loves the deep – 'like the sun I love life and all deep seas', it is because 'all that is deep shall rise up to my heights' (Nietzsche 1978b: 124). Likewise, as previously mentioned, life is described as something into which Zarathustra feels himself sinking, but from which he is also pulled out with a golden fishing rod (Nietzsche 1978b: 108). He acknowledges the deep but strives for its surface. The other has a displaced dimension which underlies and eludes metaphor. Here interpretation is not all there is, but all we have of life.

The need for a surface to disguise the depths points to a tension in relation to the other which Nietzsche discloses and denies with an ambivalence which makes him seasick (1978b: 213). There is no definitive other; only an illusion which is of his own making. Self and other dissolve in the process of self-overcoming, becoming instead the infinite Dionysian play of interpretation. 'I love those who do not want to preserve themselves. Those who are going under I love with my whole love: for they cross over' (1978b: 200).

Alternatively, interpretation needs a *difference* between self and other to claim the other as its own. Artistic creativity requires Apollonian distance to separate it from the depths – free spirit dances near but never into the abyss (Nietzsche 1974: 290).[5] It is the other's status as *illusion* which keeps the free spirit from actually drowning in his own infinity while keeping him on his stylish course upon it.

Woman represents for Nietzsche the value of appearance and the manner in which it achieves its spellbinding effect. Truth is a woman, that is the non-truth of appearance; dissimulation; a wench which cannot be won (Nietzsche 1973: 13). Woman's secrets are not there to be taken. Woman is changeability, a plastic image which has no truth to be dogmatically adhered to or believed in. She is truth precisely because she does not believe in the truth she is supposed to be, and takes herself to be no more than an image which in fact disguises nothing: 'Perhaps truth is a woman who has reasons for not letting us see her reasons? Perhaps her name is – to speak Greek – *Baubô*' (Nietzsche 1974: 38).[6]

In 'Women and their action at a distance', Nietzsche (1974: 123) uses the image of a sailboat gliding on the horizon to draw attention to the need for distance in order for this image to be appreciated *by him* as his own metaphor, his beautiful, illusory being:

> Yet! Yet! Noble enthusiast, even on the most beautiful sailboat there is a lot of noise and unfortunately much small and petty noise. The magic and the most powerful effect of women is, in philosophical language, action at a distance, *actio in distans*; but this requires first of all and above all – distance.
>
> (Nietzsche 1974: 123)

Woman is the image which reflects the style of the Dionysian spectator caught up in his own creative activity, who observes her at a distance great enough to fail to hear *her own* voice clanking with 'much small and petty noise'. While on the one hand, the falsity of an impression is what gives its recipient the space for fantasy, in this aphorism we also get glimpses and murmurs of the alterity of the other, which creates a tension within Nietzsche's own interpretation. He reveals this tension in recognizing the necessity for distance in order to make the other into his own image.

Woman's status as pure dissimilitude is important for the maintenance of Nietzsche's claim that there is no truth beyond appearance. Nietzsche is unable to propose a form of self-affirming value without first establishing that the other has no 'truth' of its own. Only then is there nothing to contest his own interpretation; that is what assures his *self*-preservation. Woman's superficiality is the condition of possibility of his own infinity. To maintain his determination of the superficiality of woman he requires distance from her, and with this distance comes the implication that something *more* than his own interpretation is being hidden by it.

Nietzsche's notion of active interpretation strains at the dependence on an independent other for the affirmation of one's own values. Nietzsche describes and dreams of a figure or power of woman who affirms herself and his own being simultaneously. This woman is the Dionysian principle of affirmative dissimulation, who dances only with those who have done with the need for an other whose value determines their own:

> perhaps this is the most powerful magic of life: it is covered by a veil interwoven with gold, a veil of beautiful possibilities, spark-

ling with promise, resistance, bashfulness, mockery, pity, and seduction. Yes, life is a woman.

(Nietzsche 1974: 272)

Woman is the life-affirming principle of the will to power, self-perpetuation, endless becoming. And having expressed his delight in her elusiveness and excess, Nietzsche's desire is to claim this excess as his own. Woman is the veil, or sail which captures and secures man's self-affirming flight across her surface. Possession of her 'veil of beautiful possibilities' guarantees his own infinite becoming. Becoming woman, becoming the mother who gives birth to himself (Nietzsche 1978b: 87) bearing oneself as a 'sea-animal' with its own sailing craft – these are all dreams of becoming *both* self and other.

Nietzsche acknowledges his dependence on the alterity of the other in his description of true friendship, whose productive value lies in the radical independence of both parties: 'in a friend one should have one's best enemy. You should be closest to him with your heart when you resist him' (1978b: 56), each inspiring the other on his own course: 'You cannot groom yourself too beautifully for your friend: for you shall be to him an arrow and a longing for the overman' (1978b: 56). Self-affirming values and the autonomy of the other go hand in hand.

Woman, however, does not have the independence necessary for friendship:

Are you a slave? Then you cannot be a friend. Are you a tyrant? Then you cannot have friends. All-too-long have a slave and a tyrant been concealed in woman. Therefore woman is not yet capable of friendship: she knows only love.

(Nietzsche 1978b: 57)

To be a slave is to be ruled by the morality of others. To be a tyrant is to be viewed by others as the law to which their will must submit itself. Slave and tyrant are figures caught within the production of reactive values. Nietzsche laments woman's capture within this structure. On the one hand, she is whipped into submissively espousing, without believing, the values and morality of others, and on the other hand, is an ideal which spurs man to seek truth beyond her appearance. Woman is both a figure or power of lying, and a figure or power of truth.[7] *Vita femina* is a third figure or power of woman as dissimilitude in the affirmative, Dionysian sense which Nietzsche dreams of embracing, but which is still caught within the 'truth' of the Eternal Feminine.

The need for Apollonian distance, veils and surfaces are witness to Nietzsche's acknowledgement that the joyous affirmation which plays without security is in fact at the mercy of an other which it both creates and would dominate, appropriate, assimilate as its own. *Vita femina* is that which eludes interpretation and is necessarily *more* than, that is, a gap in one's own self. Alterity is the spark which fires metaphors, and the quality whose denial dulls them into captured concepts and accepted, familiar truths:

> Also, and yet what *are* you, my written and painted thoughts! It is not long ago that you were still so many-coloured, young and malicious, so full of thorns and hidden spices you made me sneeze and laugh – and now? You have already taken off your novelty and some of you, I fear are on the point of becoming truths: they already look so immortal, so pathetically righteous, so boring! . . . we immortalizers of things which *let* themselves be written. . . . Alas, only birds strayed and grown weary in flight who now let themselves be caught in the hand – in *our* hand! . . . how you looked in your morning, your sudden sparks and wonders of my solitude, you my old beloved – *wicked* thoughts.
>
> (Nietzsche 1973: 201–2)

Nietzsche laments the moment of incorporation of the radically other as an accepted 'fact' of life, in which the distance between the 'you' and 'my' thoughts is no longer considered. The loss of strangeness is a loss of appreciation of the interpretative violence through which values come into being. To appreciate one's own creative powers is to also appreciate the need for an other whose strangeness and independence of will is the condition of possibility of those creative powers. One's self is not something created by the will alone, it has the instability of *conjunctions* which must be constantly negotiated.

The need for an independent other also presents difficulties for Nietzsche's doctrine of eternal recurrence. The test of the eternal return is the ability to recognize that every moment of one's life is the same moment which returns, in an infinite circle of becoming, to the will which created it and is inseparable from it. This reinterpretation of self is meant in an historical and cultural sense. Acceptance of the doctrine of eternal return implies an affirmation of the inevitable 'logic' of the will to power in all its creations. For

Nietzsche, the operation of interpretation can be construed either as a loss of confidence in any values in the face of a multitude of possibilities or, alternatively, the open-ended anticipation of another reinterpretation of self with every recurring moment. To accept that there is nothing more to existence than the eternal return of the same thing – oneself – 'how well disposed would you have to become to yourself and to life to *crave nothing more fervently* than this ultimate eternal confirmation and seal?' (Nietzsche 1974: 274).

The challenge to find this doctrine entirely acceptable is first presented to Zarathustra after he has stepped from the shore of the Blessed Isles and embarked with 'cunning sails on terrible seas' (Nietzsche 1978b: 156). The vision of the eternal return which comes to him aboard his ship brings together the dual moments of Dionysian multiplicity and Apollonian unity, and within the metaphor of Columbus, anticipates the mariner's dream of arrival at the shores of the new world, 'where only what is his and nothing alien may appear to his eyes' (Nietzsche 1974: 234).[8]

The infinity of the other is one's own Dionysian multiplicity; abandonment of security; unknown, anticipated, changing moment. Dionysus is the lightness of spirit which lives each moment for its fleetingness and because that moment is himself – his own metaphor, his autoerotic work of art. However, Nietzsche can claim his Dionysian multiplicity only by employing Apollo's veil and forgetting that he requires something irreducibly other to stand as guarantee of the *spacing* of each different apparent moment. This abyss of truth from whose imagined depths Nietzsche has hauled himself – remains *outside* of the circle of eternal recurrence. *Insistently*, Irigaray's marine lover reminds Nietzsche of what this wilful forgetfulness means for both of them. Instead, she announces her own return:

> You had fashioned me into a mirror but I have dipped that mirror in the waters of oblivion – that you call life. And farther away than the place where you are beginning to be, I have turned back. I have washed off your masks and make up, scrubbed off your veils and wraps that hid the shame of your nudity. I have even had to scrape my woman's flesh clean of the insignia and marks you had etched upon it.
>
> (Irigaray 1991: 4)[9]

The questionable alterity of *vita femina* is the tension which supports Nietzsche's vision of the overman:

If I am fond of the sea and of all that is of the sea's kind, and fondest when it angrily contradicts me; if that delight in searching which drives the sails towards the undiscovered is in me, if a seafarer's delight is in my delight; if ever my jubilation cried, 'The coast has vanished, now the last chain has fallen from me; the boundless roars around me, far out glisten space and time; be of good cheer, old heart!' Oh, how should I not lust after eternity and after the nuptial ring of rings, the ring of recurrence?

Never yet have I found the woman from whom I wanted children, unless it be this woman whom I love: for I love you, O eternity.

(Nietzsche 1978b: 230)

Although he may long for such a partner, *vita femina* must always elude him. For Nietzsche, woman acts out her indeterminacy – the non-truth of her appearance. However, she is a mask which casts the question of its possessor into doubt, and Nietzsche cannot know whether he is in possession of woman or fooled by her into believing that she is his (Spivak 1984: 22). Alternatively, he can lust after the infinity of her masks, but only by forgetting her, and claiming her appearances as his own dissimulating style. She does not figure independently of his own interpretation. She had no style of her own.

The vision of the eternal recurrence brings us back to Nietzsche's boat sweeping across the sea. Beneath the sea's surface is an abyss, an ungraspable dimension of the other which he celebrates, but ultimately prefers to gloss over, although it is the condition of possibility of each moment in the fluid eternity he claims as his own becoming. Nietzsche's affirmative being is borne by water, by a mirror surface whose incalculable depth is essential but must be pushed aside at every moment he remains afloat upon it. More precisely, Nietzsche's affirmative being is borne by his interpretations of woman. *Vita femina* is the abyss at whose edge he must strive to keep for fear of drowning. Woman is also the sail, the veil of dissimulation which spurs him on his stylish way. Finally, woman is the distant sailboat gliding over existence which he claims as the craft of his own creativity, but only by *first* maintaining that she is non-truth. Nietzsche's affirmative being clings to this determination of woman as the vessel of his own creative freedom, trying to forget that it is her alterity which gives, and robs the mariner of his infinite horizon.

NOTES

1 Although Nietzsche has been cast by some feminists as a misogynist *par excellence*, that is not the point I am making here. Rather, I am drawing attention to the fundamental ontological distinction which Nietzsche makes between the sexes. For a negotiation of this difficult terrain in feminist interpretations of Nietzsche see R. Diprose (1989) 'Nietzsche, ethics and sexual difference', *Radical Philosophy* 52 (Summer): 27–33.

2 Nietzsche's extensive use of sea imagery has been noted and taken up by many of his commentators and interpreters, for example Irigaray (1991); M. A. Gillespie and T. B. Strong (eds) (1988) *Nietzsche's New Seas*, Chicago and London: University of Chicago Press; and G. Parkes (1983) 'The overflowing soul: images of transformation in Nietzsche's *Zarathustra*', *Man and World* 16: 4.

3 As Pecora (1986) points out, the Nietzschean affirmation which 'plays without security' is not in any sense equivalent to a 'joyous affirmation of the play of the world'. To quote Pecora further: 'to the extent that "difference" has come to signify a freedom of play that does not in fact exist, and that does not seem capable of reflection upon such a condition, Nietzsche's work has only been turned into a fantastic escape from "history, nature, man himself" ': Pecora (1986) 'Deleuze's Nietzsche and post-structuralist thought', *Substance* 48: 34–50.

4 This is an allusion to the heaven in Plato's *Republic* (540b), to which the philosopher may travel only after the ideal state has been realized.

5 'One could conceive of such a pleasure and power of self-determination, such a *freedom* of the will that the spirit would take leave of all faith and every wish for certainty, being practiced in maintaining himself on insubstantial ropes and possibilities and dancing *near* [my emphasis] abysses. Such a spirit would be the *free spirit par excellence*.' Nehamas (1985: 61) uses the same emphasis to make a different point: free spirit must still employ ropes and avoid abysses, that is, that freedom does not consist in abandoning all rules and principles, but rather, in their incorporation into self.

6 *Baubô* is an obscene female demon, originally the personification of the female genitals (Nietzsche 1974: 38, Kaufmann's footnote 8). Kofman (1988) discusses the figuration of *Baubô* in Nietzsche's work.

7 See Derrida (1977: 185) for his summary of the different propositions of woman's value in Nietzsche's work. Spivak gives a critique of Derrida's analysis in 'Love me, love my ombre, elle' (1984) and in 'Displacement and the discourse of woman', in M. Krupnick (ed.) (1983) *Displacement: Derrida and After*, Bloomington, Ind.: Indiana University Press, pp. 169–95.

8 Note that Zarathustra is delivered ultimately from the sea, regaining again the *firmament* of a higher being – the overman, who has acquired the discipline to control values rather than be controlled by them.

9 For a discussion of Irigaray's (re)turning, see Frances Oppel's ' "Speaking of Immemorial Waters" ', in this volume.

BIBLIOGRAPHY

Blondel, E. (1988) 'Nietzsche: life as metaphor', in D. B. Allison (ed.) *The New Nietzsche*, Cambridge, Mass.: MIT Press.

Derrida, J. (1977) 'The question of style', in D. B. Allison (ed.) *The New Nietzsche*, Cambridge, Mass.: MIT Press.

—— (1978) 'Structure, sign and play', *Writing and Difference*, trans. A. Bass, London: Routledge & Kegan Paul.

—— (1979) *Spurs: Nietzsche's Styles*, trans. B. Harlow, Chicago, Ill.: University of Chicago Press.

Heidegger, M. (1979) *Nietzsche, Volume I: The Will to Power as Art*, trans. D. F. Krell, New York: Harper & Row.

Hume, D. (1888) *A Treatise on Human Nature*, Oxford: Clarendon Press.

Irigaray, L. (1991) *Marine Lover of Friedrich Nietzsche*, trans. G. C. Gill, New York: Columbia University Press.

Kofman, S. (1988) 'Baubô: theological perversion and fetishism', in M. A. Gillespie and T. B. Strong (eds) *Nietzsche's New Seas*, Chicago and London: University of Chicago Press.

Lingis, A. (1985) 'The will to power', in D. B. Allison (ed.) *The New Nietzsche*, Cambridge, Mass.: MIT Press.

Nehamas, A. (1985) *Nietzsche: Life as Literature*, Cambridge, Mass.: Harvard University Press.

Nietzsche, F. (1967) *The Birth of Tragedy*, trans. W. Kaufmann, New York: Random House.

—— (1968a) *The Will to Power*, trans. W. Kaufmann and R. J. Hollingdale, New York: Random House.

—— (1968b) *Twilight of the Idols and The Anti-Christ*, trans. R. J. Hollingdale, Harmondsworth: Penguin.

—— (1969) *On the Genealogy of Morals*, trans. W. Kaufmann and R. J. Hollingdale, New York: Random House.

—— (1970) 'Nietzsche contra Wagner', *The Portable Nietzsche*, New York: Viking Press.

—— (1973) *Beyond Good and Evil*, trans. R. J. Hollingdale, Harmondsworth: Penguin.

—— (1974) *The Gay Science*, trans. W. Kaufmann, New York: Random House.

—— (1978a) 'On truth and lies in a nonmoral sense', *Philosophy and Truth: Selections from Nietzsche's Notebooks of the early 1870's*, ed. and trans. D. Breazeale, Atlantic Highlands, NJ: Humanities Press.

—— (1978b) *Thus Spoke Zarathustra*, trans. W. Kaufmann, Harmondsworth: Penguin.

Spivak, G. C. (1984) 'Love me, love my ombre, elle', *Diacritics* 14(4): 19–36.

5 'Speaking of Immemorial Waters'
Irigaray with Nietzsche

Frances Oppel

The world is deep
Deeper than day can imagine.

(Nietzsche)

Beyond the horizon you have opened up, she will offer you that in
which she still lives and that your day has not even imagined.

(Irigaray)

In *Marine Lover of Friedrich Nietzsche* (1980/1991), Luce Irigaray
continues the feminist analysis of texts of western philosophy that
she began in *Speculum of the Other Woman* (1974/1985a), and at
the same time changes the direction and focus of that analysis.
Marine Lover is thus pivotal within Irigaray's ongoing project to
write about sexual difference as it has, and has not, been symboli-
cally represented in philosophical discourse. It is no accident that
this book is a turning-point for Irigaray; the nature of Nietzsche's
writing itself helped produce the change. Responsive to its rhetorical polyvalence, the narrative voices of *Marine Lover* take up positions not so much of opposition and antagonism towards Nietzsche's
texts as of contiguity and comradeship-at-arms. In the first part of
the book, 'Speaking of Immemorial Waters', Irigaray's narrator
adopts the even closer relationship to Nietzsche indicated by the
book's title.

This amorous sexual relationship seems unlikely; what, after all,
is a subtle feminist, who until this point stressed the pleasures of
lesbian love-making, doing in a relationship of amorous sexuality
with a moustachioed misogynist like Nietzsche? She is unequivocal
about the relationship, and about her own position as textual ana-
lyst; '*Marine Lover*', she said in an interview after it was written,
'is not a book *on* Nietzsche but *with* Nietzsche, who is for me a
partner in a love relationship' (1981: 295). Neither in this interview
nor in the book which is its subject does Irigaray allude to
Nietzsche's notorious sexist statements, like 'Are you visiting

women? Do not forget your whip!' from *Thus Spoke Zarathustra* (1961: 93). Her silence on the question of Nietzsche's misogyny is as significant as her statements on his use of language; both belong to the amorous partnership.

The Irigaray–Nietzsche intertextual love relationship is the subject of this chapter, and I shall return to it. However, in order not only to gauge the difference from Irigaray's earlier work that *Marine Lover* marks, but also to understand its continuity with her project overall, I shall first attempt briefly to describe this project. I use the word 'attempt' not as a trope of false modesty, but to indicate my awareness that any description, especially if it is brief, will oversimplify a highly complex body of work whose purpose is partly to throw into question the abstract intellectualized terminology required by such straightforward monologic description.[1]

Through ironic intertextual play using the tools of Freudian and Lacanian psychoanalysis and Derridean deconstruction, *Speculum of the Other Woman* reveals that the systematic unity and logical coherence of texts of Plato, Descartes, Kant, Hegel and Freud rest on a sexualized binary opposition (male/female) which in fantasy and in textual practice reduces the two poles of the opposition to one, the 'knowing subject' who is masculine and whose narrative voice produces the discourse. For Irigaray as for Lacan, this knowing, speaking subject has *nothing to do with* the biological sex of the person; it is a psychological construct. Obviously, males and females have been and are knowing, speaking subjects, but in Irigaray's view the very existence of the subject position depends upon its unconscious denial of sexual difference. She believes that the order of rational discourse is sustained by the defensive fantasy that there is only one sex – that this fantasy occurs through a complicated infantile psychic reaction to object-loss of the mother which represses the feminine and endorses a version of the female as a castrated male. She understands the repression of the other, the feminine, symptomatically: 'Does not all reabsorption of otherness in the discourse of sameness signify a desire for difference, but a desire that would always – to speak a shamefully psychological language – "be frightening?" '(Irigaray 1985b: 130). In the texts Irigaray analyses in *Speculum*, the hierarchy of psychic values privileges the male and dominates representational economy; ' "sexual difference" is a derivation of the problematics of sameness, it is, now and forever, determined within the project, the projections, the sphere of representation, of the same' (Irigaray 1985a: 27). *Speculum* argues that a language ostensibly sexually indifferent, actually a construct of fantasy that in practice privileges the male psyche, is a deadly trap, prison, net or labyrinth for the woman who desires to speak from a position of difference but who finds herself playing the part of eternal mirror to what is in effect the male ego or echo to its voice.

The ability to speak from a position of difference is crucially important to Irigaray, because she believes, with Freud in *Civilization and its Discontents*, that human beings are losing touch with their instinctual libidinal bases in the body and with nature, and that, through sublimation of erotic energies in an increasingly intellectualized culture, survival itself may be at stake. Recently she has written, 'We've reduced eros to unisex. . . . This kind of love, unisexual, destroys, in effect, human identity' (1989: 108). Humans are, as she says continuously, at least two. She concentrates her efforts on the question of language because for her language is not merely instrumental; it is 'an effect of forces and relations of power' which fundamentally constitutes 'the world and human experience as meaningful or representable' (Grosz 1989: 112).

As such, the language that Irigaray analyses in *Speculum* stands condemned. Having defined the problem, however, she moves in her next book, *This Sex Which Is Not One*, to look for a way out of the phallogocentric trap, which, in its insistence on sexual neutrality, she sees as psychically stultifying for *both* sexes:

> Yet as a matter of fact this 'masculine' language is not understood with any precision. So long as men claim to say everything and define everything, how can anyone know what the language of the male sex might be? So long as the logic of discourse is modelled on sexual indifference, on the submission of one sex to the other, how can anything be known about the 'masculine'?
> (Irigaray 1985b: 128)

She does not want to articulate a theory of woman, she writes, but 'to secure a place for the feminine within sexual difference' (1985b: 159). As for theory: 'We could not speak of (a) woman "entering into" any theory whatsoever unless the theory in question were to become an "enactment" of the copula, and not an appropriation of/by being' (1985b: 158). An 'enactment of the copula' would be, in a sense that Irigaray regards as 'difficult or even impossible to imagine' (1985b: 158), a condition of shared discourse where something she calls the feminine, as yet unknown, would find a voice, and freely mingle with something she calls the masculine – also as yet unknown.

As theory, this is vague; misty; a foreshadowing of an idea Irigaray will develop as her pessimism about the possibilities for an enactment of the copula, a discourse of sexual difference, changes, during the 1980s, to cautious optimism. During the decade, her writing becomes prophetic, oracular. Though the prophecies are often appropriately dark, veiled in obscurity, they signal an intuition that a turning-point in western culture may have been reached on account of what appears to be – she is tentative – the beginnings of the unrepression of the feminine. She detects a shift in the power relations between men and women: 'From the moment when something worthwhile about women is announced, men want to become women. . . . Why, all of a sudden, must we be in a reversal of power in a problematic of the Same? Please don't become women, men!' (Irigaray 1981: 64). In the interview published as 'Nietzsche, Freud, and women' in *Le Corps-à-corps avec la mère*, she agrees with her questioner that, in the region of sexual identities and subjectivity, 'things are trembling' (1981: 650).

Her cautiously optimistic vision is based on a close analysis of the language of more recent philosophers, beginning with Nietzsche, and including Heidegger, Levinas and Derrida. In reply to a question in a later interview, she writes in 1988 that we are witnessing

> a modification in the use of language by certain philosophers [Nietzsche, Heidegger, Levinas and Derrida] who are turning back towards the origins of their culture. . . . This return looks back to the moment at which male identity constituted itself as patriarchal and phallocratic. Is it the fact that women have emerged from the privacy of the home, from silence, which has forced men to question themselves? . . . are men seeking a way to divest themselves of these powers? I hope so. Such a desire would imply that they are inviting women to share in the definition of truth and the exercising of it with them.
>
> (Jardine and Menke 1988: 245)

The return to origins refers, in the case of Nietzsche, to his interest in the philosophies of the ancient Greek cosmologists, in whom Irigaray is also interested;[2] the 'use of language' refers to what Irigaray diagnoses as the healing of a split between poetry and philosophy – or fiction and theory, as she names these genres in the interview where she talks about her just-completed *Marine Lover*.

The 'difference' this book marks for her, she says, 'is prescribed to a certain extent by the works of Nietzsche themselves'. She continues:

> The first part ['Speaking of Immemorial Waters'] is a response to *Zarathustra*. This kind of *mise en cause*, or placing the discourse of the philosophical tradition 'on trial', by a passage to another type of language, exists in Nietzsche. Would you say that *Zarathustra* is fiction? For me, it is absolutely not fiction. . . . Would you say that Parmenides or Heraclitus is fiction?
>
> (Irigaray 1981: 44)

She finds in Nietzsche's prose a 'new kind of philosophical language' that is 'new' only because it is very old, and that the language of *Zarathustra* is 'much more oracular – that it more approaches pre-Socratic speech – than what is understood today as fiction'. She describes pre-Socratic speech as poetic language 'that does not announce the truth but which makes the truth, that acts, but not at all in a fiction/theory hierarchy' (Irigaray 1981: 45–7).

So *Marine Lover* is a book 'with' Nietzsche in several senses. Its language mimes his own refusal, as Irigaray reads it, of the fiction/theory opposition, and in doing so refuses the authorial and authoritative subject/object opposition in favour of an intertextual *corps-à-corps*. The book does not argue a hypothesis, as theory does, but more in the manner of fiction or poetry it demonstrates or enacts its effects through the use of a battery of rhetorical strategies: repetition, polyvocality, allusion, ambiguity and contradiction; a sensuous diction; mimicry, parody and irony; open-endedness: a linguistic duplicity much like Nietzsche's. Irigaray confesses her admiration for Nietzsche's prose, and her emphasis on his language indicates the value she places on its constitutive power:

> I had the feeling that in Nietzsche, there was a new kind of philosophical language because of the always very dense work of the writing, that was often connected to the critical language. That is to say, through language, through the deconstruction of language, another one could be invented. In a way, Nietzsche made me take off and go soaring. I had the feeling that I was in the middle of poetry, which made me perfectly happy.
>
> (Irigaray 1981: 45)

Irigaray's happiness in the middle of poetry, and her attention to the prose of the pre-Socratic Greeks, recalls the views of romantic theorists, and also of Julia Kristeva, that poetry is 'revolutionary';

it is capable of subverting the monological discourses of authority, law and 'truth' as one and unified, and of liberating the heterogeneity of desire.[3] Once liberated, of course, desire – the Dionysian – must be captured again in Apollonian form, but differently. *Marine Lover*'s style is 'an attempt to mark a difference' (Irigaray 1981: 48).

The book is divided into three parts. In the first, 'Speaking of Immemorial Waters', the narrator speaks as Nietzsche's fictitious marine lover – a mermaid or a sea-nymph – come to 'beguile' the philosopher with a philosophy of her own which 'weaves in and out' of his texts, 'insinuating the feminine' into them dialogically – that is through narrative perspective – and so exposing the consequences of their inevitable sexual bias.[4] The text of Nietzsche through which she swims is *Thus Spoke Zarathustra* and the 'you', addressed in the personal form 'tu', is Zarathustra, or the superman, or Nietzsche; unlike orthodox textual analysts but very like psychoanalysts, Irigaray makes no distinction between the author and his narrative voices. 'Speaking of Immemorial Waters' is the most poetic, the most fluid, the most sensuous of the three sections of the book, and it introduces themes that are relatively more systematically developed in the next two sections, 'Veiled Lips' and 'When Gods Are Born'. However, like a musical fugue, the whole book is composed of fragments that are interwoven, appearing and disappearing and then returning and repeating in a different key, until by gradual accretion the themes merge and the beginning is reached, or returned, by the ending.

Both in its themes and its formal structure, *Marine Lover* is occupied with Nietzsche's notion of eternal return. In *Speculum*, Irigaray fixed the eternal return as a metaphor for the phallogocentric economy of the Same, in which women are trapped as men's mirrors, prolonging the work of death.[5] 'Return' figures in the earlier work negatively; it is mechanical repetition. *Marine Lover* begins with the negative view of the eternal return, but – despite its apparent 'returns', or because of them, something else *also* happens in the course of the book which affirms eternal return's affirmation – with a difference.

In a series of notes on eternal recurrence in *The Will to Power*, Nietzsche writes, 'Everything becomes and recurs eternally – escape is impossible' (1967: 545). Equally impossible, as these formulations make clear, are notions of origin, end and timelessness and/or eternity as timelessness; becoming is all the being there is. If 'escape is impossible' – and here 'escape' also means 'solution', or 'meaning' guaranteed by a comforting faith in a metaphysical 'real world' that 'justifies' human endeavour – then the only empowering move possible, according to Nietzsche, is to affirm the negative, to trans-value its value, and to rejoice in the circumstances of one's fate as necessitating creativity. Nietzsche makes this affirming move in *Thus Spoke Zarathustra*, the book which begins with the announce-ment of the death of God and the prophecy of the superman – he who is strong enough to *will* the eternal return of the same.

Irigaray addresses these central concerns of *Zarathustra* in 'Speak-ing of Immemorial Waters' – waters that are elemental in female physiology, as amniotic fluid, the waters of life. After writing *Marine Lover*, Irigaray maintained that she chose to examine Nietzsche in terms of water because 'it is the element of which he is the most afraid'. She added, 'In *Zarathustra*, we hear his fear of the Deluge' (1981: 43). In *Zarathustra*, we mainly hear Nietzsche's delight in the sea;[6] Irigaray deduces this fear of the Deluge from her psychoanalytic understanding of the eternal return as a symptom:

> [*Amante Marine*] is an attempt to mark a difference, hence the choice of a marine element which evokes the amniotic fluids which thwart the eternal return. One knows of the desire Nietzsche had to be a mother, and how much he suffered from not being able to be one. The marine element is therefore both the amniotic fluids, the deepest marine element which can't simply be an appearance and to which Nietzsche will never return, which escapes him forever, and it is also, it seems to me, something which represents feminine *jouissance* quite well.
>
> (Irigaray 1981: 48–9)

In alerting readers to look for ways that the 'marine element' 'thwarts' the eternal return, this statement of intention is helpful, if somewhat surprising in the case that one hadn't considered how much Nietzsche desired to be a mother. This desire appears in *Zarathustra* as metaphor for self-creation: 'For the creator himself to be the child new-born he must also be willing to be the mother and endure the mother's pain' (Nietzsche 1961: 111). In the passage, Irigaray attributes two desires to Nietzsche: one to be a mother, and the other to return to the womb. These are two very different projects expressive of opposite wishes and thus of major ambiv-alence toward birth itself. Irigaray is reading eternal return as a defence against Nietzsche's conflicting, illicit wishes – a reading that helps make sense of 'Speaking of Immemorial Waters' and its read-ing of *Thus Spoke Zarathustra*.

At the beginning of the book, the central character, a nameless first-person female narrator, declares:

> And you had all to lose sight of me so I could come back, toward you, with another gaze.
>   And, certainly, the most arduous thing has been to seal my lips, out of love. To close off this mouth that always sought to flow free.
>
> (Irigaray 1991: 3)

Readers of this text are thrown in at the deep end – to stay with metaphors of fluidity – and required to swim. To this end, a knowledge of *Thus Spoke Zarathustra* is a great advantage, for Irigaray's language is full of echoes. This opening, for example, sounds like the opening of *Zarathustra* II:

> Then Zarathustra went back into the mountains and into the solitude of his cave and withdrew from mankind. . . . His soul, however, became full of impatience and longing for those whom he loved. . . . This, indeed, is the most difficult thing: to close the open hand out of love.
>
> (Nietzsche 1961: 107)

Gradually, reading 'Immemorial Waters', we begin to understand what Irigaray means when she says that *mimicry* is a useful 'nuptial tool' if one is 'having a fling with the philosophers' (1985b: 150). Maintaining that they have caught her in their heads as their echoes ('I was merely the drum in your own ear sending back to itself its own truth' – 1991: 3), she deliberately echoes their words, throwing them back. The effect of the mimicry is both ironic and revelatory; it opens a discursive space that can be repossessed or appropriated in new ways, to new ends. Here, a simple role reversal has taken place: rather than Zarathustra withdrawing from mankind out of love, it is a nameless 'she'; but what a difference the gender reversal makes, in fact. The word 'mankind' takes on explicit connotations of maleness when Irigaray's and Nietzsche's texts are read together; and 'she' becomes generalized femaleness, whose withdrawal from 'you all' has an entirely different significance from Zarathustra's.

In the opening two short paragraphs, Irigaray introduces us to her method, an intertextual dance; to its effect, ironic appropriation and reconsideration of Nietzsche's text and its project in the name, and from the perspective of, woman; and to a broader feminist concern, that of separatism. Irigaray had made her position clear on the subject before writing *Marine Lover*: in *This Sex* she wrote

that the ' "breaking away" of women-among-themselves seems strategically necessary, but the *staying* away will amount "finally to
the same thing" ' (1985b: 162) – that is to the same undesirable
hierarchized power structure; but she is still dealing with its implications here. The opening affirms that 'she' has left her relationship
with 'them', but on the next page, she writes: 'But I am coming
back from far, far away' (Irigaray 1991: 4) and explains that her
withdrawal has been strategic: 'had I never held back, never would
you have remembered that something exists which has a language
other than your own. That, from her prison, someone was calling
out to return to the air' (Irigaray 1991: 3).

This return is the most spectacular in the book, but we can realize
that only after reading through to the end. The elemental geography
of the return – to *air* – should not be passed over too hastily; nor
should the use of verbal tenses by which the story is narrated. 'I
am coming back': present tense. 'If I hadn't gone away': past
perfect, implied. 'You would never have remembered': present
perfect conditional. 'Someone was calling out to return': past continuous. Reconstructed in chronological order, the story events of
this narrative are (1) I was calling out for air; (2) I went away; (3)
you remembered; (4) I came back. The narrative of *Marine Lover*
is circular; the entire text after the opening is a flashback, a meditation on the reasons for this calculated disappearance from the
world of men (steps 1 and 2) which the beginning (step 4) then
supersedes, on condition that her condition (step 3) has been met.

The first chapter of Part One, 'Baptism of the Shadow', introduces themes that return throughout the piece: memory/forgetful-
ness; birth/death; inside/outside; self-reference (echoes, mirrors,
veils); horizons; abysses. As a shadow of the man, the woman is
so united to him that she almost forgets – as he does also – that
she had an existence, a birth, of her own, before her co-option as
his echo, before she was 'imprisoned' in his language. Playing on
Nietzsche's resounding affirmation at the end of *The Gay Science*
that the death of God means new and marvellous opportunities for
man – that 'the horizon appears free to us again' (Nietzsche 1974:
280) – the narrator says caustically: 'Round and round, you keep
on turning. Within yourself. Pushing out of your circle anything
that, from elsewhere, remembers. But I am coming back from far,
far away. And say to you: your horizon has limits. Holes, even'
(Irigaray 1991: 4). She has been away and during her absence has,
among other things, been baptized. But whereas traditional baptism

purifies a soul of the 'original sin' of birth, her baptism purifies her body of the taints of her former relationship with him:

> I am no longer the lining to your coat, your – faithful – understudy. Voicing your joys and sorrows, your fears and resentments. You had fashioned me into a mirror but I have dipped that mirror in the waters of oblivion – that you call life. And further away than the place where you are beginning to be, I have turned back. I have washed off your masks and make up, scrubbed away your multicolored projections and designs, stripped off your veils and wraps that hid the shame of your nudity. I have even had to scrape my woman's flesh clean of the insignia and marks you had etched upon it.
>
> (Irigaray 1991: 4)

In a general sense, *Marine Lover* explores the requirements for and the implications of her departure from, and her return to 'him', baptized as someone? as 'subject'? in her own right. Given the emphasis on water – here, the baptismal 'waters of oblivion', forgetfulness, *lethé* – the 'return to the air' would *also* be a cry for life, for 'escape' from the amniotic fluids of the mother's womb. Thus, for her, leaving her relationship with him would be like separation from the mother. But the marine element must first be returned to, for both of them: to enable her to *forget* him and to enable him to *remember* her. Both will be required to journey back, to remember their births.

Working through the crucial problem of relatedness and separation – her from him, him from her, and the prototypical separation, baby from mother – the narrator suggests that two people can be only as closely connected as mother and child-in-the-womb. Even there, a 'film' divides them: 'Between you and me [and this is a significant 'you', for it is the first time 'she' has addressed the narratee in the familiar 'tu' form; their relationship is now marked as close – perhaps it is a child she addresses, or a lover] will there not always be this film that keeps us apart?' (Irigaray 1991: 5). This film is then designated as a membrane, and the narratee is certainly Zarathustra as he appears in Book IV, at noon on his 'perfect' day, dozing blissfully in the sun. She is impatient with him because he has no desire to share his perfect moment, his 'wondrous roundness' of soul; he has forgotten her completely, and so she attacks. She warns him of the folly of his egocentricity in a series of prophetic passages:

> You fold the membrane between us in your own way. Either it is right side up and thrust out, or turned falteringly back into yourself. For holes mean only the abyss to you. And the further out you project yourself, the farther you fall. There is nothing to stop your penetration outside yourself – nothing either more or less. Unless I am there.

Sexual metaphors control the reading here: thrust out, back in, holes, penetration. There is a repetition of the narrator's critique of his open horizon which from her perspective has 'holes' in it. But holes, to him, mean 'the abyss', the most fearsome of all possibilities for contemplation, signifier of dread castration. In *Speculum of the Other Woman*, Irigaray elaborates on the notion of female 'absence' named horrific by Freud:

> [The little girl must act] *like* the little boy, feel the same urge to see, look in the same way, and her resentment at not having a penis must follow and corroborate the horrified astonishment the little boy feels when faced with the strangeness of the non-identical, the nonidentifiable. . . . a fault, a flaw, a lack, an absence, outside the system of representations and autorepresentations. Which are man's . . . a hole in man's signifying economy. A nothing that might cause the ultimate destruction, the splintering, the break in their systems of 'presence,' of re-presentation.
> (Irigaray 1985a: 50)

Zarathustra is discovered at the beginning of Book IV, contemplating an abyss: 'One day, as he was sitting upon a stone before his cave and gazing silently out – but the outlook there is of the sea and tortuous abysses . . .'; note the conjunction of sea and abyss, both female signifiers, introduced by a dash, or break, and the negative qualifier 'but'. Something is disruptive about the objects of his contemplation. Later, at noon on his perfect day, Zarathustra apostrophizes the sky: 'well of eternity! serene and terrible noontide abyss!' (Nietzsche 1961: 251, 289).

The 'Immemorial Waters' passage has several implications. One is that there is a causal connection between his tyrannical operation of the sex act ('in your own way') and the terrors of the abyss. The 'further out' he 'projects' himself, the deeper the gulf; he is using sex as a defence against his fear of castration, projecting his body into hers, and simultaneously recapitulating the ego projection by which he has captured her as his mirror and thereby denied his separation from his mother.

Another implication is that *she* is complicit in constructing the abyss; obviously, it exists only because she does, and she acknowledges that fact. It is her awareness of this complicity, and her acknowledgement of it, that is important. It gives her a choice. If she weren't 'there', he might be able to 'penetrate outside of' himself, to break through the walls of consciousness to a real awareness of what else exists, outside – or deeply within – himself. For the irony of their relationship is that they will never heal the split between them until they perform it. They must separate before they can come together as two different wholes. She has introduced this theme of the possible benefits of her absence earlier in the chapter:

> If I no longer serve as your passage from back to front, from front to back, your time will let another day dawn. Your world will unravel. It will flood out to other places. To that outside you have not wanted.
>
> (Irigaray 1991: 4)

The imagery is again sexual, fluid and apocalyptic, mimicking Nietzsche's constant reference to the dawn as a time of possibility, challenging his prophecies by telling him what, in her opinion, will bring the new day: her departure, and with it the destruction of his world as he knows it. Thus she challenges him both to remember her, to accept her difference, and to reread his own doctrines in the light of that acceptance.

The next passage presents another view of the mother–child symbiosis:

> The membrane was not yours to have. We formed it together. And if you want it for yourself, you make a hole in it just because I lack any part. And don't you make God out of that absence?
>
> (Irigaray 1991: 7)

Here, Irigaray gives theology a psychological provenance, along Freudian lines. He has taken the whole membrane – and I think the membrane, as well as carrying connotations of hymen and sexual intercourse, is also the 'film' that separates mother and embryo, the placenta – as a defensive response to his early terror at her 'absence' of a penis. As Freud has it, the (male) baby identifies totally with the mother, there is no separation, until he recognizes her sexual 'difference' at which point he imagines her castrated and, horrified and threatened, unconsciously puts something in place of the mother's penis. In 'Fetishism' (1927), Freud explains this concept, as he says, 'plainly: the fetish is a substitute for the woman's (mother's) penis that the little boy once believed in and . . . does not want to give up'. In spite of what he sees (nothing), his narcissism comes to the aid of his wishes and, 'Yes, in his mind the woman *has* got a penis, in spite of everything; but this penis is no longer the same as it was before. Something else has taken its place, has been appointed its substitute' (Freud 1961: 152–4). The narrator of *Marine Lover* audaciously suggests that this something might be God. 'God' now stands in for the other, the different against whom 'man' can define his own species; but also as the father, the familiar reassuring sexual same. As Irigaray says in *Divine Women*, 'the only thing diabolical about women is their absence of God' (1986: 6). *Marine Lover*'s suggestion is that God fills the empty place that male perceives in female, and so the male keeps his homological, homosexual system intact by incorporating the mother/female as mirror or shadow, in effect refusing to share the membrane – or to acknowledge difference.

However, the narratee of this story is Zarathustra, whose fear of the abyss on the conscious level is precisely fear of what he himself has proclaimed, God's absence. The narrator must therefore take up the implications of the death of God. Having implied in the first passage that *her* absence might help him come out of himself and 'remember' her, she now states in the second that since her 'absence' has meaning on at least two levels, it is not as simple as it looked. Women cannot simply 'break away' without consequences, and they must not do so without trying to imagine what the consequences might be. The marine lover's attempt at such imagining produces an analogy between God and a maternal fetish, which intensifies the problematic separation between her and Zarathustra. One implication of God's death is that the hole now gapes, stares a man in the face. The horizon is now, indeed, open. What does he do? The third and final passage in the series reads:

> But if your God dies, how keen is your distress. Endless is your despair and your rage to destroy even the very beginning of this nothingness. The more you seek out the source of danger and strive to control it, the more abyssal is the tomb. Before, when you gazed at the stars, at least you left earth the chance of her secret. Now you dig down into the earth to recover something

she has taken or withheld from you. But nothing is hidden from you by this ground that keeps your footsteps.

(Irigaray 1991: 7–8)

The narrator speaks here in full prophetic, apocalyptic mode. God's death will precipitate man's death – if he tries to master it by destroying the source of danger, female difference. His first mistake, from her point of view, was his mastery of the membrane that separated him from his mother – his refusal to *be* separated, in effect. His seeking to destroy the source of the nothingness, once he perceives it as 'nothingness' rather than as God, by turning ferociously inward upon himself, will hasten his own destruction. Here Irigaray agrees with Nietzsche in *On the Genealogy of Morals* (1969: 19) that nihilism, the will to nothingness, is a supreme danger. Zarathustra thinks the source is the earth, and advises his disciples to '*remain true to the earth*, and do not believe those who speak to you of superterrestrial hopes!' For Zarathustra, the earth is the mother: 'I want to become earth again, that I may have peace in her who bore me' (Nietzsche 1961: 42, 99). The earth symbolizes woman for the male, and the footstep image carries through the narrator's earlier preoccupation with woman-as-property; as he has 'marked with' or 'etched upon' her body his brands and insignia, so he impresses his 'mastery' into the earth with the weight of his body. For the marine lover, this is not good enough; she knows that the sea is the mother, the sea which preserves no footprints.

Throughout 'Speaking of Immemorial Waters' the marine lover tries to interest Zarathustra in the notion of difference. She does not preach against the earth, except in reaction to what she takes as his blindness or ambivalence toward the sea. Her principal object of attack is the eternal return, which encompasses all, object of the will-to-power, of which the superman will be the embodiment. The attack takes many forms, all of which perform a critique of his philosophy of roundness and wholeness that absorbs everything in unremitting self-referentiality, including especially the (m)other. Strategically, she emphasizes the importance of acknowledging beginnings and ends and of separating binary opposites rather than collapsing them into synthesis (a totalizing Sameness which is in fact hierarchical). The separation of binaries should begin with mother and child and end with life and death; the two pairs should not be confused.

In her own 'dance song' in the middle of Part One, 'Dance of the

Abyss', the marine lover takes up the paradoxes that Zarathustra proclaims in the 'Drunken Song' toward the end of Book IV – chiefly the life/death pair beloved of philosophers and poets from Heraclitus on. The narrator looks at it. She is not romantic, at this particular moment, and so she insists on tearing the life/death couple apart. The first sentence of this chapter underlines a valuation that runs parallel to that of sexual difference, the value of asymmetrical relationships: 'Life is never identical to itself, but death is. At least one would imagine it so: with nothing happening anymore' (Irigaray 1991: 41). The couple is split, its symmetry shattered, and death in its self-identity is linked to the eternal return. The second sentence draws our attention to and apparently endorses a linear teleology, with death as closure. 'Why equate life and death?' she asks. Why not accept death as the end? Making life equal to death means continuing to let women do the work of both – giving birth and thus sustaining death. She argues:

> By preaching the eternal recurrence, you are broken as a living man. . . . What worries you in eternity? Are you still wishing yourself some kind of God? . . .
>
> And (you) prefer not to have begun to live rather than to have received birth.
>
> And that the other has given you what escapes your creation is the source of your highest *ressentiment*. How to bring the gift of life, that is the question you ponder upon your mountain top. . . .
>
> Remaining halfway between the beginning and the end implies the will to overcome the affirmation and negation of distance, doubling them by means of your repeated flight. But, in this setting, neither the one nor the other are encountered or inhabited. And, by refusing to separate the two, you lose both.
>
> (Irigaray 1991: 41–4)

Thus Zarathustra: trapped in his eternal return with his 'only wife, eternity' (Irigaray 1991: 42), always between beginning and ending, where past and future, meeting at the gateway of This Moment, are erased, and along with them, this moment also. In this kind of environment, no one can live. Irigaray's critique of the eternal return emphasizes the deep ambivalence that it embodies toward death, toward birth, and toward sexual difference.[7]

With God now dead, as Zarathustra realizes, humans have to face death; but in facing death, as the marine lover realizes, they must also face birth, acknowledge the gift of a corporeal mother.

And in her multi-level interpretation, where sex is never far away, God's death means that Zarathustra, at least, has 'given up' his fetish, the comforting substitute for the maternal phallus, and must face the other, woman, as different, not equal to, not identical, not the same. The way is now clear, the horizon open for this epiphany; he opened it himself. But he can't manage it. His superman, his eternal return, his will, his metamorphoses of the spirit, and his faithfulness to earth – all are responses to the gaping hole caused by God's death. His marine lover puts it to him: rather than trying to fill the hole with other sublimations in a heroic creative effort, why not *share* the pain with your human other, work together toward solutions, and avoid the crisis that her departure altogether might cause?

The marine lover, however, herself creative and heroic, seems to admit that this 'sharing', this acknowledgement of difference which means letting the other go, cannot or will not happen – ironically – until she becomes the 'same' (as he), a subject in her own right. She must follow him down that path, and she could hardly ask for a better teacher and model of subjectivity than Zarathustra. What she holds against him – as self-serving, self-referential and ultimately self-destructive – she adopts for herself. When she is on her own, having been baptized in the waters of oblivion, and therefore subject of her own reflection, she gives the eternal return a different value. Describing her experience of liberation, she becomes lyrical about its intoxicating pleasures, and those of self-love, auto-eroticism. A few quotations taken from different places in Part One:

> I had been taught that a woman who belonged to no one was nothing. . . . Nothing? This whole that always and at every moment was thus becoming new? Nothing? This endless coming into life at each moment? (5)
>
> Whole (I) shall be at every moment, and every whole moment. (11)
>
> And what matter if it be ebb or flow? As long as, at each moment, (I) move as a whole. And, for me, ebb and flow have always set the rhythm of time. . . . One moment is worth absolutely no more than the other, for the whole is present in each. At each hour comes fortune, multiple in the unwinding of its becoming. (14)

An endless coming-into-life at each moment is one way to think the eternal return; but the narrator is clear that her experience of

eternal return is not like Zarathustra's. Since their relationship is
not symmetrical – they are not the same – her experience of eternal
return can be free of resentment. *Her* time never repeats, and she
never turns in a circle. *He* is closed, self-enclosed, but she is 'spread
out and open in this endless becoming' (14).

Irigaray takes up Zarathustra's story almost where Nietzsche
leaves it off, breaking into *Thus Spoke Zarathustra* near the end of
its narrative. The function of this particular point of entry is
revealed in a refrain the marine lover sings three times. It tells of
ripeness, echoing Zarathustra's celebration of his own mellow state
from 'The Drunken Song' when he chants, 'What has become
perfect, everything ripe – wants to die!' (Nietzsche 1961: 331). Her
refrain goes:

> But since I have never mellowed, I still want to live. And if
> your hour ends when mine begins, that gives me no pleasure.
> For I love to share whereas you want to keep everything for
> yourself. (19)

He is ripe, and his time is ending, perhaps; however, her time is
only beginning. The refrain – and the fact that it *is* a refrain –
evokes general cultural resonances of the future of relations
between male and female.

There is a sense of possibility, of 'almost there', of excitement
as before a goal not quite reached, throughout 'Speaking of
Immemorial Waters'. Zarathustra has come a long way, and the
marine lover acknowledges it:

> He who has gone through pain, is free of heaviness. Miraculous is
> the motion of him who, beyond nostalgia, goes on walking. . . .
>   The man who discovers what such ills are made of, and
> resolves their enigma himself rather than laying their burden on
> the other, is suddenly moving in a world with no boundaries but
> those of his living body. (29)

That point, she continues, echoing Zarathustra's commandment,
'Become what you are!' (Nietzsche 1961: 252), is 'the beginning of
the man whose highest achievement is to be what he is. With no
evasion'. She celebrates this achievement for him, and appropriates
it as a goal for herself, but finds that his perfection, reached pain-
fully at the end of four books, leaves something to be desired:
herself. At this point she enters the narrative and tells him to 'now
begin again, you have yet to begin to live' (20).

The problem is that Zarathustra, teetering at the edge of the abyss ('and where does man not stand at an abyss? Is seeing itself not – seeing abysses?' [Nietzsche 1961: 177]), gets vertigo. The marine lover says:

> On the edge of this precipice, you seek the secret of your birth and of your death. The strength of your reaction brings you resources to restore you. To wrap you all over again in fallacious reserves and illusory certainties. So you can go far off again, motivated by *ressentiment*. (55)

On the very brink of the new day that he announces, Zarathustra withdraws into the same resentment against life/death that he thinks produced God in the first place. The strength of his reaction to the abyss produces the sublimation of eternal return, and a blindness to the falseness of his own dichotomies. Addressing Nietzsche rather than Zarathustra at the end of Part One, the narrator confronts Nietzsche with his two antithetical personae, the masks of Dionysus and Christ. 'Were they', she asks, 'really different? Did they not, secretly, have the same birth within your universe?' This is only a 'sham, phony contradiction'; the real one, the 'origin of your *ressentiment*', the genuine antagonism, is with her, his only worthy opponent (72).

The marine lover suggests, however, that Zarathustra's idea of self-overcoming might be read as something other than a doctrine of self-identity. During a meditation on overcoming directed to superman, she puts to him the question Zarathustra puts to the 'wisest of men'. Zarathustra asks, 'What urges you on and arouses your ardour, you wisest of men . . . ?' His answer is the will to power, the secret of life that says, 'Behold, I am that *which must overcome itself again and again*' (Nietzsche 1961: 136, 138). She asks, 'Who is it that you must overcome?' and answers that he has confused his rivals, fighting himself when his real wish is to 'master that dark place where you find birth' (67). Still, the struggle-to-the-death with himself in an eternal self-overcoming might generate enough energy to release difference:

> A worthy opponent? Are you calling for the destruction of the power of the mirror? Taking stock of your hatred, and going beyond it? Estimating the power of your *ressentiment* and, by loosing such energy, heralding a future other than a time of revenge? (68)

It is a future she longs for. Her own vision of paradise regained for the two of them, beyond their necessary separation, beyond her own auto-erotic pleasures, is different from Zarathustra's celebration of ripeness in the moment, when opposites meet in paradox and 'midnight is also mid-day, pain is also joy' (Nietzsche 1961: 331). At that moment, Zarathustra perfects himself alone. Ironically, her future will be a return, too; not an eternal return to the present moment, but a journeying back to the future:

> Let it be a return to something that has never taken place. The embrace of earth and air and fire and water, which have never been wed. (21)

> Why are we not, the one for the other, a resource of life and air? Celebrations and springing out of or into the same. (31)

In the air, where humans live, they are different, and as such should be each other's resource; but they spring out of or into the same maternal source, which should also be a resource, of life.

Irigaray is as paradoxical as Nietzsche, but if their differences weren't clear, Irigaray makes them so at the end of *Marine Lover*. The final part, 'When Gods Are Born', declares that Nietzsche's 'insoluble fate' is 'paralyzing him his dionysian becoming'. 'Sensing the impotence to come', Irigaray writes – alluding to the last letters Nietzsche wrote in which he signed himself 'The Crucified' (Middleton 1969: 345) – 'Nietzsche declares he is the crucified one. And is crucified. But by himself' (Irigaray 1991: 188). These sentences illustrate Irigaray's characteristic ambiguity: they mean both that Nietzsche is the agent of his own crucifixion, both subject and object, murderer and victim; *and* that he is alone. This is Irigaray's point: that in denying the difference of woman, in incorporating all potential subjects as objects into his all-absorbing subjectivity, Nietzsche condemns himself to the return of the Same which is death: 'The lonely fading away of a gesture which was motivated also by the other' (189). As for this other, the 'she' who bore him, she must now go her own way. For Irigaray, the inscription of God on the Cross may be interpreted 'go beyond', and she says to women, 'To interpret him [the Crucified] therefore means "go beyond" if possible without return. Not be satisfied with such a love. Leave it to the men of *ressentiment*, and try to create another world' (189).

So in the end she departs: a clean, linear move; a refusal to share, out of a desire to share, because there was no sharing. It is a move which, as we know, makes her return possible. And it is Nietzsche, or his books, with whom she breaks, and to whom she returns, because of his contemplation of the abyss, the fearful but exhilarating unknown; his 'strength to say "yes" ' to himself (16); and his 'new kind of language' that made her take off and go soaring, because it is the language of risk and of desire. For her his books hold possibilities for women, and for men, and for both together, and thus they herald the kind of future Irigaray would like to create.

ACKNOWLEDGEMENTS

I am grateful to a research grant from the Faculty of Humanities, Griffith University, which enabled me to have most of Irigaray's *Amante Marine* translated, and to Dr Maureen Aitken, of Women's College, University of Queensland, for her careful translation, made before Gillian C. Gill's (1991) translation was published. I should also like to thank Carol Smith and the Institute for Research on Women, Douglass College of Rutgers University, for providing the best possible working conditions during the final drafting of this chapter; and Anne Freadman, Sylvia Lawson and Paul Patton for their helpful editorial comments.

NOTES

1 The interpretation of Irigaray's work is also highly contested. For a recent article summarizing central arguments of the considerable body of Irigaray criticism, see Berg (1991).
2 See Grosz (1989: 169) for an account of this interest.
3 For a romantic statement, see P. B. Shelley's 'A defence of poetry', in C. Woodring (ed.) (1961) *Prose of the Romantic Period*, Cambridge, Mass.: Riverside Press; for Kristeva, see excerpts from *Revolution in Poetic Language*, trans. M. Waller, in T. Moi (ed.) (1986) *The Kristeva Reader*, Oxford: Basil Blackwell (first published 1974). In *This Sex Which Is Not One* (first published 1977), Irigaray, in an apparent uptake on Kristeva's notion of the 'semiotic' as traces of pre-Oedipal drives articulated in the rhythms of poetic language (*Revolution*, 112), speaks of the 'covering up' of the 'forcefulness, of force itself [of desire, of pleasure] under the lawmaking power of discourse' (Irigaray 1985b: 163) and of the need for a language which 'jams the theoretical machinery itself' to release the force of desire (1985b: 79).
4 I stress Irigaray's fictitious framework, because there has been some confusion about the identity of the marine lover. In 'An interview with Luce Irigaray', Amsberg and Steenhuis (1983: 194) say that *Amante Marine* 'sets out from a book by Nietzsche about his lover'. The quotations in this sentence are from Burke (1987: 105).
5 For instance, in her reading of Freud's essay on 'Femininity', Irigaray says that woman is charged by Freud

> with preserving, regenerating and rejuvenating the organism, notably through sexual reproduction. . . . To being still the restoring, nourish-

ing mother who prolongs the work of death by sustaining it. . . .
'Woman' can function as place – evanescent beyond, point of departure
– as well as time – eternal return, temporal detour – for the sublimation
and, if possible, mastery of the work of death.

(Irigaray 1985a: 53–5)

6 For examples, see Cathryn Vasseleu's 'Not drowning, sailing' in this
volume, which, in substantial agreement with Irigaray, makes clear
Nietzsche's ambivalence toward the sea.
7 The interpretation of eternal return as a classic Freudian fetish is made
by Pautrat (1990: 167).

BIBLIOGRAPHY

Amsberg, K. and Steenhuis, A. (1983) 'An interview with Luce Irigaray',
trans. R. van Krieken, *Hecate* 9(1–2): 192–202.
Berg, M. (1991) 'Luce Irigaray's "Contradictions": poststructuralism and
feminism', *Signs* 17(1): 50–70.
Burke, C. (1987) 'Romancing the philosophers: Luce Irigaray', *Minnesota
Review* 29 (Fall): 103–14.
Freud, S. (1961) *The Future of an Illusion, Civilization and its Discontents,
and Other Works*, Standard Edition, vol. XXI, ed. J. Strachey, London:
Hogarth Press and the Institute of Psycho-analysis.
Grosz, E. (1989) *Sexual Subversions: Three French Feminists*, Sydney:
Allen & Unwin.
Irigaray, L. (1980) *Amante Marine: de Friedrich Nietzsche*, Paris: Les
Editions de Minuit.
—— (1981) *Le Corps-à-corps avec la mère*, Montreal: Les Editions de la
plein lune.
—— (1985a; orig. 1974) *Speculum of the Other Woman*, trans. G. C. Gill,
Ithaca, NY: Cornell University Press.
—— (1985b; orig. 1977) *This Sex Which Is Not One*, trans. C. Porter with
C. Burke, Ithaca, NY: Cornell University Press.
—— (1986; orig. 1985) *Divine Women*, trans. S. Meuke, Sydney: Local
Consumption Occasional Paper no. 8.
—— (1989) *Le Temps de la différence: pour une révolution pacifique*, Paris:
Libraire Générale Française.
—— (1991) *Marine Lover of Friedrich Nietzsche*, trans. G. C. Gill, New
York: Columbia University Press.
Jardine, A. and Menke, A. M. (eds) (1988) 'Exploding the issue: "French"
"Women" "Writers" and "the Canon"?', *Yale French Studies* 75: 229–58.
Kristeva, J. (1986) *The Kristeva Reader*, ed. T. Moi, Oxford: Basil
Blackwell.
Middleton, C. (ed.) (1969) *Selected Letters of Friedrich Nietzsche*, Chicago
and London: University of Chicago Press.
Nietzsche, F. (1961) *Thus Spoke Zarathustra: A Book for Everyone and
No One*, trans. R. J. Hollingdale, Harmondsworth: Penguin.
—— (1968) *The Will to Power*, trans. W. Kaufmann and R. J. Hollingdale,
New York: Vintage.

—— (1969) *On the Genealogy of Morals*, trans. W. Kaufmann, New York: Vintage.

—— (1974) *The Gay Science*, trans. W. Kaufmann, New York: Vintage.

Pautrat, B. (1990) 'Nietzsche medused', in L. Rickels (ed.) *Looking After Nietzsche*, Albany, NY: State University of New York Press.

Woodring, C. (ed.) (1961) *Prose of the Romantic Period*, Cambridge, Mass.: Riverside Press.

6 *Das Weib an sich*
The slave revolt in epistemology

Daniel W. Conway

Philosophy reduced to 'theory of knowledge' . . . that is philosophy in its last throes, an end, an agony, something inspiring pity. How could such a philosophy – *dominate*!

(BGE 204)[1]

INTRODUCTION

In his discussion of the ascetic ideal in *On the Genealogy of Morals*, Nietzsche warns us not to invest our redemptive hopes in science. Rather than provide or enable an alternative to the ascetic ideal, contemporary science in fact represents

the *best* ally the ascetic ideal has at present, and precisely because it is the most unconscious, involuntary, hidden, and subterranean ally!

(GM III: 25)

Nietzsche exposes the 'will to truth' that drives scientific inquiry as sheltering an unacknowledged faith in the redemptive capacity of truth, a faith that he proposes as complicit with the ascetic ideal. Rather than liberate us from the thrall of the ascetic ideal, the 'will to truth' of contemporary science continues the millennia-long assault on the body and the affects: '*All* science . . . has at present the object of dissuading man from his former respect for himself, as if this had been nothing but a piece of bizarre conceit' (GM III: 25).

Nietzsche's warning against the ascetic kernel of contemporary science provides an instructive backdrop against which we might assess the current debate among feminist theorists over the epistemic status of objectivity. Can the project of feminist epistemology accommodate a reconstituted notion of objectivity, and if so, how should this reconstituted notion be positively characterized? The two most currently authoritative parties to this debate are postmodern feminist epistemology, of which I propose the work of Donna

Haraway as representative, and feminist standpoint theory, as championed by Sandra Harding.

I contend that Nietzsche's perspectivism not only adumbrates the postmodern strategies of feminists like Donna Haraway, but also issues a pre-emptive warning against the version of feminist standpoint theory espoused by Sandra Harding. Because Harding's epistemological project unwittingly serves the 'will to truth' emblematic of contemporary science, her feminist standpoint theory ultimately discounts those immediate, embodied experiences of women that it presumes to subject to theoretical analysis. If the project of feminist epistemology is to incorporate the radically situated knowledges of women and other subjugated agents, then its practitioners must take the 'postmodern' turn outlined by Nietzsche and implemented by Haraway.

NIETZSCHE'S PERSPECTIVISM AS A MODEL FOR FEMINIST EPISTEMOLOGY

Nietzsche's perspectivism, an epistemic thesis conveyed via a host of masculinist and residually misogynist images, might seem like an unlikely precursor of feminist epistemologies. But in fact Nietzsche provides an epistemic framework that both accommodates and prizes the radically situated experiences of women. In the following passage, which contains Nietzsche's most detailed and sustained discussion of the position now known as 'perspectivism', he both warns us to beware of traditional epistemology and points us in a more promising direction:

> let us be on guard against the dangerous old conceptual fiction that posited a 'pure, will-less, painless, timeless knowing subject'; let us guard against the snares of such contradictory concepts as 'pure reason', 'absolute spirituality', 'knowledge in itself'; these always demand that we should think of an eye that is completely unthinkable, an eye turned in no particular direction, in which the active and interpreting forces, through which alone seeing becomes seeing *something*, are supposed to be lacking. . . . There is *only* a perspectival seeing [*perspektivisches Sehen*], *only* a perspectival 'knowing'; and the *more* affects we allow to speak [*zu Worte kommen*] about one thing, the *more* eyes, different eyes, we can use to observe one thing, the more complete will our 'concept' of this thing, our 'objectivity' be.
>
> (GM III: 12)

In this brief passage, Nietzsche makes several points with which feminist theorists have expressed agreement. First of all, he warns us to beware of the traditional interpretation of objectivity as disinterested contemplation. The goal of disinterested contemplation presupposes 'conceptual fictions' and 'contradictory concepts', and furthermore requires us to posit a disembodied, disinterested knowing subject, 'an eye turned in no particular direction'. Nietzsche's perspectivism thus attempts to account for those affective components and determinants of knowledge that traditionally have been ignored or discounted by epistemology. His reconstituted notion of objectivity (consistently noted by his use of quotation marks) suggests that knowledge is a function of the embodied expression of our affective investment in the world. His perspectivism thus presupposes an account of subjects as radically situated, that is affectively invested, in the world and in their bodies.

Second, if we interpret these 'eyes' as perspectives, whose 'interpretative forces' are sustained by a suffusion of affect, then we see that for Nietzsche, perspectives are not disembodied points of view that hover disinterestedly over the world. Indeed, Nietzsche's perspectivism is strategically designed to recuperate the metaphorics of vision that have dominated (and perverted) representational epistemology.[2] In order to appropriate the metaphorics of vision for his reconstituted notion of objectivity, Nietzsche glides effortlessly between the twin sensory images of 'eyes' and 'voices':

> the *more* affects we allow to speak about one thing, the *more* eyes, different eyes, we can use to observe one thing, the more complete will our 'concept' of this thing, our 'objectivity', be.

Eyes and affects, knowing and feeling, seeing and speaking, conception and perception, situation and expression: the pursuit of objectivity requires us to deconstruct these binary oppositions and integrate the supposedly antagonistic terms within each. Nietzsche's reconstituted notion of objectivity encourages a maximal expression of affective investment in the world – a chorus of radically situated 'voices' – and thus stands 180 degrees removed from the traditional epistemological goal of disinterested, disaffected contemplation. In fact, he concludes his warning against disinterested contemplation by graphically likening the pursuit of objectivity to an act of self-directed castration: 'to suspend each and every affect, supposing we were capable of this – what would that mean but to *castrate* the intellect?' (GM III: 12).

'There is *only* a perspectival knowing' thus means that knowledge is possible only if one's affective engagement with the world is both recognized and expressed. If it is not, then one can at best lay claim to a desiccated, bloodless simulacrum of knowledge. Nietzsche's recuperation of the metaphorics of vision enables us to understand perspectives as *bodies*: suffused with affect, inextricably situated in the world, and inscribed with the pain and torment inflicted by normalizing mores and institutions.[3] Nietzsche consequently reconstitutes the notion of objectivity as an aggregation of radically situated perspectives (or bodies) – none of which affords us an epistemically pure glimpse of the world. The task of the *Wissenschaftler* who aspires to objectivity is to compile as exhaustive an aggregation of radically situated perspectives (or bodies) as possible, to assemble an unprecedented chorus of affective voices.

Third, Nietzsche recommends his perspectivism not for its epistemic purity, but for the strategic advantage that accrues to his reconstituted notion of objectivity. His discussion of 'perspectivism' appears within the context of his analysis of the ascetic ideal, with which he associates the traditional understanding of objectivity as disinterested contemplation. Nietzsche frequently contends that the pursuit of objectivity requires a concomitant assault on the affects, which in turn leads, paradoxically, to a diminution of our knowledge, to the subordination of situated knowledges to lifeless simulacra of knowledge. The strategic advantage of objectivity lies, he believes, in 'the ability to *control* one's Pro and Con and to dispose of them, so that one knows how to employ a *variety* of perspectives and affective interpretations in the service of knowledge' (GM III: 12).

Fourth, Nietzsche willingly accepts the self-referential implications of his endorsement of situated knowledges. He readily acknowledges that his own perspectivism too is situated, that it reflects the peculiar political interests of its author. 'Perspectivism' is itself perspectival in nature, for it is the product of the partial perspective and embodied affect peculiar to Herr Nietzsche. Rather than stake an illicit claim to epistemic purity, Nietzsche quite openly voices the hostility and resentment that inform his own political campaign against the ascetic practices of traditional epistemology. It is no coincidence that Nietzsche's most illuminating articulation of his perspectivism appears in *On the Genealogy of Morals*, a book in which he announces and foregrounds his own vested political interests in compiling a genealogy of morals.

Nietzsche's perspectivism thus provides a promising epistemological model for feminist theorists. But let us be clear about the opportunity cost of embracing Nietzsche's perspectivism: If we accept this reconstituted notion of objectivity, and seek a maximal aggregation of radically situated perspectives, then we must abandon the quest for a privileged, epistemically pure, God's-eye perspective on the world. We need not disavow our cultural, genealogical or political preferences for certain perspectives, but we must be careful to situate these preferences within a discernible political agenda. The privilege of a particular perspective will derive entirely from its situation within the political agenda it expresses, and not from its internal coherence or privileged access to the real world.

THE LEGACY OF NIETZSCHE'S PERSPECTIVISM IN POSTMODERN FEMINIST EPISTEMOLOGY

Virtually all feminist theorists, and at any rate those with whom I am primarily concerned here, follow Nietzsche in rejecting the traditional philosophical ideal of objectivity. Feminist theorists have long maintained that the achievement of objectivity would require agents to accede to a disembodied, trans-perspectival, patriarchal standpoint – a chimerical gambit that Donna Haraway calls 'the God trick'.[4] This 'view from nowhere' acquires the privilege and cachet of a 'view from everywhere', and effectively devaluates the experiences of those agents whose knowledges of the world are most obviously and ineluctably situated. Feminist theorists thus argue that this ideal of disinterested, detached objectivity is pursued at the expense and exclusion of the situated knowledges of women, especially women of colour. Traditional (patriarchal) epistemology thus delivers only a simulacrum of objectivity, for its emphasis on disinterested detachment precisely discounts the partiality that accrues to a radically situated perspective.

At the same time, however, feminist theorists are understandably reluctant to abandon the *notion* of objectively valid knowledge as the goal of philosophical inquiry. A reconstituted notion of objectivity would provide a standard whereby they might claim, for instance, that one scientific theory is better or more complete or more promising than another. In this light, we might think of the goal of feminist epistemology as the reconstitution of the notion of objectivity, such that feminist theorists might continue the critical enterprise of science without subscribing to its most pernicious concepts.

With respect to the positive content of this reconstituted notion of objectivity, a debate currently rages among feminist theorists.

Donna Haraway, whose writing I shall treat as representative of the project of postmodern feminist epistemology, contends that the objectivity of a perspective is a function of its *partiality*:

> The moral is simple: only partial perspective promises objective vision. . . . Feminist objectivity is about limited location and situated knowledge, not about transcendence and splitting of subject and object. In this way we might become answerable for what we learn and see.[5]

The partiality that Haraway prizes is achieved not through the disinterested detachment of subjects from the world, but through the radical situation of subjects in the world. Her suggested reconceptualization of 'feminist objectivity' therefore devolves from her more fundamental reconceptualization of the world we seek to know in terms of the world in which we live. Haraway considers the pursuit of objectivity a feminist project because women have traditionally been excluded from the male fantasy of detached, disinterested contemplation of disembodied truth. As a consequence, women have traditionally had no choice *but* to cultivate the objectivity that accrues to their situations. We might think of postmodern feminism as attempting to recover the situated knowledge involuntarily acquired by subjugated women, and subsequently turning it to their own political advantage. Postmodern feminism thus aims to assemble the epistemic resources of subjugated standpoints, so that the residents of these standpoints might eventually liberate themselves.

A perceived weakness of this reconstituted notion of objectivity is that postmodern feminists like Haraway cannot (and do not) assign a purely epistemic privilege to the subjugated standpoints of women and excluded others. More precisely, in accordance with her reconstitution of the notion of objectivity, Haraway appropriates the epistemic privilege traditionally assigned to the objectively valid perspective of detached, disembodied standpoints and relocates it in the partial perspective of radically situated standpoints:

> I would like a doctrine of embodied objectivity that accommodates paradoxical and critical feminist science projects: feminist objectivity means quite simply *situated knowledge*.[6]

Haraway's brand of feminism conveys a postmodern sensibility in large part because she has abandoned the quest for an epistemically pure, foundationally innocent standpoint. Indeed, a primary aim of her writing is to disabuse feminists of the perceived need for an untainted, originary, epistemically pure standpoint from which to launch their various political campaigns. Partiality thus stands as the sole determinant of objectivity, and there exists no verifiable epistemic relation between objectivity and standpoints informed by positions of exclusion, oppression or victimage:

> A commitment to mobile positioning and to passionate detachment is dependent on the impossibility of innocent 'identity' politics and epistemologies as strategies for seeing from the standpoints of the subjugated in order to see well.[7]

Postmodern feminists register a preference for the standpoints of excluded, subjugated women not because such standpoints are epistemically pure, but because 'they seem to promise more adequate, sustained, objective, transforming accounts of the world'.[8]

This preference is clearly political in nature, and Haraway makes no pretence of aspiring to epistemic purity or foundational innocence. For Haraway, any epistemic privilege necessarily implies a political (i.e. situated) preference. Her postmodern orientation elides the boundaries traditionally drawn between politics and epistemology, and thus renders otiose the ideal of epistemic purity. All perspectives are partial, all standpoints situated – including those of feminist theorists. It is absolutely crucial to Haraway's postmodern feminist project that we acknowledge her claims *about* situated knowledge as *themselves* situated within the political agenda of postmodern feminism; postmodern feminists must therefore accept and accommodate the self-referential implications of their own epistemic claims.

The political agenda of postmodern feminism thus assigns to (some) subjugated standpoints a political preference or priority. Haraway, for example, believes that some subjugated standpoints may be more immediately revealing, especially since they have been discounted and excluded for so long. They may prove especially useful in coming to understand the political and psychological mechanisms whereby patriarchy discounts the radically situated knowledges of others while claiming for its own (situated) knowledge an epistemic privilege that divorces objectivity from partiality:

> The standpoints of the subjugated . . . are savvy to modes of denial through repression, forgetting, and disappearing acts – ways of being nowhere while claiming to see comprehensively. The subjugated have a decent chance to be on to the god-trick and all its dazzling – and therefore blinding – illuminations.[9]

But these subjugated standpoints do not afford feminists an epistemically privileged view of the world independent of their political agenda. Feminist theorists who subscribe to Haraway's agenda must therefore resist the temptation to claim for subjugated standpoints the same type of privilege that patriarchy claims for itself. The epistemic 'privilege' of subjugated standpoints must be understood in terms of the feminist reconceptualization of objectivity and revision of epistemology.

A subjugated standpoint may shed new light on the ways of an oppressor, but it in no way renders superfluous or redundant to science the standpoint of the oppressor. Because neither standpoint fully comprises the other, the aggregation of the two would move both parties (or a third party) closer to a more objective understanding of the world:

> The science question in feminism is about objectivity as positioned rationality. Its images are not the products of escape and transcendence of limits, i.e., the view from above, but the joining of partial views and halting voices into a collective subject position that promises a vision of the means of ongoing finite embodiment, of living within limits and contradictions, i.e., of views from somewhere.[10]

If some feminists have political reasons for disavowing this project of aggregation, or for adopting it selectively, then they must pursue their political agenda at the expense of the greater objectivity that they might otherwise have gained. The decision to discount the situated knowledge of another is always a political decision with political consequences, and feminists should beware of appealing to epistemic purity to defend such decisions.

SANDRA HARDING'S FEMINIST STANDPOINT THEORY

Sandra Harding articulates and defends what she calls 'feminist standpoint epistemologies', which she presents as superior to the theory known as 'feminist empiricism'. The hallmark of feminist standpoint epistemologies is that they 'direct us to start our research and scholarship from the perspectives of women's lives'.[11] The goal of the standpoint epistemologies is to collect the immediate, but 'scientifically inadequate' data from women's experiences, and to construct viable scientific theories based on – but not reducible to – these experiences.

Despite her endorsement of feminist standpoint theory, Harding expresses a general agreement with the deconstructive designs of postmodern feminism, and she explicitly applauds Haraway's campaign to reconstitute objectivity in terms of situated knowledges.[12] Harding thus agrees that the pursuit of objectivity is a patriarchal exercise that systematically excludes the experiences of women. In a rhetorical question to which she implies that an affirmative response is in order, Harding asks,

> If it is the experience of subjugation that provides the grounding for the most desirable inquiries and knowledges, then should not the experience of . . . women who have suffered from racism provide the grounding for . . . feminist scientific and epistemological projects, not to mention ethics and politics?[13]

As an alternative to the traditional notion of objectivity, Harding proposes what she calls 'strong objectivity', which requires the scientist (or epistemologist) to situate herself or himself 'on the same critical, causal plane as the object of his or her inquiry'.[14]

Harding apparently believes, however, that 'strong objectivity' is gained not (merely) through an aggregation of the partial perspective of radically situated standpoints, but also by privileging within this aggregate a cluster of standpoints distinguished by their experiences of oppression, exclusion and victimage:

> Epistemologically, the standpoint theories argue that it is an advantage to base thought in the everyday lives of people in oppressed and excluded groups.[15]

Subjugated standpoints are not merely important additions to the aggregate of perspectives that feminist epistemologists are assembling, but actually afford us a more accurate ('less distorted') glimpse of the world:

> The logic of the standpoint epistemologies depends on the understanding that the 'master's position' in any set of dominating social relations tends to produce distorted visions of the *real regularities and underlying causal tendencies in social relations* – including human interactions with nature. The feminist standpoint epistemologies argue that because men are in the master's position *vis-à-vis* women, women's social experience – conceptualized through the lenses of feminist theory – can provide the grounds for a less distorted understanding of the world around us.[16]

Harding apparently believes that the perspective of the 'slave' is privileged in so far as the 'slave' understands not only what it is like to be a 'slave', but also what it must be like to be a 'master'. In order simply to survive, presumably, the 'slave' has managed to discern and correct for the distortions imposed on the world by the perspective of the 'master'. So the 'slave' not only sees the world differently, but also sees the world more clearly and with a better understanding than the 'master', whose own perspective is rendered redundant and superfluous by the epistemic privilege of the 'slave'.

Harding's version of feminist standpoint theory is fraught with conceptual problems. First of all, Harding's epistemological model actually precludes our access to the radically situated knowledges that she proposes as constitutive of 'strong objectivity'. In order to defend the scientific basis of her version of feminist standpoint theory, Harding draws a distinction between 'women's experiences' and 'women's lives'.[17] Whereas the former 'would not seem to be reliable grounds for deciding just which claims to knowledge are preferable',[18] the latter provide 'an objective location . . . from which feminist research should begin'.[19] The implementation of any such distinction would require us to enlist the services of a competent epistemologist, who could convey better than these women the objective meaning of their 'scientifically inadequate' experiences. This mediatrix would presumably decipher the raw data of women's experiences and translate them into the reliable, objective data of women's lives. As we have seen, Harding is confident of her own capacity to relate and disseminate the situated knowledges of subjugated standpoints without imposing additional distortion.

By legislating the intercession of the epistemic mediatrix, however, Harding actually seals us off from the radically situated knowledges that she associates with 'strong objectivity'. Instead of the 'scientifically inadequate' experiences of disfranchised women of colour, we receive theorized interpretations of subjugated standpoints, filtered through the epistemically privileged, composite standpoint of the mediatrix herself. Harding's epistemology thus engenders an *absurdum practicum*, for it renders inaccessible the radically situated knowledges that it proposes as constitutive of 'strong objectivity'. Rather than deliver 'strong objectivity', Harding serves up a 'strongly edited objectivity': (ostensibly) based on the visceral experiences of women of colour, but *interpreted by* the mediatrix.

Second, Harding simply stipulates the epistemic privilege that she claims for the subjugated standpoint of the 'slave'. Although (or perhaps because) this alleged privilege serves as the cornerstone of the political agenda that she derives from feminist standpoint theory, Harding makes no recognizable attempt to verify it or articulate the conditions under which it obtains. Indeed, the alleged privilege that accrues to the 'slave' functions within Harding's theory as an unchallengeable axiom or tenet of faith; without it, Harding would have an even more difficult time defending the epistemic merits of her version of feminist standpoint theory.

Third, Harding presents an overly idealized characterization of the privilege she assigns to the partial perspective of the 'slave'. Her investment of the 'slave' with an epistemic privilege not only is romantic, but also trivializes the situation of victimage that gives rise to the 'strong objectivity' she prizes. The standpoint of the 'slave' is riddled with just as many unknown snares and prejudices as that of the 'master'; the former standpoint may warrant Harding's political allegiance, but it is just as complicated (and problematic) epistemically as the latter standpoint.

Haraway alerts us to the precise error that Harding commits. Immediately after registering a preference for the partial perspective afforded by subjugated standpoints, Haraway reminds us of the need for feminists to situate politically their own claims about situated knowledge. In an admonition apposite to, though not explicitly directed toward, Harding's feminist standpoint theory, Haraway warns against

> the serious danger of romanticizing and/or appropriating the vision of the less powerful while claiming to see from their positions. To see from below is neither easily learned nor unproblematic, even if 'we' 'naturally' inhabit the great underground terrain of subjugated knowledges. The positionings of the subjugated are not exempt from critical re-examination, decoding, deconstruction, and interpretation; that is, from both semiological and hermeneutic modes of critical enquiry. The standpoints of the subjugated are not 'innocent' positions.[20]

Postmodern feminists must consequently resist as misleading the unsituated claim that subjugated standpoints promise a better or clearer glimpse of the world. Residents of subjugated standpoints 'see' the world differently, and their experiences of the world are currently of immense political value to feminist epistemology, if only by virtue of their systematic historical exclusion and devaluation.

Fourth, Harding's imputation of an epistemic privilege to the 'slave' unwittingly reintroduces the recently retired notion of objectivity, and exposes the residual realism that undergirds her version of feminist standpoint theory. If the 'master' 'tends to produce distorted visions of the real regularities and underlying causal tendencies in social relations', then the 'master' fails even on the terms of traditional, patriarchal epistemology. According to Harding's model, there *is* a real world, after all, which competing standpoints can capture with varying degrees of distortion. Hence there *is* a privileged, 'less distorted' standpoint (or cluster of standpoints), and the task of science is to gain command of these foundational standpoints on the world. If we extend the logic of Harding's theory, then science should consider as its basis the standpoint of the Ultimate Victim, i.e. whomever feminist standpoint theorists determine to be minimally empowered and maximally oppressed.

Rather than extricate epistemology from the snares of patriarchy, Harding serves up an inverted, matriarchal version of patriarchal objectivity. Having set out to validate knowledge in terms of embodied, radically situated knowledges, Harding concludes by discounting the relative value of those standpoints that fall short of maximal victimage. She summarily banishes the 'view from above' prized by the scientific patriarchy, only to install its antipode, the 'view from below' as the new foundation of knowledge. Harding's version of feminist standpoint theory thus enshrines the objectively valid perspective of *das Weib an sich*, and therefore remains trapped within the traditional epistemological paradigm it means to supplant.[21]

Fifth, Harding's residual commitment to the notion of patriarchal objectivity betrays a basic confusion that lies at the heart of her version of feminist standpoint theory. Despite her avowed intention to ground epistemic privilege in situated knowledges rather than in epistemic purity, she in fact claims both types of privilege for her articulation of the standpoint of the 'slave'. As a consequence, we find two notions of objectivity at work in her theory. Although Harding endorses the pursuit of 'strong objectivity' via situated knowledges, she does not sufficiently or consistently situate her own (second-order) claims about situated knowledge. She consequently confuses her own political preference for the subjugated standpoints of women of colour with the epistemic purity of such standpoints.

When speaking *about* these subjugated standpoints, Harding (usually) accounts for their privilege in terms of her situated political preference; but when speaking *from* these standpoints, which she is presumptuously and unjustifiably inclined to do, she accounts for their privilege in terms of an epistemic purity that the distortions of the 'master' compromise. Harding's own composite standpoint, which purports to integrate the visceral experiences of dispossessed women of colour with the suspiciously 'masterful' theorizing of an educated, economically privileged, white college professor, is a detached, disembodied abstraction, a vestige (and perversion) of the antepostmodern patriarchal quest for objectivity. Whereas Haraway and other postmodern feminists have accepted the opportunity cost of a reconstituted notion of objectivity, Harding has not. Despite acknowledging the epistemological and political advantages of postmodern feminism, Harding clings to the idea that the standpoint of the 'slave' affords us an epistemically pure glimpse of the real world. Harding consequently breaks only incompletely and irresolutely with patriarchal epistemology, and thus declines Haraway's invitation to take the postmodern turn.

Sixth, Harding's failure to situate her own claims about situated knowledges, and thus own up to the political agenda that informs her version of feminist standpoint theory, admits of grave repercussions for feminist politics. Haraway warns of a 'dream' to which some feminists continue to subscribe:

> The permanent partiality of feminist points of view has consequences for our expectations of forms of political organization and participation. We do not need a totality in order to work well. The feminist dream of a common language, like all dreams for a perfectly true language, of perfectly faithful naming of experience, is a totalizing and imperialist one.[22]

This 'dream' of foundational innocence is not only epistemically bankrupt, but also politically disastrous, for it imposes upon feminist politics conditions of justification that are impossible to meet. Haraway's campaign to expose and debunk this 'dream' effectively absolves feminists of any perceived responsibility for grounding or justifying a political agenda by appeal to epistemic criteria. Haraway regards both epistemology and politics as serious endeavours, but she does not require of the latter that it acquire its justificatory and motive force from the former – especially if the former retains its familiar patriarchal cast. The 'privilege' of any postmodern feminist agenda must and will be purely political; the desire or need for a further, epistemic privilege will only frustrate feminist political activity.

Harding would appear to subscribe to this totalizing dream, for she attempts to ground her political agenda in the epistemic privilege of those subjugated standpoints that afford us a less distorted view of the real world. Harding's weakness for this 'totalizing dream' thus betrays the degree of her complicity in the traditional patriarchal epistemology that she ostensibly seeks to dismantle. Harding has unwittingly embarked on a quest for epistemic purity, for the 'totalizing and imperialist' standpoint demanded (but never achieved) by traditional, patriarchal epistemology.

Because she can neither defend nor verify this epistemic privilege, however, feminist standpoint theory must place its political agenda in abeyance. Before feminist standpoint theorists can act politically, they must first excavate and recover a chimerical point of epistemological origin. Before challenging patriarchy head on, they must first fashion (or invent) for themselves an unassailable epistemic foundation. Feminist standpoint theory thus runs the risk of indefinitely postponing political activity while Harding attempts to defend the mysterious epistemic privilege of *das Weib an sich*, which she claims for victims and slaves. So long as feminist standpoint theorists continue their quest for the Holy Grail of epistemic purity, the reign of objectivity continues uninterrupted, and the political needs of women remain largely unaddressed.

THE SLAVE REVOLT IN EPISTEMOLOGY

From a Nietzschean perspective, Harding's terminological predilections appear uncannily honest, for her dubious investment of the standpoint of the 'slave' with an epistemic privilege neatly recapitulates the strategies of slave morality, as documented in *On the Genealogy of Morals*. According to Nietzsche, the ascetic priest catalyses the 'slave revolt in morality' by supplying the slaves with metaphysical ammunition for use against the nobles – and ultimately against themselves. Under the tutelage of the ascetic priest, the slaves claim to prefer the punishment meted out to them, thus reinterpreting their suffering as a sign of their goodness. The slaves may eventually succeed in disarming the nobles, but only by consigning themselves to perpetual enslavement – herein lies their sole strategic advantage.

Harding valorizes the position of the 'slave' precisely as Nietzsche's analysis of slave morality would lead us to expect: she essentially transforms victimage into virtue. Fomenting what amounts to a 'slave revolt in epistemology', Harding decrees that certain disadvantaged and subjugated agents command a privileged standpoint precisely because they are victims. At first glance, Harding's strategy might appear to reprise Haraway's: both endeavour to turn the conditions of victimage to the advantage of the victims, to 'seize the tools to mark the world that marked them as other'.[23] But unlike Haraway, who openly situates her own epistemological inquiries in the political agenda of postmodern feminism, Harding fails to situate her own claims about (and upon) situated knowledges. Like its predecessor revolt in morality, then, the 'slave revolt in epistemology' empowers the 'slaves' only by displacing their agency and ensuring their continued enslavement.

In the *Genealogy*, Nietzsche offers us a sketch of the ascetic priest that instructively illuminates the political consequences of Harding's slave revolt in epistemology:

> He brings salves and balms with him, no doubt; but before he can act as a physician, he first has to wound; when he then stills the pain of the wound *he at the same time infects the wound* . . . in [his] presence everything necessarily grows sick, and everything sick tame.
>
> (GM III: 15)

Like the ascetic priest, Harding presents herself – *qua* epistemologist – as the theoretical spokesperson for various subjugated standpoints, which she describes as instantiating the position of the 'slave'. Attempting to empower these disadvantaged agents *as* 'slaves', Harding resorts to a quick fix. In order to alleviate the pain and alienation of their victimage, she promises these 'slaves' the (illusory) epistemic privilege that derives from a 'less distorted' perspective on the world. These subjugated standpoints, she insists, afford their otherwise dispossessed residents a more accurate glimpse of the world as it really is.

Nietzsche's psychological profile of the ascetic priest indicates that Harding's version of feminist standpoint theory treats only the 'symptoms' of gender-based oppression, and not the underlying 'illness' itself (GM III: 17). If Nietzsche is right, then Harding's groundless assurance of a privileged standpoint on the world is more likely eventually to alienate women further from their own experiences than to affirm and validate these experiences. The world appears alien and inhospitable to the 'slaves' in part because they do *not* understand the logic and motives that inform the standpoint of the 'master'. To lead the 'slave' to believe otherwise, as Harding does, verges upon cruelty. The quick fix that Harding provides will consequently prove disastrous in the long run, for it ultimately prevents women from gaining the liberation that genuine objectivity might supply.

If Nietzsche's analysis is applicable, then Harding's version of feminist standpoint theory not only empowers women *qua* victims, but also empowers Harding herself *qua* victims' theoretical spokes-person – much as the ascetic priest empowers the slaves *qua* sufferers and himself *qua* sufferers' advocate. In order to maintain the privilege of her own composite feminist standpoint, from which she presumes to speak both about and for dispossessed women of colour, Harding must ensure their continued victimage. This is not to say, of course, that Sandra Harding personally oppresses women of colour or consciously sabotages their pursuit of enfranchisement. But because she fails to situate her own (second-order) claims about their situated knowledges, and fails to appreciate the danger that her theorizing might further devaluate their situated knowledges, she potentially stands in their way and further distorts their voices.[24]

By virtue of its very constitution, trading on a problematic distinction between 'women's experiences' and 'women's lives', Harding's version of feminist standpoint theory cultivates in these victims a dependency on the mediatrix to express in a 'scientifically adequate' fashion their experiences of victimage. Although Harding's distinction between 'women's experiences' and 'women's lives' is designed to subject the speech of *all* women to scientific rigour,[25] its implementation would be especially devastating for those oppressed women who *already* are not allowed or empowered to speak for themselves. Those women of colour whose voices remain muffled, unheard, unarticulated – and therefore 'scientifically inadequate' – would become further enslaved to the mediatrix who offers to derive theoretically the objective meaning of their experiences. Not-withstanding her unimpeachably noble intentions, Harding poten-tially contributes to the victimage of those dispossessed women of colour whom western culture – and now feminist science – discour-ages from speaking for themselves.[26]

We should therefore not be surprised if, like the ascetic priest, Harding displaces the agency and responsibility of the subjugants for whom she speaks. She tends on occasion to impute agency to concepts, categories, designations, sentences and other linguistic constructs/implements. She claims, for example, that

> The concept 'African' tends to paper over the vast differences between the histories and present projects of the hundreds of indigenous African cultures.[27]

The imputation of agency to a concept, rather than to the person(s) responsible for wielding or popularizing the concept, only reinforces the victimage of the victim, who now must beware of autonomous, adventitious concepts as well as the extra-linguistic oppression of the 'master'. By displacing agency into the linguistic realm, Harding 'papers over' the fact that victims too are agents, that victims can resist their victimage by deflecting pernicious concepts and designations with empowering concepts and designations of their own design. As agents, however, subjugated women of colour would presumably speak for themselves, and no longer depend for their theoretical expression on the composite feminist standpoint of the mediatrix.

Harding's version of feminist standpoint theory thus runs the risk of further discouraging dispossessed women of colour from speaking in their own 'scientifically inadequate' voices. If ultimate liberation from victimage entails even a modicum of self-expression, then feminist standpoint theory promises liberation only for the mediatrix and her 'scientifically adequate' elite. For all others, it promises only continued victimage. Nietzsche's analysis of the psychology of the ascetic priest thus indicates that the mediatrix required by feminist standpoint theory might unwittingly sustain the privilege of her own (abstract) composite standpoint by compounding the victimage of subjugated agents.

CONCLUSION

As an antidote to the dream of foundational innocence, by which Sandra Harding is perhaps enthralled, Donna Haraway proposes various imaginative exercises designed to liberate feminists from the perceived need for an originary, epistemically pure standpoint. As an enabling narrative for postmodern feminists, Haraway offers the myth of the cyborg, a composite, hybrid creature that embodies the irresolvable tensions and dualities that characterize late modernity.[28] The cyborg represents the embodiment of purely prospective agency, an unhistorical mutant to which the past – along with the allure of innocence, origin and redemption – is irretrievably lost. If feminists can imagine themselves in their political activity as cyborgs – which, in reality, women have always been – then they can perhaps exorcize the immobilizing spectre of *das Weib an sich*, which continues to haunt their practices.

Here too Haraway follows Nietzsche. The original cyborg, I propose, is none otherx than Zarathustra, the consummate micropolitical agent of late modernity. I read the *Bildungsgang* of Zarathustra as something like a cyborg myth: operating in the shadow of the dead God, consigned by his crepuscular destiny to a belief in idols that he can neither respect nor reject, Zarathustra must somehow neutralize his romantic dreams of return and redemption. Zarathustra eventually 'becomes what he is' by turning that which oppresses him – his destiny, his fatality – to his own strategic advantage. He is ineluctably both free spirit and ascetic priest, and he implements both strands of this dual heritage to found a micro-community of higher men (Z IV: 2–9). This community is unstable and ephemeral, lacking altogether in theoretical justifications, institutional reinforcements, and foundational myths. This community of higher men is exclusively prospective in its orientation; it has no laws, no history, and no goal above and beyond the survival of European nihilism.

Zarathustra founds this cyborg community, supplying it with a minimal micro-political infrastructure in the form of an inaugural 'Ass Festival' (Z IV: 17–18), but eventually withdraws from it. He comes to realize that his dual heritage renders him both life-giving and life-destroying. Although he has consecrated this micro-community in the *Twilight of the Idols*, he has also enslaved his companions and encouraged them to invest their redemptive hopes in him. Sensing that he has enslaved his companions and usurped the station of the dead God – having become someone for the sake of whom 'living on earth is worthwhile' (Z IV: 19) – he banishes the higher men and dissolves the micro-community he founded.

The final scene of *Zarathustra*, framed in cyclical imagery that suggests a closed system, captures the purely prospective agency that characterizes the cyborg. Restless in his sheltering solitude but chastened by the prospect of reprising the logic that doomed his previous political endeavours, Zarathustra rises none the less to greet the dawn. Bereft of hopes for ultimate success, armed solely with the will to survive the decadence of late modernity, Zarathustra 'goes under' once again to found yet another, equally ephemeral, cyborg community.

NOTES

1 With the exception of occasional emendations, I rely throughout this chapter on Walter Kaufmann's editions/translations of Nietzsche's works for Random House and Viking Press. Numbers refer to sections rather than to pages, and the following key explains the abbreviations for my citations. BGE: *Beyond Good and Evil*; GM: *On the Genealogy of Morals*; TI: *Twilight of the Idols*; Z: *Thus Spoke Zarathustra*.

2 Donna Haraway suggests a similar reclamation project:

I would like to proceed by placing metaphorical reliance on a much maligned sensory system in feminist discourse: vision. Vision can be good for avoiding binary oppositions. I would like to insist on the embodied nature of all vision, and so reclaim the sensory system that has been used to signify a leap out of the marked body and into a conquering gaze from nowhere.

(Haraway 1991: 188)

3 My interpretation deviates sharply from the many recent attempts to identify Nietzsche's perspectivism with a privative anti-essentialism. Two recent books representative of the anti-essentialist reading of Nietzsche's perspectivism are Nehamas (1985) and Rorty (1989).

4 Haraway (1991: 189).

5 Ibid. 190.

6 Ibid. 188.

7 Ibid. 192.

8 Ibid. 191.

9 Ibid. 191.

10 Ibid. 196.

11 Harding (1991: 249).

12 Ibid. 11.

13 Harding (1986: 191).

14 Harding (1991: 161).

15 Ibid. 271.

16 Harding (1986: 191, emphasis added). In her most recent work, Harding confirms her commitment to this residually realist model: ' "The winner tells the tale", as historians point out, and so trying to construct the story from the perspective of the lives of those who resist oppression generates less partial and distorted accounts of nature and social relations' (1991: 126).

17 Harding (1991: 123).

18 Ibid. 123.

19 Ibid. 123.

20 Haraway (1991: 191).

21 Discarded drafts of *Beyond Good and Evil* indicate that Nietzsche at one time intended to include a separate Part entitled *Das Weib an sich*. Vestiges of this intended Part are found in Sections 231–9 of *Beyond Good and Evil*. Because Nietzsche models *Das Weib an sich* on the Kantian *Ding an sich*, we can assume with some confidence that the ridicule he heaps on the latter applies to the former as well. Nietzsche's point here is that both *Das Weib an sich* and the Kantian *Ding an sich* are metaphysical inventions to which no human perspective or standpoint corresponds.

22 Haraway (1991: 173).

23 Ibid. 175.

24 Harding (1991) glosses this criticism of feminist standpoint theory:

But it is not the experiences and the speech [of women] that provides the grounds for feminist claims; it is rather the subsequently articulated observations of and theory about the rest of nature and social relations – observations and theory that start out from, that look at the world from the perspective of, women's lives. And who is to do this 'starting out'? With this question it becomes clear that knowledge-seeking requires democratic, participatory politics.

(Harding 1991: 124)

25 As Harding (1991: 123) explains, 'Moreover, women (feminists included) say all kinds of things . . . that are scientifically inadequate. (Women, and feminists, are not worse in this respect than anyone else; we too are humans.)'
26 According to Harding (1991: 123) 'So while both "women's experiences" and "what women say" certainly are good places to begin generating research projects in biology and social science, they would not seem to be reliable grounds for deciding just which claims to knowledge are preferable'. Why Harding believes this is not at all clear; presumably biologists and social scientists must also subject the raw data of women's experiences to theoretical conceptualization.
27 Harding (1986: 173).
28 Haraway (1991: ch. 8) 'A Cyborg Manifesto'.

BIBLIOGRAPHY

Haraway, D. J. (1991) *Simians, Cyborgs and Women*, London: Free Association Books.
Harding, S. (1986) *The Science Question in Feminism*, Ithaca, NY: Cornell University Press.
—— (1991) *Whose Science? Whose Knowledge? Thinking from Women's Lives*, Ithaca, NY: Cornell University Press.
Nehamas, A. (1985) *Nietzsche: Life as Literature*, Cambridge, Mass.: Harvard University Press.
Nietzsche, F. (1966a) *Beyond Good and Evil*, trans. W. Kaufmann, New York: Random House.
—— (1966b) *Thus Spoke Zarathustra: A Book for All and None*, trans. W. Kaufmann, Harmondsworth: Penguin.
—— (1967) *On the Genealogy of Morals*, trans. W. Kaufmann, New York: Random House.
—— (1968) *Twilight of the Idols*, trans. R. J. Hollingdale, Harmondsworth: Penguin.
Rorty, R. (1989) *Contingency, Irony and Solidarity*, Cambridge: Cambridge University Press.

7 *Ressentiment* and power
Some reflections on feminist practices

Marion Tapper

Nietzsche's remarks on *ressentiment* and power and Foucault's analytics of power form the backdrop to this chapter. My concern is with certain feminist discursive and non-discursive practices, primarily in those institutions in which feminists have achieved a degree of success – bureaucracy, educational institutions and the professions. The question is: in what strategies of power are these practices participating and with what conception of power are they operating?

The thesis is that some feminist practices, in so far as they are motivated by the spirit of *ressentiment*, have been preoccupied with power as control and that this involves a double-edged danger. On the one side it risks playing into the hands of, rather than resisting, the modern mechanisms of power that Foucault identified as operating by techniques of surveillance, normalization and control. On the other, it involves a blindness to or forgetfulness of other forms of the will to power which are positive, those active forms concerned with self-formation and autonomy. In particular, I hope to identify what I shall call the logic of a psycho-politics that seems to be emerging in a specific feminist configuration of power/knowledge. It shifts from identifying and seeking to redress injustices to finding 'evil' everywhere, and not only in actions and practices but also in the 'soul' – of individuals and types of individuals, of language, discourse, culture and sexuality. It then requires and produces experts to detect the 'evil' and special discourses to expose it.

My procedure will be to outline some instances in which I think we can see a shift from wanting equal power within existing institutions to attacking those institutions themselves, from criticizing practices and discourses to finding everything 'evil'. I then ask whether this makes sense in terms of the structure of *ressentiment* and, if so, what implications this has for our understanding of and participation in relations of power. Again I consider some instances of feminist practices in institutions. In conclusion I discuss some ways in which some feminist practices, rather than resisting power, might be complicit in it.

> One desires *freedom* so long as one does not possess power. Once one does possess it, one desires to overpower; if one cannot do that (if one is still too weak to do so), one desires *'justice'*, i.e. *equal power*.
>
> (Nietzsche 1968: 784)

Let me start by saying that I take it as given that men have had and in many respects still do have power over women, however differently it may be exercised in different places and times and for different classes. But it does not follow from this that women were powerless; in any case, this is certainly not true now.

In response to this women have engaged, and quite properly so, in much of what Nietzsche might call nay-saying: insisting on the extirpation of sexism from language, of harassment from everyday relations, of exploitation from economic practices, of sexist bias from theories and discourses, of objectification from represen- tations, and so on. And also much yea-saying: for control over our bodies, for safe movement, for equal opportunity, affirmative action, legal changes, and for representation in positions of power.

On the face of it it would be hard to deny that these are all worthwhile as actions extending the principles of freedom, equality and justice to include women. Also, on the face of it, we would have to admit that these actions have been reasonably successful though by no means completely. (In any case at least it is clear what further would be required to fulfil the intentions of these actions.) In the academies, for example, women have by and large achieved equality. That there is not equal representation has a largely historical explanation in that it is only relatively recently that women have been undertaking postgraduate degrees and apply- ing for jobs in large numbers. Women can now get jobs and pro- motions if they produce the amount and quality of work that men do; most if not all committees require female representation; there is an enormous growth in publishing by and about women; and academies now have procedures to deal with instances of sexual harassment and other grievances such that few academics would dare to behave in ways which only a few years ago were the cause of justifiable complaint. My interest is in why and in what ways women have not been satisfied with this level of institutional reform. Let me consider some examples.

In the 1970s (in Australia) the struggle to introduce women's studies courses and majors in the academies generated considerable debate as to whether or not, and why, it would be better to have separate women's studies courses or to have the study of women incorporated into other courses; and in parallel, whether or not, and why, it would be better to have separate women's studies departments or women's studies taught through the various departments of established disciplines. In most, if not all, institutions various of these options have been adopted with varying degrees of strength and success. But curiously this has not proven to be enough. At least some feminist academics now want all courses and preferably all appointments, at least in arts faculties, to incorporate or evidence a concern for women's issues (Matthews and Broom 1991: 14). And mention is even made of the need to retrain male staff about disciplinary masculinism (Allen 1991: 10).

A related matter and one which contributes to the likelihood of the occurrence of the above-mentioned shift from wanting a place in that academy to wanting power in the academy is a shift in the critical feminist discourses within disciplines and perhaps with the critique of 'western patriarchal discourse' as such. Take, for example, art history. Earlier art historical critiques were concerned to establish that women artists were ignored, excluded from institutions and from recognition through critical appraisal and the formation of canons. In the process they discovered or retrieved and documented the work of women artists and argued that they should be included in the canon. It is worth noting that the fact that this was possible showed that, despite being excluded and ignored, women artists were not rendered powerless, much less non-existent. Since the early 1980s the focus of attention has shifted from getting women included in the canon to questioning the process of canon formation. More specifically it is claimed that the problem is not so much that the history of art and the practice of art history excludes women artists. The problem concerns the reason why art criticism and art history need to assert a feminine stereotype, sensibility and art. The ideology of the language of art, it is said, is 'made by a dominant group which affirms men's dominance and power and reproduces their supremacy' (Parker and Pollock 1981: 80).

Similarly with philosophy. For some years feminist philosophers catalogued the absurdly sexist remarks made by male philosophers about women and re-read the canon to reveal sexist bias in even those texts that said nothing explicit about women. This practice, perhaps in part because it has been completed, has given way to much more broadsweeping claims. Lloyd, for example, suggests that 'our ideals of Reason have historically incorporated an exclusion of the feminine, and that femininity itself has been partly constituted through such processes of exclusion' (Lloyd 1984: x). Jones states that 'this definition of authority as rules normalises an androcentric view of authority' (Jones 1988: 122). These random examples occur in carefully argued and detailed analyses. Others make much wilder claims that philosophy itself – logic, metaphysics, epistemology, philosophical forms of argument and analysis – is patriarchal. Whatever the meaning and validity of such claims, and whatever the author's intentions in making them, they seem to have had a baneful effect. Some women students, for example, use them to justify refusing to read the classics of philosophy on the ground that they are written by men and hence patriarchal. If challenged, for example by saying that Anselm's ontological proof of the existence of God is one of the most beautiful and elegant pieces of writing, they too easily resort to the claim that logic is masculine; or that Plato or Sartre have been proven to be sexist. We now have a form of discourse in which it is enough to say that a text is written by a man to dismiss it. The reverse side of this is the construction of a canon of feminists' texts which operates by the same process of exclusion of all canons: Plato, Hobbes, Rousseau, Hegel and so on are excluded in favour of the feminist critiques of political theory.

In a different domain Joan Cocks traces a similar shift with respect to feminist political and theoretical concerns with the body and sexuality. What began as an attempt to reclaim female sexuality and bodily pleasure from its denunciation and denial has been transformed into a radical rejection of sexual desire and pleasure as nothing but a social construct of male power. And what began as a necessary and legitimate struggle against sexual harassment and abuse of women and children has extended into a suspicion of all bodily contact, gesture and movement as possibly expressive of male power. As Cocks says, this broadens 'the meaning of the body's violation and the scope for authoritarian rule' (Cocks 1991: 154).

In general we might say that early liberal feminists, and their contemporary counterparts, saw themselves as arguing within a theory of justice and social practices for the transformation of those practices so that women could also share in the good things available while the bad things were removed. In contrast some contemporary radical feminists tend to proclaim themselves against the whole of western discourse and society. We find wholesale denunciations of men, patriarchy, sex, language, philosophy, and so on. We find claims that men have all the power and women none and that men use that power to repress women; differences are acknowledged between women and men and between women, but not between men; everything considered unacceptable is associated with men; and monolithic univocal explanations of this are proposed: either by such concrete things as 'the nature of men' or more abstractly, the institution of 'compulsory heterosexuality'.

The question I want to raise about this is whether it might be motivated and thereby explained by the spirit of *ressentiment*? A number of features which are pertinent here characterize this spirit. First, an inability to 'let go', to forget, it cannot have done with anything (Nietzsche 1969: 58). It is both a backward-looking spirit – it needs to keep on remembering past injustices – and an expansive spirit – it needs to find new injustices everywhere. In the kinds of institutions I am concerned with, those in which women have roughly achieved equal power, it can be expressed in the following kind of phenomenon. Where those with institutional power cannot justifiably claim that they are being discriminated against at the level of actions and practices they can maintain their political integrity, their claim to ideological purity and sense of powerlessness by resorting to finding 'evil' and injustice in wider and wider circumstances and at deeper and more concealed levels. The issue is no longer just what men say about and do to women but the very nature of language, discourse, culture and society. The enemy is no longer someone with whom you disagree and hence with whom you can argue, but a type – man – who is uncomprehending and unable and unwilling to try, a type whose very being is recalcitrant to virtue, who is evil.

The person motivated by the spirit of *ressentiment* looks for 'evil', needs to recriminate and distribute blame, to impute wrongs, distribute responsibilities and to find sinners. As Nietzsche says, they want others to be evil in order to be able to consider themselves good (Nietzsche 1969: 39). As Deleuze says, the man of *ressentiment* feels 'the corresponding object as a personal offence and affront because he makes the object responsible for his own powerlessness' (Deleuze 1983: 116). There seems to be two elements here. One is the need to see the other as powerful and responsible for my powerlessness, and then the transformation of this thought into the thought that my powerlessness is a proof of my goodness and the other's evil. And this works by a revaluation of the enemy's values – an act of the most spiritual revenge, as Nietzsche says (Nietzsche 1969: 34). This makes sense of two aspects of feminist thought. First, the need to see women as helpless victims, as abused, misrepresented, as powerless in the face of such an onslaught of sexist, patriarchal, male power in every dimension of life and thought. Second, in the now frequently asserted claims of women's moral superiority: that women are caring, nurturant, their relations non-hierarchical, and so on. And seeing ourselves as good gives us a right to demand that others conform to our values.

One further aspect of *ressentiment* worth mentioning here is the inability to admire and respect. In contrast with envy, which allows for the possibility of admiring the work and qualities of those we envy, *ressentiment* allows for no such thing. If a man gets a job or promotion or a publication it is explained away by the fact that he is a man, using old boys' networks and so on. And now that women are getting jobs and so on we can see the same type of response on the part of men: she got it only because of affirmative action policies or because of her sexual behaviour.

However, in the discussion of *ressentiment* I do not mean to be attributing particular psychological states to particular individuals, but rather to be diagnosing the spirit of some current feminist discursive and non-discursive practices. The issue is why it is that now that women have achieved considerable formal and substantial equality – at least in the institutions I am concerned with – this has not proven enough. My concern is not with *ressentiment* as individual psychology but with the way this is played out politically. Women have quite reasonably wanted power, but perhaps, entangled in the spirit of *ressentiment* (quite unsurprisingly given our oppression throughout history) we have failed to be sufficiently critical about what it was that we wanted in wanting power. We wanted what it was that we believed the others had: power over.

In his Preface to the English translation of *Nietzsche and Philosophy* Deleuze says that Nietzsche is misunderstood if the will to power is interpreted as 'wanting or seeking power' and if the Nietzschean 'slave' is understood as someone who finds himself dominated by a master, and deserves to be (Deleuze 1983: xii). We could not disagree if this is all that Nietzsche is meant to mean by will to power and slave. But Deleuze also tells us that to want or seek power is a form of the will to power – its lowest degree, 'its negative form, the guise it assumes when reactive forces prevail in the state of things' (Deleuze 1983: xi). In other words wanting power over is only one form of the will to power, and a reactive, negative form. Deleuze also says that '*ressentiment* and bad conscience are expressions of the triumph of reactive forces in man and even of the constitution of man by reactive forces: the man-slave' (Deleuze 1983: x). When reactive forces prevail they prevail with both the dominators and the dominated: 'totalitarian regimes are in this sense regimes of slaves, not merely because of the people they subjugate, but above all because of the type of "masters" they set up' (Deleuze 1983: x).

In this context it is interesting, if not also reasonable, to understand the extent to which the spirit of *ressentiment* may be shaping the form and direction of feminist struggles and successes. May it not be that, under the sway of reactive forces, we have been too inclined to seek power, to want to become masters of the type appropriate to a regime of slaves, to want to dominate? That this might be so would be invisible to us while we think of power as power over, while we think that whatever men do is exercising power or control over us such that if we are to become powerful we will have to gain control. *Ressentiment* makes it look as if power over is the only kind of power such that gaining power over seems the only escape from powerlessness. This would blind us to the possibilities of other, positive, active forms of the will to power. It would also, given that we are always enmeshed in relations of power, make it difficult to see how the ways in which we are exercising power may be complicit in larger strategies of power that we might otherwise object to, such that instead of resisting domination we are creating another form of it.

To claim that some feminists have been seeking power over men, and in some institutions are gaining it, is not to claim that women have in fact gained the sort of power that those who manage institutions have. Clearly very few women are senior managers, professors, deans or heads of department. What I mean can be better understood in the light of Foucault's account of the modern forms of power which operate by structuring the possible field of actions of others (Foucault 1982: 221). It is a form of power which makes individuals subjects; the crucial questions are: what sorts of subjects and by what techniques is this achieved? My suggestion is that feminists do not have to be in 'positions of power' to set up a situation in which certain things are not sayable and not do-able, where certain discursive and non-discursive practices are not acceptable. This can be done by establishing a norm for both discourse and behaviour and using the rules and regulations of the institution to achieve this. If this is how power works we might well say why should feminists not do this? After all, all relations are embedded in relations of power in this sense and the whole point of feminism is to rule out oppressive ways of structuring fields of action while, or in order to, opening up other fields, other possibilities. I shall return to this question after having examined some ways in which feminists are now exercising power. Let me consider some cases.

A fairly straightforward example can be found in the academies. What started out as a campaign to get women appointed and promoted, to introduce women's studies courses and to eliminate sexist bias from teaching practices and course content has now become somewhat different – and in accordance if not collusion with broader changes in the academies. These broader changes involve an increasing bureaucratization which operates with definite techniques of surveillance and normalization – with pervasive and constant procedures of appraisal in which each individual must monitor themselves to ensure that they conform to the standardized expectations of what it is to be an academic (as set out by bureaucratic committees) in order to pass the appraising eye of the supervisor with acceptance. Feminists are co-opting these procedures. The academic must now establish that they teach, research and administer not only in a way in general acceptable to bureaucrats but also in a way which is deemed satisfactory to feminist bureaucrats (whether academic or professional), as must the whole administration of the academy. Course content must be relevant to women, teaching materials must not be sexist, students' essays must not include sexist language, all committees must include at least one woman, and so on. Whether or not any of these are good or bad in themselves is one issue, another, and the one that most concerns me, is the form and use of power involved and the underlying strategies.

Let's consider an aspect of this in more detail: the insistence on women's agenda being incorporated into policy guidelines for selection committees. I mean by this the requirements to call for the references of at least some women applicants, to have some women on the short list and so on, and to explicitly justify not doing so where this is not done, and to explain what steps have been taken to ensure that good women candidates did apply. In some respects this is quite ineffective, and in some respects damaging to the cause of women's interests in getting appointed. If a selection committee, or a majority of it, does not want to appoint a woman it can go through all the proper procedures and still find some reason or another for not considering her to be the most suitable or best candidate for the position. Of course if there is a man they do not wish to appoint they can always find some reason for not doing so. Only now, in the case of women, committees can claim that they have done it legally and morally, for now they can claim that they have not ignored women candidates, they can claim that they have given women more consideration than they otherwise or previously might have.

In the context of discussing problems faced by the Women's Studies Program at the Australian National University, Matthews and Broom consider a number of options for improving the situation of women and women's studies. One is for 'all future appointments in the faculty of Arts to require expertise in women or gender' (Matthews and Broom 1991: 14). Apart from their specific problems this could be seen as a solution to the problem I discussed above. But again this would seem to me to be either ineffective, except in the short term, or dangerous in several respects. It would be ineffective in that before too long every ambitious candidate, or anyone with any sense, will tack on to whatever else they do a project concerning women's issues. And once again the committee's proceedings can continue as before, possibly resulting in men who have little sympathy with women's interests being appointed. I do not take it that just because someone has published on feminism that they are sympathetic, and in the proposed context it would be even less likely. One would have to assume that to write on feminism would bring about a conversion and this is obviously false as shown by the existing writers on feminism who are virulently opposed to it. Short of adopting a positive discrimination policy, which would not exclude those women who are hostile or indifferent to feminism, the only way to avoid this outcome would be to ensure that the 'right kind' of people get on to selection committees so that the candidates with the 'right kind' of research projects are selected. And who are the 'right kind' of people and which are the 'right kind' of research projects? Us and ours – whoever we may be; that is whoever can control the committees. Men might have dominated the academies and the disciplines but they were not always this hegemonic, at least they allowed for some pluralism among themselves. In any case, surely we do not want to repeat this pattern.

There is also a danger in the implicit demand that all research activities have a women's issues component or that all researchers have this as a component of their interests. Matthews and Broom

(1991) restrict their proposal to Arts faculties but, as Allen (1991) and others who refer to 'disciplinary masculinism' even in the sciences and engineering make clear, there is no reason to stop there. The danger I see is that of a kind of intellectual authoritarianism, or at least an excessive privileging of some interests. We could, for instance, agree that nuclear research should be correlated with social and political concerns – for the health and safety of nuclear plant workers and the surrounding population, for the implications for world peace and so on – without thinking that it should be the direct concern of the scientists themselves, and without claiming that the matter is of special concern to women. Some research areas have no immediate socio-political implications, much less any particular relation to women as a group, mathematics and some areas of philosophy for example. And those areas which clearly or arguably do have a direct relation to or impact on women would probably fall into one or two categories: if they did not discuss women's issues they would not be good research, or, the technical aspect of the research might be considered a legitimately separate activity though we might also consider it deplorable that the researcher was not also interested in the implications of the research.

This demand *vis-à-vis* research and appointments is so far only at the stage of a proposal. But a similar demand *vis-à-vis* teaching, coming from Equal Opportunity Offices, is much closer to being implemented in some universities. At the University of Melbourne, for example, there is a document on Gender-Inclusive Curriculum which covers teaching methods and assessment, language and content, as well as the environment in which this occurs. This will, I suspect, have similar effects to the proposal concerning appointments: non-compliance with the spirit if not the letter of the law; its exploitation by those who seek job security or promotion while at least some of those who already bring feminist concerns to their teaching practices and content might find themselves disadvantaged; or an increasing control and surveillance of what we teach and how.

This last point brings me back to the issue that concerns me most here: the unreflective complicity in the modern forms of power. It concerns me most because ethically I am not opposed to the idea that in the present context special consideration should be paid in and to the appointment of women and that attention should be given to the exclusion of women's interests and needs from research and teaching. But the question is: what are feminists doing in the *way* in which we are attempting to redress such injustices?

The first general point to be made is that these practices are playing into and extending the strategies of control that the administrators of the academies are already implementing. Universities, at least in Australia, no longer seem to be satisfied with the power to hold their staff accountable for what they do. They also require a new kind of person, one prepared to engage in constant self-monitoring and to accept frequent external appraisal where the criteria of acceptability, as distinct from accountability, are determined by the administrators in the university and government. Some feminist bureaucrats and academics are providing them with further criteria of acceptability and avenues for surveillance and in the process gaining further power for themselves. For who will determine that acceptable procedures of appointment and promotion or dismissal have been fulfilled? Who will decide what an androcentric perspective is such that they can determine that a curriculum is gender-inclusive? Who will decide that a safe learning environment has been provided – that visual harassment has not occurred? Who will assess which of the current research in women's studies is to be the standard against which the content of a curriculum is to be reviewed?

In undermining the autonomy of individual academics and the processes of peer review and debate these new procedures will establish a profile of the normal, acceptable academic and institute systems of surveillance and judgement. First, a certain kind of individual will be required, and not just one with the right statements, but also one with the right thoughts, movements and gestures. Power, says Foucault, structures the possible field of action of others and the modern form of pastoral power does so in ways which make individuals subjects: 'subject to someone else by control and dependence, and tied to his own identity by a conscience or self-knowledge' (Foucault 1982: 212). And in its modern form it does so as both 'a government of individuality and a form of government by individualisation' (Patton 1989: 265). Second, the university administrators themselves may not care whether academics follow research in women's studies, develop gender-inclusive curricula or use non-sexist language, but it can only be pleasing to them to have others supporting and proposing criteria and techniques of surveillance and appraisal. Foucault says:

> in thinking of the mechanisms of power, I am thinking of its capillary form of existence, the point where power reaches into the very grain of individuals, touches their bodies and inserts

itself into their actions and attitudes, their discourses, their learning processes and everyday lives.

(Foucault 1980: 39)

Feminists can and do use this kind of understanding of the mechanisms of power to expose the effects of power on women's bodies and lives (see Bartky 1988 for an example). But do we want to use them ourselves?

As with other areas of disciplinary power which employ experts to label us and make us conform, these new procedures will require and produce a new set of experts and a new regime of power/knowledge. As Foucault says relations of power require the production of discourses which involve an ensemble of rules according to which the true and the false are separated and which have specific effects of power attached to them (Foucault 1980: 131–3). And this is what we are already beginning to see. Arguments from authority – a feminist text says that Plato is sexist, so he is, that logic is masculine, so it is; women's studies research shows that multiple choice tests disadvantage females and that males and females employ different learning styles, so they do. Will the content of a course be challenged because its text is sexist and so the teaching of it discriminatory? Will certain methods of teaching and assessment be banned? Women claim that if they feel harassed then they have been harassed, and if need be will call in a range of feminist experts to assert that this is so.

It might be argued that there is an alternative description and theoretical analysis of these phenomena. Rather than seeking power over, women in the academies are trying to establish discursive spaces for the expression of feminine specificities, expressions that have been denied by the dominant patriarchal discourses and social and political structures. And that in the process women may have to use the tools of the enemy. The aim, it may be said, is for 'autonomy, self-determination and a viable place which women can occupy as women in the theoretical and socio-political universe' (Grosz 1986: 195). Let us grant that this is the motivation and that if it were achieved the result would be highly desirable. My worry is that as this is being practised in the institutions like universities it is having a different effect. This may be partly because if we are going to establish and respect autonomy then there will have to be some ground rules according to which we operate. We cannot claim autonomy for ourselves while denying it in others; worse, such a denial undermines our own autonomy (Poole 1975: 13). If we reject as patriarchal any discourse that is committed to truth and objectivity or any model of intellectual inquiry that requires formal logic or aims for unambiguous, precise modes of articulation (Grosz 1986: 199, 203) then it is not clear how such feminists could conduct themselves in the academy without denying the autonomy of most of its members. If feminism started out with the laudable intention of increasing the kinds of individuality available and acceptable, and to dissociate them from forms of domination, it is now, I suggest, in danger of doing the opposite. The use of feminist discourse, the specific power effects it has induced, and its deployment in and use of existing structures of power in institutions is not acting as a 'road block' to repression but introducing a new form of it.

ACKNOWLEDGEMENTS

I would like to thank Paul Patton for his patience, Kimon Lycos for discussing drafts of this chapter and the example on Anselm, and Graham Little for the point about envy.

BIBLIOGRAPHY

Allen, J. (1991) 'Women's studies in the 1990s: problems and prospects', *Australian Universities' Review* 34(2).
Bartky, S. L. (1988) 'Foucault, femininity, and the modernisation of patriarchal power', in I. Diamond and L. Quinby (eds) *Feminism and Foucault: Reflections on Resistance*, Boston, Mass.: Northeastern University Press.
Cocks, J. (1991) 'Nietzsche and contemporary body politics', *Differences* 3(1).
Deleuze, G. (1983) *Nietzsche and Philosophy*, trans. H. Tomlinson, London: Athlone Press.
Foucault, M. (1979) *The History of Sexuality, Volume 1: An Introduction*, London: Allen Lane.
—— (1980) *Power/Knowledge: Selected Interviews and Other Writings 1972–1977*, ed. C. Gordon, New York: Pantheon Books.
—— (1982) 'The subject and power', in H. L. Dreyfus and P. Rabinow (eds) *Michel Foucault: Beyond Structuralism and Hermeneutics*, Brighton, Sussex: Harvester Press.
Grosz, E. (1986) 'What is feminist theory?', in C. Pateman and E. Grosz (eds) *Feminist Challenges: Social and Political Theory*, Sydney: Allen & Unwin.
Jones, K. B. (1988) 'On authority: or, why women are not entitled to speak', in I. Diamond and L. Quinby (eds) *Feminism and Foucault: Reflections on Resistance*, Boston, Mass.: Northeastern University Press.
Lloyd, G. (1984) *The Man of Reason: 'Male' and 'Female' in Western Philosophy*, London: Methuen.

Martin, B. (1988) 'Feminism, criticism and Foucault', in I. Diamond and L. Quinby (eds) *Feminism and Foucault: Reflections on Resistance*, Boston, Mass.: Northeastern University Press.

Matthews, J. and Broom, D. (1991) 'Orphans of the storm: the attrition of the ANU women's studies program', *Australian Universities' Review* 34(2).

Nietzsche, F. (1968) *The Will to Power*, trans. W. Kaufmann and R. J. Hollingdale, New York: Vintage.

—— (1969) *On the Genealogy of Morals*, trans. W. Kaufmann, New York: Vintage.

Parker, R. and Pollock, G. (1981) *Old Mistresses: Women, Art and Ideology*, London: Routledge & Kegan Paul.

Patton, P. (1989) 'Taylor and Foucault on power and freedom', *Political Studies* 37(2).

Poole, R. (1975) 'Freedom and alienation', *Radical Philosophy* 12 (Winter).

University of Melbourne (1991) *Gender Inclusive Curriculum: Some Considerations*, Melbourne: Equal Opportunity Unit.

8 Politics and the concept of power in Hobbes and Nietzsche

Paul Patton

INTRODUCTION

A widespread conception of power regards it as necessarily external and opposed to the freedom of individuals. Another approach understands freedom in less negative terms, in such a manner that individuals are more or less free depending upon the kinds of action and forms of social being effectively open to them. For the latter tradition, there is no externality between power and freedom. On the contrary, as Foucault's work has emphasized, the forms of social being and action available in a given society must themselves be seen as effects of power. The basis for this historical approach to human agency in Foucault's work is a conception of human being in terms of power.

Hobbes and Nietzsche also treat forms of human individuality or social being as consequences of a more fundamental desire or will to power. Any such conception of power and its working in human society will have implications for possible forms of political community. Hobbes' *Leviathan* is a particularly clear example. Moreover, his description of life in the absence of sovereign government (*bellum omnium contra omnes*) is sometimes taken as a model for the form of social life which would result from the overcoming of slave moralities and the reappearance of 'noble' human beings. This analogy reflects a widely shared view that Nietzsche's heroic politics of human self-overcoming seek to promote an individualism which is ultimately incompatible with any form of recognizable political community. The aim of this chapter is to challenge this view of the political implications of Nietzsche's conception of power, by comparing it with that of Hobbes. This comparison is intended to show that, just as Hobbes derives a conception of political society from his conception of human powers, so Nietzsche's conception of human being in terms of will to power might have different implications for possible forms of political society. There are, after all, significant differences between them: they do not have the same conception of power nor of its historical dynamic. While both envisage an inbuilt tendency on the part of human beings to seek to increase their power, the process takes quite different forms and leads to very different outcomes in each case. Finally, I shall argue with reference to Nietzsche that a conception of human being based upon power does not imply the inevitability of domination or oppression.

At the beginning of the Second Essay in *On the Genealogy of Morals*, Nietzsche raises the hypothesis that a possible outcome of human cultural development might be the creation of a new type, a sovereign individual, defined as one with the right to make promises: 'To breed an animal with the right to make promises – is not this the paradoxical task that nature has set itself in the case of man?' (Nietzsche 1969: 57). For Nietzsche, this right is no juridical concept but a matter of effective capacity. There is no opposition between power and freedom here but an internal connection between them: the freedom to enter into promises exists only because of the individual's power to stand security for his or her own future actions. Among the consequences of this power over oneself and fate, Nietzsche singles out two: feelings of honour and trust towards one's peers, along with a superiority and a mastery over those 'more short-willed and unreliable creatures' who promise without the right to do so. These are at least some of the elements of a social relation to others, not the forms of dissociation from others which would be involved in a war of all against all.

By contrast, Hobbes' account of political community does not assume the existence of individuals with the capacity to enter into contracts and keep them, regardless of what others might do. On the contrary, it assumes that human nature is such that it would be folly to enter into contracts which rely upon expecting others to perform their part: 'he which performeth first, does but betray himself to his enemy' (Hobbes 1991: 96). It becomes rational to keep promises only once there is established a common power sufficient to compel the performance of others. In other words, for Hobbes, it is only when individuals are constituted as civil subjects by their subjection to sovereign power that there is a basis for trust. In Nietzschean terms, Hobbes' commonwealth is a community of slaves. It is not the existence of sovereign individuals but the fact of individuals being subject to a sovereign which constitutes the possibility of social relations among equals. The precondition of individual freedom is not the power of the individuals concerned but the power effectively wielded over them by the sovereign.

HOBBES

In order to see how Hobbes is led to this extreme solution to the problem of political community, we must examine his theory of human nature and the concept of power upon which it depends. Hobbes defines the power of a man as 'his present means to obtain some future apparent good' (Hobbes 1991: 62). He defines goods as simply the objects of human appetite or desire, and the end of human life as the constant pursuit of such objects of desire. Happiness or felicity consists in 'continual success in obtaining those things which a man from time to time desireth' (Hobbes 1991: 46). It is important that success be continual, for the overriding object of man's desire 'is not to enjoy once only, . . . but to assure for ever, the way of his future desire' (Hobbes 1991: 70). The pursuit of this end is also governed by the dictates of reason, which according to Hobbes are not so much laws as 'Conclusions, or Theoremes concerning what conduceth to the conservation and defence of themselves' (Hobbes 1991: 111). In other words, human life is governed by two overriding aims: the first is to preserve or to maintain itself in existence, the second is to ensure as far as possible continued success in attaining the objects of its desires.

It follows from this conception of human being, along with certain other assumptions Hobbes makes about the objects and nature of human desire, that the pursuit of power itself becomes a 'general inclination of all mankind, a perpetuall and restlesse desire of Power after power, that ceaseth only in death' (Hobbes 1991: 70). Further, Hobbes claims that this desire for power itself gives rise to an intersubjective dynamic whereby individuals are constantly driven to increase their power: the only way in which they can assure even their present power and means to live well is to acquire more power. In short, for Hobbes, human beings are both subjects of power and subjects constantly driven to increase their power. In order to see why this is so, we need to consider his assumptions about the objects of human desire, such as property, as well as those about the natural powers of human beings themselves. In *Leviathan*, Chapter 13, Hobbes asserts (1) that there is a rough equivalence among the natural powers of people such that none can consider themselves immune to threat from others; (2) that this equality of natural endowments gives rise to 'equality of hope in the attaining of our ends', so that where desires conflict in the sense that both cannot be satisfied at once, individuals become enemies to one another; (3) that there are some who take pleasure in acts of conquest. Taken together, along with the view of human nature as a desire-satisfying machine, these assumptions support Hobbes' view that life in the state of nature would be characterized by universal diffidence or mistrust. In the absence of any other way of overcoming this mistrust, the rational response is to seek to secure oneself by enhancing one's own power to such a degree that one is protected from any foreseeable threat. Of course, the rationality of subjects in general means that life in the state of nature is subject to an endless escalating competition for power. The resultant insecurity and accompanying fear of death are what motivate acceptance of the contract. Individuals are driven to subject themselves to sovereign power because their very lives are under constant threat. In doing so, they establish over themselves a superior power whose natural right extends to the life of its citizen-subjects. In this manner, Hobbes' contract of government is a means by which the threat of death is deferred or displaced. It constitutes a community of citizens whose equality rests upon their relative powerlessness before the sovereign.

It is apparent that Hobbes' claim that life in the absence of government would be a state of universal war forms a crucial premise of his argument for the necessity of sovereign power. Yet, C. B. Macpherson argues that Hobbes is already committed to this competitive dynamic because of prior assumptions he makes about the nature of power among men (Macpherson 1968: 33–5). Macpherson draws attention to the fact that Hobbes defines men's natural powers not in terms of any absolute level of bodily endowments but in terms of the eminence of those faculties (Hobbes 1991: 62). In other words, the power of a body depends upon its differences from other bodies, and an individual is more or less powerful to the degree that his or her capacities exceed those of others. To read Hobbes in this way is to align his conception of power with that of Foucault, for whom the power of a body resides not 'in a certain strength we are endowed with', but in the fluctuating field of relations to other bodies. On this view, the power even of a single body is dispersed in such a manner that 'power is everywhere, not because it embraces everything, but because it comes from everywhere' (Foucault 1978: 93). However, Macpherson's concern is not with the deconstructive potential of this conception of power but with its underlying motivation. He takes this assumption of the differential character of power neither to be self-evident nor to follow from anything Hobbes has said up to this point in *Leviathan*. Rather, he argues, it follows from an additional premise set out earlier in Hobbes' *Elements of Law*: 'because the power of one man resisteth and hindereth the effects of the power of another: power simply is no more, but the excess of the power of one above that of the other' (Hobbes 1928: 26). It is on this basis, Macpherson argues, that Hobbes is able to treat the power of individuals in society as effectively equivalent to their command over the power of others. Thus, in *Leviathan*, Chapter 10, Hobbes assumes that once beyond the natural endowment of individuals (strength, forme, prudence, arts, eloquence, liberality or nobility), the only means to increase power are those which give one power over the power of others. These he calls instrumental powers and they include 'Riches, Reputation, Friends, and the secret working of God, which men call Good luck' (Hobbes 1991: 62). The remainder of his discussion proceeds to list the various ways in which one gains power over the power of others. For example, to have servants or friends is to have power, 'for they are strengths united'. Riches joined with liberality is power 'because it procureth friends, and servants' (Hobbes 1991: 62). Similarly, nobility is power in those commonwealths where privileges are attached to noble rank, 'for in such privileges consisteth their power'. So too are all the signs of 'favour' in a commonwealth, for such favour is power (Hobbes 1991: 65).

It is by no means certain, however, that Hobbes reduces power in society to power over others because of the assumption that human powers are conflictual. At least one of his examples of an instrumental power seems to contradict this assumption, namely friendship. While a person's capacity to inspire friendship from another may indeed enhance their power, because it enables them to call upon the resources of such friends, it can do so only on the condition that the use of those resources does not harm the interests of the friends concerned. Friendship is a voluntary relation, and on Hobbes' principles of human behaviour, no one can voluntarily seek to reduce their own power. More generally, it can be argued that friendships, alliances and other non-conflictual confluence of powers occur precisely because the powers and the aims of those concerned do not conflict but on the contrary complement one another. If friendship may be considered a means to enhance one's power, then it does so only in so far as the effect is reciprocal: the enhancement of one's own powers proceeds only through the enhancement of those of the other. Reciprocity here does not imply equality of power between the parties concerned. Nietzsche no less than Hobbes was aware that using one's power to increase the powers of others is a means of exercising power over them. In this manner, he comments, we maintain others in a certain dependence upon ourselves, or show them how advantageous it is to be in our power so that they will be inclined to return the favour (Nietzsche 1974: 86).

Hobbes' argument in *Leviathan*, Chapter 13, from the equality of men's powers to the equality of their expectation of attaining the objects of their desires does provide reasons for thinking that men's powers will be conflictual under certain conditions. However, these have as much to do with the nature of certain objects of desire as they do with the nature of human powers: conflict arises when the object of desire is such that satisfaction cannot be obtained by both parties at once, as in Hobbes' example of property in land (Hobbes 1991: 87). The conflictual character of human powers cannot therefore be identified as the crucial assumption behind Hobbes' reduction of power to power over the powers of others. His discussion in *Leviathan* may well assume that human powers will be different, but difference does not imply opposition. Macpherson's readiness to take this step is perhaps influenced by his own concern to find the model of market society at the base of Hobbes' social thought. Yet even within a commodity market alliances or mergers between different producers may occur on the basis of mutual interest. Perhaps it is not the supposedly conflictual character of human powers which determines the form of Hobbes' response to the problem of political community. Rather, as the market analogy suggests, the problematic character of Hobbes' conception of power may lie in the assumption that power is an essentially quantitative phenomenon.

In order to speak of an individual's power as the excess of that person's powers over those of another, or to speak of sovereign power as compounded of the powers of many individuals united by their common consent, Hobbes appears to assume a quantitative essence common to all the means by which agents seek to attain their objectives. It is this one-dimensional conception of power which allows him to assume that an individual's power is increased simply by accumulating or incorporating the existing powers of others. However, this is an implausible conception of power on several grounds, including the incomparability of qualitatively different means of action, as well as the dependence of such means on appropriate conditions for their effective exercise (Hindess 1989: 34–6). Its implausibility is starkly displayed by the attempt to imagine the effective capacity of the sovereign to govern (enforce laws, raise taxes, etc.), as opposed to its right to govern, as composed of the combined powers of the subjects themselves. Nevertheless, this one-dimensional conception of power is an important presupposition of Hobbes' argument for the necessity of sovereign power. Although he begins with a quite general conception of power as capacity – 'present means to obtain some future apparent good' implies nothing about the precise nature of those means – his subsequent account reduces an individual's power in the state of nature to the amount of the power of others he or she can command. This conception of power as primarily a matter of power over others then feeds into the account of the pre-political state of universal insecurity and war, for the only means to augment one's own power is 'to master the persons of all men [one] can . . . such augmentation of dominion over men, being necessary to a man's conservation, it ought to be allowed him' (Hobbes 1991: 88). Such a conception of power sustains a conception of society as naturally hierarchical, whether organized into commonwealths or not.

Moreover, Hobbes' solution to the problem posed by this universal drive to increase power at the expense of others follows the same model of simple linear increase. Having set out the laws of nature which show that the natural conduct of life demands that individuals should set aside their natural right to all things which it lies within the scope of their powers to obtain, on condition that others do likewise, Hobbes introduces the crucial third law of nature: 'that men perform their convenants'. In the absence of some means to enforce compliance, this crucial condition cannot be met, for 'covenants without the sword, are but words' (Hobbes 1991: 117). The argument for the necessity of sovereign power turns upon the claim that this third law of nature can be followed only on the condition that a superior power is established to enforce the keeping of contracts. The covenant by which a commonwealth is instituted thereby establishes a basis for trust. However, although it transforms the individuals concerned into civil subjects, this transformation is entirely external to their existence as moral subjects. It involves no more than the transfer of part of their existing power to the sovereign: a transfer of right and a renunciation of the right to act without restraint other than their limits of their own power. Hobbes' contract to establish political community is conceived entirely within the framework of his quantitative conception of power.

In fact, Hobbes does admit another possible means by which men may be held to their word. Besides the fear of the consequences of breaking their word, which is the motive on which sovereign power is founded, he admits as a possible motive 'a Glory or Pride in appearing not to need to break it'. However, this possibility is raised only to be put aside on the grounds that such pride entails 'a Generosity too rarely found to be presumed upon, especially in the pursuers of Wealth, Command or, sensual Pleasure; which are the greatest part of mankind. The passion to be reckoned upon, is Fear' (Hobbes 1991: 99). Although he recognizes men's preference for governing themselves rather than allowing themselves to be governed by others – 'there are very few so foolish, that had not rather governe themselves than be governed by others' (Hobbes 1991: 107) – Hobbes does not consider the possibility that such self-government might extend to self-transformation. He does not therefore consider the possibility that the forms of exercise of power over others or over the self might produce the kinds of qualitative change in the nature of the subject that Nietzsche calls 'self-overcoming'. As a result, he does not consider the possibility envisaged by Nietzsche that the human animal in general could become 'an animal with the right to make promises'.

NIETZSCHE

Nietzsche's conception of human being is conditioned by his theory that 'in all events a *will to power* is operating' (Nietzsche 1969: 78). In some passages in *The Will to Power*, this takes the form of a cosmological theory. Whatever the final scope of the will to power hypothesis, it follows from its application to the field of organic matter that life *is* will to power. This was, in part, the secret revealed to Zarathustra by Life herself (Nietzsche 1961: 137–8), and the claim is repeated many times throughout Nietzsche's writings. But what does it mean? In particular, when applied to the social realm, does Nietzsche's hypothesis offer anything more than Hobbes' image of human life as involving a perpetual and restless desire of power after power? There are passages, such as the following from paragraph 259 of *Beyond Good and Evil*, which appear to suggest that Nietzsche has a thoroughly Hobbesian conception of nature as a struggle for survival through mastery over others:

> One has to think this matter thoroughly through to the bottom and resist all sentimental weakness: life itself is essentially appropriation, injury, overpowering of the strange and weaker, suppression, severity, imposition of one's own forms, incorporation and, at the least and mildest, exploitation.
>
> (Nietzsche 1973: 175)

Nietzsche undoubtedly means what he says when he calls this the 'primordial fact of all history'. Nevertheless, he says much else besides about human being and its history which implies that we should not too readily take this as his final vision of human 'nature', much less his vision of the form of social life which might emerge as a result of overcoming present types of human beings. His view of human nature and social being is more complex than this, ultimately because nature itself is more complex, but also because he does not have the same one-dimensional conception of power.

To think of power in terms of 'overpowering the strange and weaker', incorporation and exploitation, is to think of power essentially in terms of the hostile exercise of power over others. 'Hostile' because not all forms of overpowering involve appropriation, injury and exploitation of those over whom power is exercised. On the one hand, it is undeniable that in so far as human life remains a form of animal or biological life it does not escape the web of such hostile relations to other forms of life. On the other, while such forms of exercise of power may be an essential dimension of life, they are not for Nietzsche the essential dimension of power. Rather, power is primarily a matter of activity, of expenditure of the force or energy with which a given body is endowed: 'Every animal . . . instinctively strives for an optimum of favourable conditions under which it can expend all its strength and achieve its maximal feeling of power' (Nietzsche 1969: 107). As such, Nietzsche's conception of power must be differentiated from the concept which underpins either a Hobbesian or a Darwinian conception of life. The difference lies in the fact that for Nietzsche the fundamental principle is not the goal but the process, not the momentary stasis attained by the satisfaction of need or desire but the expenditure of energy itself. In paragraph 13 of *Beyond Good and Evil*, he remarks that we should beware of superfluous teleological principles such as the drive to self-preservation. His own principle is more general, encompassing not only the drive to self-preservation but also the drive to self-destruction or self-overcoming: 'A living thing desires above all to vent its strength – life as such is will to power – self-preservation is only one of the indirect and most frequent consequences of it' (Nietzsche 1973: 26; cf. Nietzsche 1974: 291–2).

Nietzsche's conception of power is thus not limited to the hostile forms of exercise of power over others. As we have seen, neither is Hobbes' conception of power in terms of present means to obtain future apparent goods, even though he quickly reduces this latter to the former kind of power. However, Nietzsche's conception of power is different from that of Hobbes in a further important respect which emerges when we consider that the dynamic underlying power for Hobbes is one of preservation or increase in the capacities of a given body, or preservation *through* increase of the body's capacities. Nietzsche has a more general conception which includes all forms of activity directed at the maintenance or increase of the power of the body in question, as well as forms of activity which might lead to its destruction or to its transformation into a different kind of body. The difference between him and Hobbes may be understood in terms of Nietzsche's distinction between active and reactive expressions of will to power. Power understood in terms of self-preservation is reactive rather than active power, it is the manner in which power is typically exercised from a position of weakness: 'the wish to preserve oneself is the symptom of a condition of distress' (Nietzsche 1974: 291). Power understood as present means to obtain some future apparent good is still power defined with reference to objects initially outside or beyond a given body, with reference to what that body lacks. To the extent that this conception takes as given the nature of that body, and therefore the distinction between those things which hinder and those things which enhance its power, it is also a reactive conception of the nature of power. By contrast, Nietzsche offers an active conception, in which power is defined only with reference to the activity of which a given body is capable. The active body is one whose activity is not defined by what it lacks but by what it is capable of doing. The difference between these two conceptions corresponds to the different orientations involved in slave and master modes of valuation:

> in order to exist, slave morality always first needs a hostile external world; it needs physiologically speaking, external stimuli in order to act at all – its action is fundamentally reaction. The reverse is the case with the noble mode of valuation: it acts and grows spontaneously.
>
> (Nietzsche 1969: 37)

A sovereign individual is clearly an active or noble being in these terms, one defined by reference to an effective capacity to promise. By contrast, the subject of Hobbes' contract of government is defined by its lack of security, and by its need to ensure self-preservation. Thus, so far as their respective implications for political community are concerned, we can say that Hobbes' conception of power implies a community of 'slaves', while Nietzsche's conception implies the possibility of a community of 'masters'.

However, Nietzsche's conception of life as will to power must be distinguished from Hobbes' view not only because his conception of power is significantly different, but also because his conception of life is more complex. As a result, Nietzsche has a much more sophisticated view of the forms which the exercise of power might take. For Hobbes, there is no difference in principle between human being and the rest of animate nature: it is all a matter of seeking means to satisfy desires, to attain goods and avoid evils. The only mode of increase of power is quantitative, and the typical means of increase is by incorporation in some form or other; in other words, by gaining power over the power of others. In this sense, human beings are no different from large-scale amoeba. Human powers are inevitably led to conflict, and life in the Hobbesian state of nature corresponds to the account of life in the passage from paragraph 259 of *Beyond Good and Evil* cited above. Nietzsche would not deny that human life is inextricably caught up in the web of mutually hostile relations to other forms of life. However, he would deny that its forms and possibilities for action are completely constrained by this 'primordial fact'. Unlike Hobbes, he does not have an essentialist and a-historical conception of human nature, but rather understands this as something achieved or produced by the operation of the will to power in the contingent historical circumstances in which human history is played out. In *On the Genealogy of Morals*, Nietzsche offers a speculative account of the development of 'consciousness' among human beings. His hypothesis is that human beings first became conscious of others and then of themselves after being enclosed within 'the walls of society and of peace'. This establishment of a form of state and settled social existence was not the outcome of any contract but the result of conquest. Yet it produced a change of the utmost importance in those conquered: turning back their own 'instincts of freedom' upon themselves, thereby giving rise to what Nietzsche calls 'the gravest and uncanniest illness, from which humanity has not yet recovered, man's suffering of *man, of himself*' (Nietzsche 1969: 85). Herein lie the origins of a cultural dynamic which gives rise to both contemporary nihilism and the means for its possible overcoming (humankind as a way, a bridge, a promise). Ultimately, the basis of the human capacity for self-transformation lies in the very nature of will to power as Nietzsche understands it; that is as a law of life in terms of which 'all great things bring about their own destruction through an act of self-overcoming' (Nietzsche 1969: 161). This is the second element of the secret revealed to Zarathustra by Life herself: 'I am that *which must overcome itself again and again*' (Nietzsche 1961: 138).

This conception of human being as instinctive animal life transformed by the addition of consciousness changes everything with regard to the human will to power. For on this basis, Nietzsche proposes a conception of human agency as governed not simply by the drive to increase power but by the drive to maximize the *feeling* of power. Thus, in *The Anti-Christ*, he defines the good for humankind as 'all that heightens the feeling of power', and happiness as 'the feeling that power *increases* – that a resistance is overcome' (Nietzsche 1968a: 115). Given the self-conscious, interpretative element in every human act of will, it follows that humankind is the one animal in which the feeling of power is divorced from any direct relation to quantity of power. For relatively simple creatures such as higher mammals there may be a direct relationship between increase or decrease in the animal's power and the appropriate affective state: activity which enhances the animal's power leads to happiness or joy, while activity which weakens it leads to unhappiness or distress. For human beings, the situation is more complex. As a result, the link between heightened feeling of power and actual increase of power is broken. Not only is there no necessary connection in principle, but also there is a long history of magical and superstitious practices for which there is no connection in fact. This introduces the possibility that what is experienced as an increase or enhancement of power may in fact not be, while conversely what is experienced as a decrease or frustration of power may in fact be a means to its enhancement. It is precisely in order that the latter possibility not be lost sight of that Nietzsche insists upon the value (for life) of suffering, and therefore upon the short-sightedness of those conceptions of an ideal social life which involve the elimination of all forms of suffering (Nietzsche 1973: 135). (To say this is not of course to recommend the maintenance of any particular extant forms of suffering.) Similarly, the hypothesis which underpins *On the Genealogy of Morals* is precisely the thought that perhaps those activities which have hitherto most contributed to heightened feelings of power – all forms of activity directed towards the Good as this is defined by the slave moralities of Christianity – do not enhance but undermine the power of the 'type man' (Nietzsche 1967: 20).

If Nietzsche's conception of human being as governed by the

drive to enhance its feeling of power breaks the link to actual increase of power, then it also dissolves any necessary connection between the expression of the human will to power and hostile forms of exercise of power over others. Of course, as a matter of historical fact, Nietzsche allows that the varieties of cruelty practised upon others in the course of entertainment, homage to the gods or punishment, have been among the chief means by which humans have sought to excite the feeling of power in themselves: 'cruelty is one of the oldest festive joys of mankind' (Nietzsche 1982: 16). So pervasive does he regard this practice of taking pleasure in causing suffering that he insists that 'almost everything we call "higher culture" is based upon the spiritualization and intensification of *cruelty*' (Nietzsche 1973: 140). Such passages appear to confirm the view that Nietzsche regards cruelty as an ineradicable human impulse. In turn, this suggests that the desire for ever renewed feelings of power would be satisfiable only by some at the expense of others, and that political community without domination would be inconceivable (cf. *inter alia* Read 1989; Miller 1990).

However, this conclusion overlooks Nietzsche's own implicit evaluation of the means by which the feeling of power is obtained. On the one hand, he suggests that the 'higher' means of attaining the feeling of power by exercising power over others are precisely those means which do not involve doing harm to others. For example, the question posed in paragraph 422 of *Daybreak* implies that enhancing the feeling of power of others is itself the highest means of attaining the feeling of power in oneself: 'Why is making joyful the greatest of all joys? Because we thereby give joy to our fifty separate drives all at once' (Nietzsche 1982: 422). Similarly, in *The Gay Science*, he states unequivocally that doing harm to others is a lesser means of producing a feeling of power in oneself than are acts of benevolence towards them:

> certainly the state in which we hurt others is rarely as agreeable, in an unadulterated way, as that in which we benefit others; it is a sign that we are still lacking power, or it shows a sense of frustration in the face of this poverty.
>
> (Nietzsche 1974: 86)

This remark implies that social relations founded upon assistance or benevolence towards others will be 'more agreeable' than relations founded upon cruelty or domination. And 'more agreeable' here implies that relations of this type enhance the feeling of power to a greater degree than do relations which involve violence towards others. There are of course many ways of assisting or benefiting others which may enhance the feeling of power of those assisting, but at the expense of the feeling of power of those assisted. Christian charity is one of Nietzsche's favoured examples; varieties of welfare payment are perhaps the modern secular equivalent. The difficulty for the active and powerful individual, the type endowed with the 'gift-giving' virtue, is to find ways of doing good to others which also enhance their own feeling of power. This problem is manifest throughout the drama of Zarathustra.

On the other hand, as the remark from *The Gay Science* quoted above implies, Nietzsche views the desire to hurt others as a means of obtaining the feeling of power characteristic of those in a position of relative weakness. Rather than seeking conditions under which it can expend its own strength, the slave seeks above all to deprive others of the possibility of expending theirs. In this manner, the slave obtains its feeling of power primarily by causing harm to others, by seeking to render others incapable of action. While there is an 'injustice' or cruelty towards others implicit in the situation of masters, it is not the same cruelty since it does not necessarily intend harm towards those others. The master or noble type is not by its nature committed to harming others in the manner of the slave: 'The evil of the strong harms others without giving thought to it – it *has* to discharge itself; the evil of the weak *wants* to harm others and to see the signs of the suffering it has caused' (Nietzsche 1982: 373). Undoubtedly, there has been a history of cruelty towards others on the part of such 'noble' or master types. However, this may be taken to indicate the relatively weak and uncultured state of those early forms of nobility. In so far as the history of culture has involved a history of cruelty towards others it is precisely a history of slavish human beings, of that type of human being whose primary mode of acting is reactive and negative. In *Daybreak*, Nietzsche suggests that it is precisely the relative weakness of human beings that has made the feeling of power one of the most subtle human capacities:

because the feeling of impotence and fear was in a state of almost continuous stimulation so strongly and for so long, the *feeling of power* has evolved to such a degree of *subtlety* that in this respect man is now a match for the most delicate gold-balance. It has become his strongest propensity; the means discovered for creating this feeling almost constitute the history of culture.
(Nietzsche 1982: 24)

However, Nietzsche views the history of human culture as a process of continual 'self-overcoming' of man, a progress in the *elevation* of the type 'man' (Nietzsche 1973: 173). In the course of this progress, the forms in which power is exercised bring about changes in the nature of those exercising power. Power is exercised not only upon others but also upon the self, and as a result the forms of human self-hood are transformed. This is why Nietzsche attaches so much importance to the long history of asceticisms, and to the 'pathos of distance' between classes of people which in turn gives rise to increased distance 'within the soul itself' (Nietzsche 1973: 173). The effect of such activity is to bring about qualitative changes in the means by which human beings attain a feeling of power in acting upon one another and upon themselves. The higher forms of nobility are defined not by their power over others but by their power over themselves; not by their willingness to diminish but by their willingness to enhance the feeling of power in others: 'in the foreground stands the feeling of plenitude, of power which seeks to overflow, the happiness of high tension, the consciousness of a wealth which would like to give away and bestow' (Nietzsche 1973: 176).

On this basis, Nietzsche is able to envisage a solution to the problem of the constitution of political community directly antithetical to that proposed by Hobbes. Limited by his quantitative and one-dimensional conception of power and the possible forms of its increase, Hobbes is incapable of imagining qualitative transformation in either the means by which power is exercised or the nature of the subjects exercising power. He cannot envisage a community made up of persons with the effective capacity to promise. The 'glory' which he considers only to reject as a possible motive for the keeping of contracts is equivalent to Nietzsche's 'feeling of power': he defines it as that 'exultation of the mind' which arises from 'the imagination of a man's own power and ability' (Hobbes 1991: 42). However, in Hobbes' view, the feeling that one is sufficiently strong to wish not to be seen breaking one's word is a rare occurrence. Conversely, the feeling that one's power is so fragile as to need protection against insult is so common that glory figures along with competition and diffidence as one of the three principal causes of conflict among men. Hobbes' solution to endemic conflict is the institution of a sovereign power defined primarily in terms of its power to make and enforce laws. His conception of human powers and the means of their increase thus leads to a conception of political community founded upon the juridical and political power of a state.

By contrast, Nietzsche's conception of human powers and their increase or enhancement through a dynamic of qualitative self-transformation allows him to envisage the possibility of a sovereign individual 'conscious of his own power and freedom . . . with the actual *right* to make promises' (Nietzsche 1969: 59). Instead of arguing for the necessity of a sovereign ruler whose capacity to encourage trust is founded upon the sad passion of fear, Nietzsche invites us to imagine a political community founded upon the capacity for autonomous action shared by its members. Such individuals possess a heightened sense of their own power, a feeling of power which Nietzsche supposes to be justified. Capable of taking responsibility for their own actions, these sovereign individuals will stand in a relation of mutual respect to one another which Nietzsche calls *honour*. The political content of such respect, the rights which the sovereign individual grants to others, will be 'concessions' to the sense of power of those others, made on the basis of its own sense of power (Nietzsche 1982: 67). Far from implying a Hobbesian state of war, Nietzsche's will to power hypothesis thus poses a series of problems for political theory: what are the conditions necessary in order for such a community to exist? What would be the nature of such a form of association? His own scattered remarks sketch no more than the barest outlines of the form that a community of sovereign individuals would take. On the one hand, it will be made up of self-legislating and responsible individuals; on the other, it will entail a community so conscious of its own power that it might even leave unpunished those who cause it harm. To imagine a community of such individuals is not to suppose that injury toward others will never occur. However, it is to imagine a community in which there is no need of an absolute sovereign power to enforce contracts and punish criminals. Such a form of state power will be unnecessary either because the criminal will call himself to account 'in the proud feeling that he is thus honouring the law which he himself has made' (Nietzsche 1982: 109), or because the justice that punishes will have come to an end 'as does every good thing on earth, by *overcoming* itself' (Nietzsche 1969: 73).

ACKNOWLEDGEMENTS

I am grateful to Moira Gatens, Barry Hindess and Keith Ansell-Pearson for their helpful comments on earlier drafts of this chapter.

BIBLIOGRAPHY

Ansell-Pearson, K. (1990) 'Nietzsche: a radical challenge to political theory?', *Radical Philosophy* 54.

—— (1991a) 'Nietzsche on autonomy and morality: the challenge to political theory', *Political Studies* 39(2).

—— (1991b) 'The significance of Michel Foucault's reading of Nietzsche: power, the subject, and political theory', *Nietzsche-Studien*, Band 20.

Benn, S. (1972) 'Hobbes on power', in M. Cranston and R. S. Peters (eds) *Hobbes and Rousseau: A Collection of Critical Essays*, New York: Anchor.

Foucault, M. (1978) *The History of Sexuality, Volume I: An Introduction*, trans. R. Hurley, London: Allen Lane.

Hindess, B. (1982) 'Power, interests and the outcomes of struggles', *Sociology* 16(4).

—— (1989) *Political Choice and Social Structure*, Aldershot: Edward Elgar.

—— (forthcoming) *Power: A Subversive View*, Oxford: Blackwell.

Hobbes, T. (1928) *Elements of Law, Natural and Politic*, ed. F. Tönnies, Cambridge: Cambridge University Press.

—— (1991) *Leviathan*, ed. R. Tuck, Cambridge: Cambridge University Press.

Macpherson, C. B. (1968) 'Introduction' to T. Hobbes, *Leviathan*, ed. C. B. Macpherson, Harmondsworth: Penguin.

—— (1973) 'Problems of a non-market theory of democracy', in *Democratic Theory: Essays in Retrieval*, Oxford: Clarendon Press.

Miller, J. (1990) 'Carnivals of atrocity: Foucault, Nietzsche, cruelty', *Political Theory* 19(3).

Nietzsche, F. (1961) *Thus Spoke Zarathustra*, trans. R. J. Hollingdale, Harmondsworth: Penguin.

—— (1969) *On the Genealogy of Morals and Ecce Homo*, trans. W. Kaufmann and R. J. Hollingdale, New York: Random House.

—— (1968a) *Twilight of the Idols and The Anti-Christ*, trans. R. J. Hollingdale, Harmondsworth: Penguin.

—— (1968b) *The Will to Power*, trans. W. Kaufmann and R. J. Hollingdale, New York: Random House.

—— (1973) *Beyond Good and Evil*, trans. R. J. Hollingdale, Harmondsworth: Penguin.

—— (1974) *The Gay Science*, trans. W. Kaufmann, New York: Random House.

—— (1982) *Daybreak*, trans. R. J. Hollingdale, Cambridge: Cambridge University Press.

Patton, P. (1989) 'Taylor and Foucault on power and freedom', *Political Studies* 37(2).

—— (1992) 'Le sujet de pouvoir chez Foucault', *Sociologie et Sociétés* 24(1).

Read, J. H. (1989) 'Nietzsche: power as oppression', *Praxis International* 9(1/2).

Schutte, O. (1984) *Beyond Nihilism: Nietzsche without Masks*, Chicago, Ill.: University of Chicago Press.

Warren, M. (1988) *Nietzsche and Political Thought*, Cambridge, Mass. and London: MIT Press.

9 'Is it not remarkable that Nietzsche . . . should have hated Rousseau?'

Woman, femininity: distancing Nietzsche from Rousseau

Penelope Deutscher

Sarah Kofman, Jacques Derrida and Paul de Man have all suggested curious similarities between the work of Rousseau and Nietzsche.[1] This chapter uses that circumstance as a springboard from which to argue that the Rousseauist and Nietzschean conceptions of femininity, while apparently similar, are radically opposed when assessed by Nietzschean criteria.

I deliberately slant the comparison such that Nietzsche's conception starts to be distanced from Rousseau's misogyny, and thus the discussion ends with Nietzsche as the more appealing of the pair, an unmasker of an arch-Rousseauist 'idealism' of women and an apologist for '*proud women*'. Of course, the fact that Nietzsche's account of women can be distinguished from Rousseau's does not preclude its being otherwise misogynist. Nevertheless, through setting them against extremely like passages in Rousseau, I reinterpret many of those Nietzschean passages which have been most disturbing to various feminist readings, so that the comparison between Rousseau and Nietzsche offers an opportunity to reconsider our understanding of a Nietzschean sexual difference, sexual distance and sexual antagonism.

APPARENT SIMILARITIES BETWEEN ROUSSEAU AND NIETZSCHE

Nietzsche despised Rousseau, jeering that he was a 'moral tarantula' and an 'abortion' (Nietzsche 1982: 3), 'sick with unbridled vanity and unbridled self-contempt' (Nietzsche 1968a: 101). But Jacques Derrida has commented that he finds Nietzsche's antipathy for Rousseau most surprising. He reminds us of Rousseau's account of sexual difference whereby a man should be strong and active; and a woman weak and passive. Then he interrupts, 'Is it not remarkable that Nietzsche, sharing this conception of femininity, of the degradation of culture and of the genealogy of morals as servitude to the slave should have hated Rousseau?' (Derrida 1976: 342, trans. modified).

Certainly, there is a strong resemblance between the Rousseauist and Nietzschean conceptions of women: both denounce the equality of the sexes, both recommend that men keep their distance from women, both argue for a certain 'resistance' between the sexes. So, can we distinguish these conceptions?

One thing to note is that superficial resemblances between Rousseau and Nietzsche often prove the 'marker' of a deeper conceptual antipathy between the two. For example, where – as Derrida suggests – both philosophers praise the vigorous ancient Greek and Roman epochs and denounce their degradation into a modern, softened culture, and both discuss this degradation in terms of a genealogy of morality, in fact for Rousseau the cultural degradation is the degeneration of virtue and pity whereas for Nietzsche the genesis of morality and pity is the cultural degradation. Nietzsche himself is very precise that it is on the basis of this kind of difference that he is 'contra Rousseau': 'You have', he says, 'the choice of concluding with Rousseau that "this pitiable civilisation is to blame for our bad morality", or against Rousseau that "our good morality is to blame for this pitiableness of our civilisation"' (Nietzsche 1982: 100).

Furthermore, when Nietzsche declares that he, 'like' Rousseau, speaks of a 'return to nature', he tells us how to interpret the kind of superficial resemblances one encounters between the two philosophers. Where he describes Rousseau's return as a 'going-back', he calls his own return a 'going-*up*' (Nietzsche 1968a: 101). He describes Rousseau's nature as 'idealistic', as 'idyll and opera' (Nietzsche 1968b: 72), his own as 'frightful' although 'high and free'. Where Emile might be an example of Rousseau's 'return to nature', Nietzsche cited *Napoleon* as a piece of 'return to nature' as he understood it.

For Nietzsche it is important to ask what sense each philosopher gives to the terms 'nature' and 'return', and to *sniff*[2] the instincts each expressed. Rousseau's return to nature, he affirms, reeks of reactivity, self-loathing and *ressentiment* against the aristocratic culture (Nietzsche 1968b: 61–2). So, in the case of an apparent similarity, Nietzsche particularly recommended that in order to distinguish the two philosophers, we should listen more carefully to the details, ask whether each had given the same meaning to a term both employed, and listen to the instincts each seemed to express – active or reactive? We can apply these criteria to the proposal that the Rousseauist and Nietzschean conceptions of femininity are akin.

FORESHORTENED AND TYPOLOGICAL NIETZSCHEAN READINGS

If we must examine the meanings each philosopher gives to his terms, we should certainly bear in mind Nietzsche's very particular style of interpretation. For example, Nietzsche's attention is directed to the instincts Rousseau manifests, rather than to the details of his argument, about which he is particularly vague, as we see when he denounces Rousseau as a personification of the subsequent French Revolution (Nietzsche 1968a: 102) and speaks of a Rousseauist 'return to nature' despite Rousseau's insistence that one could not 'return' to the mythological state of nature (Rousseau 1987a: 34). However, if we juxtapose Nietzsche's understanding of the term 'Rousseau' with his understanding of the term 'feminism' we begin to understand the roughness of detail as part of a sustained interpretative mode. Again, Nietzsche sketches with very broad strokes – vaguely claiming that emancipists idealize women, preach chastity, and imitate men (Nietzsche 1969a: 267; 1966: 163–4). It could even be said that when Nietzsche denounces what he terms 'feminism', there is little difference between the sense that Nietzsche has given to the term 'feminism' and the sense that Nietzsche has given to the term 'Rousseau'. Antithetical when represented in terms of their precise content, they nevertheless take on almost the same meaning in Nietzsche's texts: reactivity, idealism and egalitarianism.

Thus, Nietzsche's terms are often so radically '*foreshortened*'[3] that what is foregrounded and relevant is *only* the presence of reactivity, idealism, egalitarianism. No sense can be made of his denunciation of 'Rousseau' or 'feminism' unless the foreshortened meaning of these terms is read with the denunciation. In other words, when Nietzsche denounces 'Rousseau', and when he denounces 'feminism', what he is denouncing *is* reactivity, *ressentiment*, idealism, egalitarianism.

We can further demonstrate the need to read Nietzsche in terms of the meaning of a term at the point of its denunciation if we examine two passages. First, in the opening to *Daybreak*, Nietzsche denounces God, virtue, truth, justice, all the ancient ideals, every kind of faith, as, 'the whole of European feminism,[4] (or idealism if you prefer that word)' (Nietzsche 1982: 4).

The passage is comprehensible only if read as a foreshortening of the terms 'idealism' and 'feminism' to the point of their being interchangeable for Nietzsche. This can be read with a second passage, a posthumous fragment where Nietzsche aligns 'Rousseau' with 'feminism'. One might presume that this occurs because 'idealism' and 'feminism' are again interchangeable terms – but no. In this passage, 'feminism' signifies femininity, described as 'rule of feeling, sovereignty of the senses', and Rousseau is being seen to express that feminine sensibility (Nietzsche 1968b: 59). Again, the shifting between these terms, and the fact that when mobilized they may mean no more than 'sensibility', 'reactivity' or 'idealism', is such that it is essential to read a Nietzschean comment *with* the foreshortened sense of such terms.

Lastly, we see the same problem when, although Nietzsche seems to condemn feminism on the grounds that it contravenes the eternal feminine (Diprose 1989: 32) he *also* denounces feminism for invoking an idealized 'eternal feminine', a 'woman-in-herself' inherently capable of rational pursuits if immersed in different social practices. This is apparent when Nietzsche mocks women who idealize the notion of a 'woman-in-herself' (*Weib an sich*)[5] in their fight for the emancipation of women (Nietzsche 1969a: 267):

> Woman wants to become self-reliant: and for that reason she is beginning to enlighten man about 'woman-in-herself' [*Weib an sich*].
>
> (Nietzsche 1966: 162, trans. modified)

> woman adduces Madame Roland, or Madame de Staël or Monsieur [*sic*] George Sand . . . as if they proved anything in favour of 'woman-in-herself' [*Weib an sich*].
>
> (Nietzsche 1966: 164, trans. modified)

We can set against this the grounds on which Rousseau denounces sexual equality. Rousseau considers that the confusion of sexual difference which occurs when women take to literature and public speaking is a corruption of their *essential nature* as man's complement – the soothing, pleasing, domestic helpmeet. While Nietzsche seems to resemble Rousseau in denouncing sexual equality, the very terms of Nietzsche's denunciation would rather *apply* to Rousseau. Indeed, he is just as scathing of men who, he says, are all-too-ready to believe in this, 'malignant idealism', the 'eternal feminine' (Nietzsche 1969a: 267), which he describes as an 'entirely imaginary value'[6] (1972: 271) which manages to idealize women's servility[7] (Nietzsche 1974a: 18). So, in Nietzschean terms, feminism and Rousseau can also be equated in so far as they both, on his reading, idealize an eternal feminine.[8]

WOMEN AS WEAK, WOMEN'S PITY FOR THE OTHER

It follows that when we discover that both Rousseau and Nietzsche associate women with weakness, and with a sensibility to pity, we must first ask what each philosopher means by 'pity' in order to unravel the apparent resemblance. We need also to remember the device of foreshortening through which Nietzsche makes his references to women as representatives of a weak type, and that this device distinguishes the structure of his own comments about women from those of Rousseau.

First, we should note that while both philosophers associate women with pity, pity has a very different connotation for each. Rousseau elevates pity as a natural virtue awoken in man in the mythical state of nature by his imagination, which allows him to identify with the other's weakness and suffering (Rousseau 1966: 32). This facilitates a sensibility to the other which is responsible for all the social virtues: generosity, mercy, benevolence and friendship, all these being, as Rousseau explains, 'the products of a constant pity' (Rousseau 1987a: 54). Now Nietzsche agrees that pity is a basis for all the social 'virtues' – see, for example, his comments on the 'morality of pity' (Nietzsche 1969a: 19) – and he agrees that it is a particular 'sensibility' to the other's demand. However, on this basis Nietzsche does not elevate but rather denounces pity, precisely because he associates that sensibility to the other with weakness, with the weak type. Rousseau makes the weakness and sensibility to the other which pity involves a virtue – but Nietzsche *unmasks* that virtue. He denounces pity on at least two grounds. First, it is a 'self-ishness',[9] an appropriation[10] of the other to the ends of our own satisfaction with ourself, 'dressed-up' as a 'self-*less*ness' (Nietzsche 1982: 83–5). Second, it is a weakness when it derives from our own inability to withstand the 'appeal' from the weak[11] (Nietzsche 1969a: 228).

If we ask what Rousseau and Nietzsche each mean by associating women with a particular propensity for pity, we find that where Rousseau is elevating women for their weak susceptibility,[12]

Nietzsche is denouncing women on these same grounds (Nietzsche 1982: 89; 1969a: 232). We must then remember our supplementary problem, of what Nietzsche means when he says *in this context*, 'woman'. As has often been pointed out (Derrida 1979: 97; Kofman 1986: 228; Diprose 1989: 27), there are multiple versions of women in the Nietzschean texts. Rather than denouncing women for their propensity to pity, Nietzsche seems rather to use women in this instance as a device through which to denounce pity. For, although he does (in *Ecce Homo*) use women to represent the weak type, he does also (elsewhere) use women to represent an ideal strong type. He also uses so much – indeed *all* of a contemporary culture to represent the weak type, that it does seem that Nietzsche's attack is directed more consistently at weakness and pity, than consistently at women, and that women are attacked only where Nietzsche has foreshortened 'women' so extremely that their connotation is the the pity and reactivity that he attacks.

WOMEN AT A DISTANCE

The question of Nietzsche's desire to keep a certain distance from the weak, who are sometimes represented by women, leads us to the similarity that both Nietzsche and Rousseau recommend that a certain distance be kept from women. It is particularly in relation to their recommendation that man 'respect' a sexual distance, phrased in terms of a respect for women's 'modesty' that Sarah Kofman has argued that the texts of Rousseau and Nietzsche are 'joined' (*se communiquent*) (Kofman 1988: 201). In *Nietzsche et la scène philosophique*, Kofman argues that Nietzsche's idea of respect for women's distance or 'veil' expresses a fear of women, a castration anxiety. Woman's modesty, she interprets, 'permits the male to desire a woman without being petrified (*médusé*); it is a veil . . . , a spontaneous defense' (Kofman 1988: 191). While her assertion of the similarity between this account in Nietzsche and Rousseau is confined to a brief remark in a footnote, Kofman does indeed, in her *Le Respect des femmes*, present us with an analogous interpretation of the Rousseauist investment in a 'respect' for woman's '*pudeur*'. In working through the different senses of the Rousseauist and Nietzschean notions of 'sexual distance' we shall also have an opportunity to clarify the question of the similarity asserted by Kofman.

Now, for both Rousseau and Nietzsche, the notion of keeping women at a distance has both a positive and a negative sense. For

Rousseau, the need for a distance between the sexes refers both to the sexual division between the public and private spheres, and it also refers to a certain threat of contamination that women pose to men. He explains this in his 'Letter to M. D'Alembert', where he states that man's sexual identity is jeopardized by excessive contact with women, for man is rendered effeminate by such contact, thus: 'The two sexes ought to come together sometimes; and to live separated ordinarily . . . by a commerce that is too intimate . . . the women make us into women' (Rousseau 1960: 100). Thus, in so far as Rousseau sometimes presents women as elevated objects to be idolized at a respectful distance, Sarah Kofman argues in *Le Respect des femmes* that this is a kind of Rousseauist ruse which protects men from contamination by women under the guise of a respectful admiration (Kofman 1982: 66).

Certainly, Nietzsche sometimes recommends that the strong keep their distance from the weak, so as not to become overly contaminated by their rancour and *ressentiment*. In so far as he sometimes represents women as weak and rancorous, we could say that this is the pejorative sense in which Nietzsche seems to be like Rousseau in recommending that a distance be kept from women because of the threat of contamination. We see this when Nietzsche exclaims:

> Finally women! One half of mankind is weak, typically sick, changeable, inconstant – woman needs strength in order to cleave to it; she needs a religion of weakness that glorifies being weak . . . or better, she makes the strong the weak – she rules when she succeeds in overcoming the strong!
>
> (Nietzsche 1968a: 460)

Before we see the two philosophers as akin in their account of woman as weak and contagious, we need to ask what each considers is in danger of being contaminated. For Rousseau, the threat is to sexual identity, to masculinity. He confesses, in fact, indirectly, to the instability and fragility of masculinity, to its dependence on a distance from women. Rousseau also indirectly confesses to the fragility of man's position as 'natural master' of woman, quite apart from his overt and sustained view that nature also intends domestic woman to be the private 'manager' of man. This latter view is not meant to preclude the account of man as the 'natural master', for, claims Rousseau, 'There is quite a difference between arrogating to oneself the right to command and governing him who commands' (Rousseau 1991: 408). Yet Rousseau nevertheless seems to consider that man's commanding position is very easily jeopardized. Man, we find, can be subjugated by woman by excessive mingling with her, and also by desiring her, or loving a particular woman, or by marrying a woman of a higher social class. Man must constantly be on his guard against this threat – if not, 'then the woman, pretending to authority, acts as a tyrant toward the head of the house, and the master becomes a slave and finds himself the most ridiculous of creatures' (Rousseau 1991: 408).

For Nietzsche, the threat posed is not to man's sexual identity,[13] but rather to what he terms active forces and the 'Great Health' of the strong (Nietzsche 1974b: 346). He asserts, rather than indirectly confessing to, the fragility of active healthy forces in a contemporary, reactive society. This means that he is not obliged to resort to covert means in order to maintain an account of the superiority of the strong. In other words, he does not claim that the strong are 'really' the natural masters, and yet suggests that they had better not let the weak claim authority for a moment, neither love the weak too particularly, nor spend too much time in their proximity, or they'll find out that the weak have metamorphosed into the strong! True, the weak represent a danger to, may tyrannize or even jeopardize the health of the healthy. But while the weak type may tyrannize the strong type (Kofman 1988: 179), the threat they pose is never that they might thereby metamorphose into a strong type (Nietzsche 1969a: 121–5). Thus, the strong are not driven to dress up the weak in *moral* lofty colours, to elevate them on to a pedestal such that one would not approach the weak too closely while speaking 'most respectfully' of them. When Nietzsche recommends a 'pathos of [guarding a] distance' from the weak, and thus sometimes from women, this is not a covert attempt to uphold a most fragile masquerade in the distribution of values. For the threat posed is not that the weak may become, or are really the strong, but rather that they may weaken the strong. It is for this reason that Nietzsche sometimes advises the strong to distance themselves from them.

There is, furthermore, the second, positive Nietzschean understanding of a necessary distance between the sexes. Here he affirms women's art 'of grace, of play, of chasing away worries, of lightening burdens and taking things lightly – and her subtle aptitude for agreeable desires!' (Nietzsche 1966: 163). This tallies, of course, with the particular version of woman seen passing at some distance, where Nietzsche speaks of woman's 'action at a distance', her most magical and powerful effect. In the well-known metaphor, he likens women to mysterious sailing ships seen gliding by. 'In these quiet regions', he says, 'even the loudest surf turns to quiet and life itself into a dream about life' (Nietzsche 1974b: 123–4).

But despite the fact that Nietzsche is like Rousseau in emphasizing women's gaiety, their laughter and delightful, soothing and charming effect on men (Rousseau 1991: 358, 363), Nietzsche makes it clear that in order for women to have this effect, women must be at a necessary distance from men. While if Rousseau approaches too closely to women, he will find his masculinity jeopardized, if Nietzsche approaches too closely, he will find that woman takes on a different perspective. Approaching closely to women, man may find a jangling hubbub. 'Yet! Yet!', he reminds, 'Noble enthusiast, even on the most beautiful sailboat there is a lot of noise and unfortunately, much small and petty noise' (Nietzsche 1974b: 124).

Here, it seems that Nietzsche's irony is directed not so much at the effect of women's 'action at a distance' (he seems to agree that this effect is magical, rather than ridiculing it as 'illusory') but rather at the 'noble enthusiast' who might be overly carried away with his beautiful sailing vision. For Nietzsche reminds us that man *longs* for the 'happiness and seclusion' that women seem to offer, that he is 'apt' to think – in other words, that he has a certain investment in thinking – that nearer to women the tumult would cease and that there abides his 'better self'.

Now, what these comments suggest is that while both Rousseau and Nietzsche speak of the pleasing effect of woman, where woman is constructed as man's 'better self', nevertheless each philosopher accounts rather differently for the masculine investment in elevating woman such that she has this delightful effect. I want to make several points here.

First, although Nietzsche criticizes Rousseau on a number of points, he does not specifically refer to his conception of woman. Nevertheless, he offers a critique of a masculine investment in women's 'action at a distance' which strikes us as particularly applicable to the Rousseauist construction. Where Nietzsche reminds us that man longs for the happiness and seclusion which he seems to see faraway in women, that man is *apt* to think that alongside women abides his better self, we think irresistibly of Rousseau's version of a harmonious, peaceful complementarity between the sexes, and the Rousseauist vision of woman as the distanced, gentle companion. Nietzsche suggests that men like to conceive of women as ideals and celestial objects. Thus Nietzsche speaks of 'man's belief that a fundamentally different ideal is wrapped up in women' (Nietzsche 1966: 148), saying

Men have hitherto treated women like birds which have strayed down to them from the heights.

(Nietzsche 1966: 147)

Man created woman – but out of what? Out of a rib of his God, of his 'ideal'.

(Nietzsche 1968a: 23)

Here, we can't but think of the relationship that Sarah Kofman has pointed out (Kofman 1982: 68–9): the striking resemblance between Rousseau's conception of man's stance before woman and his stance before God. When Rousseau is before Mme de Warens, when Saint-Preux is before Julie and when Emile is before Sophie, man's relationship is that of respectful adoration, a humble abasement of man before an object that one would not profane by attempting to approach too closely. When Rousseau describes the appropriate relation to God, we see the same economy of respectful distance and humble self-abasement:

Seized with respect, [man] halts and does not touch the veil, content with the knowledge that the immense Being is beneath it.

(Rousseau 1969: 1,137)

Some difference between Rousseau and Nietzsche's conception of women delighting men at a distance seems to be implied by Nietzsche's wariness of man's desire to excessively elevate and idealize woman. Pursuing this, we might say, second, that there seems to be significant difference between Rousseau and Nietzsche in terms of what they take to be behind what they both term the 'veil' – the 'veil' referring to the impediment of voluntary distance erected between man and woman, or between man and God, or between man and truth or indeed between man and nature's secrets.

Rousseau's respect is for an ideal which he believes lies *behind* the veil. Nietzsche says that the charming and tranquil effect of women is produced by their distance. It is the veil itself, rather than the ideal one believes is behind the veil, which produces the charming effect. Yet although Nietzsche is rather mocking of the noble enthusiast who wants to believe in the ideal behind the veil, we should nevertheless note that he does not denounce the effect itself as an *illusion*. Because, for Nietzsche, as again has frequently been pointed out by Kofman among others, there is no last truth lying behind a veil that a philosopher might hope to uncover:

> We no longer believe that truth remains truth when the veils are withdrawn . . . . Today we consider it a matter of decency not to wish to see everything naked, or to be present at everything, or to understand and 'know' everything.
>
> (Nietzsche 1974b: 38)

What this means is that the magical effect which women have on the noble enthusiast is not an illusion – rather the only illusion is his confusion of that powerful effect of the veil with a 'behind' of the veil. In other words, denying the last truth behind the veil, Nietzsche denies the truth of woman. Introducing his passages on women, Diprose reminds us that Nietzsche '*qualifies*',[14] 'These are after all only – *my* truths' (Nietzsche 1966: 162) – and it is entirely compatible with this that his metaphor for truth is woman. 'Supposing truth is a woman', he writes, dogmatic philosophers have been so inexpert with woman, so awkward and improper, as to approach her with 'gruesome seriousness and clumsy obtrusiveness' (Nietzsche 1966: 2). But, he comments elsewhere, 'perhaps truth is a woman who has reasons for not letting us see her reasons' (Nietzsche 1974b: 38).

So we see here the slippage between the question of whether there is a truth of woman (I would say that Rousseau thinks so, while Nietzsche does not) and whether there is truth itself behind the veil for which woman is a metaphor (again I would say that Rousseau thinks so, and Nietzsche doesn't). In other words, the slippage between the status of 'truth itself' and that of the 'truth of woman' occurs in both Rousseau and Nietzsche's texts. The slippage occurs because both philosophers give a feminine connotation to both nature and truth. We have already seen the feminine connotation that Nietzsche gives to truth – supposing truth is a woman, he says, we should respect her modesty, we should not, as scientists, attempt to unveil her, because her modesty is necessary. Instead of woman being the 'Emperor' wearing no clothes, rather there is nothing *behind* her clothes, her veil. We see again, the slippage between Rousseau's notion of respect for women, and his notion of respect for 'nature's secrets', or the 'eternal wisdom' for whom his metaphor is a woman, in the following passages from his 'Discourse on the sciences and the arts':

> This is how luxury, dissolution and slavery have at all times been the punishment for the arrogant attempts that we have made to leave the happy ignorance where eternal wisdom had placed us. The heavy veil with which she covered all her operations, seemed

to give us sufficient warning that she had not destined us for vain enquiries . . . . Peoples, know then once and for all that nature wanted to protect you from science, just as a mother wrests a dangerous weapon from the hands of her child; that all the secrets she hides from you are so many evils from which she is protecting you.

(Rousseau 1987b: 10)

But while the slippage between the 'truth' of woman and woman as a metaphor for truth is common to Rousseau and Nietzsche, the reasons *why* one must respect feminine modesty, whether of woman, or of truth, are entirely opposed. This is where we can interrogate Kofman's interpretation that the texts of Rousseau and Nietzsche are 'joined' on this point. I want to suggest that we should be sensitive to the differences in the Rousseauist and Nietzschean investment in a distance between the sexes, and the difference in their conceptions of the 'veil'. For, whereas the Nietzschean respect is for the truth that there is no ultimate truth behind the veil, the Rousseauist respect is precisely for the truth behind the veil.

So let's return to the suggestion from Kofman and Derrida that Nietzsche's economy of 'respect' for the distance of woman stems from an economy of *fear* of (castrating) woman, and thus Kofman's suggestion about the alliance between Rousseau and Nietzsche on this point. We note first that in the case of Derrida's *Spurs*, man's fearful wariness of what's (not) behind woman's veil is only one aspect of a three-part version of woman. Derrida's triad of Nietzschean women is a triad of masculine versions of woman, in which woman is either denounced as dissimulator by credulous man in the name of truth, or else denounced for manipulating effects of truth (here the abyss of non-truth behind the masquerade is terrifying) or affirmed as dissimulator, in the name of the absence of truth. In the latter, non-truth remains an 'abyss', but is *affirmed* as such (Derrida 1979: 97). Nietzsche's various masks include his interpretation of women in all these different terms, at various times. So we could interpret Kofman's suggestion about the alliance between Nietzsche and Rousseau in terms of the fact that at least *one* of Nietzsche's masculine versions of women is a 'Rousseauist' version. This is the version in which women's distance must be 'respected' in order to avert the threat posed by women. We might say that Nietzsche's temporary face here is the Rousseauist man – a man elevating women to a distanced, charming ideal in order to stave off the threat she poses to him.

But while both Rousseau – and one of the Nietzschean masks – defer with 'respect' the threat posed by women, the threat is still very differently understood. Rousseau staves off the threat posed by women in the name of the truth identified by Derrida in the first of the three Nietzschean 'propositions' about women. Rousseau is the credulous man of the first proposition. We see his belief in truth expressed in his fear that woman may be deceiving man, his disapproval of all things artificial and deceptive, his refusal to approach nature's secrets in the name of the truth behind the veil. While Nietzsche *identifies* the 'credulous' man threatened by the perversion of truth, he also articulates a second threat: that of non-truth, the abyss, and the manipulation by woman of non-truth in her seductive truth-effect, and he *also* manages to go beyond the perspective of woman as threatening.

And this is why it is important to acknowledge, as Kofman does, that Derrida insists on the 'enigmatic but necessary congruence between [Nietzsche's] "feminist" and "anti-feminist" claims' (Kofman 1988: 201). For a necessary congruence suggests that we read Nietzsche's occupation of a credulous [Rousseauist] mask *with* his identification of non-truth as potentially threatening, and yet also with the affirmative mask that ridicules both the credulity in truth and the fear of non-truth. Put bluntly, Rousseau proposes no such critique of his own credulity or his own fears about women.

Finally, we have seen that for Rousseau, man should respect the veil over truth because he should be content to live in a 'happy ignorance'. When affirmative, Nietzsche's 'respect' is no fearful humility. It is not a recommendation to men that they live in a happy ignorance but rather the *opposite* – that they be *courageous* enough to face the absence of ultimate truths, and for that reason, not attempt to unveil all. It is in this context that we must read the apparent proximity of the following affirmations.

Rousseau:

one would say that nature had taken precautions to conceal this fatal secret from us.

(Rousseau 1987b: 66)

Peoples, know then once and for all that nature wanted to protect you from science.

(Rousseau 1987a: 10)

Nietzsche:

One should have more respect for the bashfulness with which

nature has hidden behind riddles and iridescent uncertainties. Perhaps truth is a woman who has reasons for not letting us see her reasons?

(Nietzsche 1974b: 38)

Again, it is Nietzsche's own proposal for how to interpret more carefully the apparent similarities between himself and Rousseau which is instructive here. His proposal suggests that we pay attention, not only, as we have done, to the question of what each philosopher means by the 'veil', but also that we pay attention to the instincts each expresses in recommending that we not approach it too closely. We might say that Rousseau's 'respect' is a voluntary self-abasement, a stunting of forces, a desire for contented ignorance, for a benevolent protectionism (as Nietzsche once described the Rousseauist nature), a stance of 'humility' before his ideal. Nietzsche was not wrong to denounce Rousseau precisely for his idealism and his self-abasement. It may be that one of the Nietzschean masks expresses a *ressentiment* toward women, and this would be the elevation of women into a glorious ideal where this expresses a fear of the non-truth of women and an aversion to close and dangerous proximity to her.[15] However, it is most important that we sniff no 'humility', no self-abasement in the *affirmative* pleasure Nietzsche does describe in the enjoyment of woman at a 'magical' distance (if that perspective is affirmed *as* a perspective) given that such a humility could only be, in Nietzsche's terms, a stunting and abasement of his own forces and the expression of a weak and reactive type.

THE RESISTANCE BETWEEN THE SEXES

So, I want to use this question of what instincts are expressed and whether forces are stunted or strengthened, to assess the ways in which Rousseau and Nietzsche affirm the need for a 'resistance' between the sexes. We have seen that for Nietzsche, woman's soothing, delightful effect is sustained only by her distance from men. So, what does man find when he approaches more closely to women? Certainly, he does not find the truth of woman, for as we know, there is no truth of woman. Nevertheless, he finds another, different effect, or we could say, another, different perspective. Now, we have already encountered one of these different women, and this is the woman who represents rancour, *ressentiment*, reactivity and feminism as Nietzsche understands it. While we also know that there is at the very least a 'third' woman, the third woman I wish to discuss here is the woman of turbulence and resistance. This is the woman of 'antagonism between the sexes', as Nietzsche puts it, and in fact, this is one of the various accounts in which Nietzsche speaks 'positively' about women.

Nietzsche describes this antagonism separating man and woman as 'most abysmal', as the necessity of an eternally hostile tension (Nietzsche 1966: 147), as, 'harsh, terrible, enigmatic and immoral' (Nietzsche 1974b: 319). He describes procreation as depending on the duality of the sexes and involving perpetual strife, with only periodically intervening reconciliation (Nietzsche 1967: 33), where 'something new is born from two enemy principles'[16] (Nietzsche 1978: 187). Nietzsche's comments about the relations between the sexes being a case of 'love thy enemy' (Nietzsche 1972: 377) are not as sarcastic as they sometimes sound, because of his revaluation of the notion of 'enemy relations'.[17]

Now I want, of course, to juxtapose this account with the ideal of a harmonious complementarity between the sexes as envisaged by Rousseau.

First, we know that both Rousseau and Nietzsche oppose egalitarianism of the sexes in the name of what each calls '*natural*' relations between the sexes. Thus, both Rousseau and Nietzsche defend their versions of sexual difference against denunciations of the 'contra-nature', for example Rousseau condemns Plato's 'civil promiscuity which throughout confounds the two sexes in the same employments and in the same labours', as a subversion of nature (Rousseau 1991: 363). Nietzsche condemns the emancipation of women as a 'malignant idealism' and a 'contra-nature', aiming to poison 'the good conscience, what is natural in sexual love' (Nietzsche 1969a: 267–8).

But Nietzsche has already warned us to ask 'What is this nature Rousseau speaks of?' and cautioned us about the difference between Rousseau's 'good', 'benevolent' nature, and his own terrible nature; we need to apply this distinction to their respective reliance on conceptions of 'natural' relations between the sexes. While Rousseau's 'natural' relations offer an ideal alternative to the contemporary state of degraded relations between the sexes in which Rousseau thinks that man develops a *fear* of women, in Nietzsche's version of a 'natural' relation between the sexes it is precisely fear that man should bear woman. While fear between the sexes is for Rousseau a contra-nature, for Nietzsche, fearful relations are affirmed in his 'terrible' nature. Nietzsche explains

that the terrible man will accord woman her 'due tribute of contempt and fear'[18] (Nietzsche 1968b: 526).

What does Nietzsche understand by sexual antagonism? In
Beyond Good and Evil it is described as the man of 'depth' being
'obliged' to think of woman in something described as the 'oriental
way' thus: 'he must conceive of woman as a possession, as property
that can be locked, as something predestined for service' (Nietzsche
1966: 167). Nietzsche's 'sexual antagonism' is always described as
a matter of how man likes to, or is obliged to, or 'must' see woman
– as tantalizing savage creatures to capture and enclose. However,
we are told that woman resists man's idea of her, she combats these
affronts and is dangerous (Nietzsche 1966: 169–70, 87, 88), and it
may be for this reason that when Zarathustra holds forth to the
Old Woman on the subject of women, that she cautions him not
to go near them without his whip (Nietzsche 1969b: 93).

In reading Nietzsche's account of how men 'must' see woman –
as a potentially servile object – we must remember that Nietzsche
exposes the man who elevates woman to a divine ideal as a means
of rendering her *servile*. While Nietzsche argues that man pursues
woman as an object, 'pre-destined for service', he also seems to
incorporate into that notion woman's resistance to this attempt to
ensnare her. This resistance seems to play a part in the notion of
antagonism between the sexes as enemy principles.

Furthermore, it is to be remarked that this 'man of depth' is
described as having 'that depth of benevolence [*Wohlwollens*] which
is capable of severity and hardness and easily mistaken for them'
(Nietzsche 1966: 167). For benevolence has a particular, revalued
sense for Nietzsche. In *Ecce Homo* he explains that attacking one's
enemy is a kind of 'benevolence' [again, '*Wohlwollens*'][19] and of
'gratitude': it is a mark of 'respect', of 'distinction' and 'recognition'
of the other as a 'worthy' and 'equal'[20] enemy (Nietzsche 1969a:
231–3). So Nietzsche's conception of enemy relations should be
read as insisting on the recognition and distinction of the other as
the enemy which he considers is involved. It is a recognition that
he would not think Rousseau accords the other, precisely because
Rousseau conceives of the other in terms of pity, and for Nietzsche
pity is among other things an appropriation of rather than a recognition of the other.

However, in *The Gay Science*, Nietzsche again describes 'sexual
antagonism'. Here he describes the difference of the sexes in love.
This, he says, is a relationship where woman gives herself to man
in a complete gift, in a 'total abandon' [*vollkommene Hingabe*] 'and

not mere surrender', of soul and body, without reserve, to man –
and where man's forces thereby accumulate (Nietzsche 1974b: 319).
What is difficult to reconcile with the notion of enemy, antagonistic
relations between the sexes is Nietzsche's presentation of what
seems to be an extreme *docility* on the part of women. It is hard
to see – if man desires that woman give herself completely[21] and if
woman does indeed make herself over to him as an 'absolute gift'
– why Nietzsche should describe these relations as '*terrible* and
enigmatic': indeed, we seem to be brought back to a harmonious
complementarity, to a Rousseauist sexual difference.

In this regard, perhaps we should note first, that curiously, on
the Rousseauist account, woman does *not* give herself over to man
as a perfect gift. For Nietzsche, when woman gives herself, she
does so without restriction and without reserve. But Rousseau's
woman 'properly' resists man. The resistance is a strategic and
temporary reserve followed by a modest consent.[22] For Nietzsche,
there is no modesty, no chaste self-governing in the sexual antagonism and the unrestrained gift of the woman. Perhaps he would
argue that both men's and women's forces are weakened in the
Rousseauist relations between the sexes, since man abases himself
before woman, and since women modestly inhibit their own desires
in their resistance to man, and then 'let themselves be vanquished'
(Rousseau 1960: 86). Again, that the point is always the instincts
expressed by the account of woman, rather than the 'details' of
that account, is particularly apparent in the fact that Nietzsche
disparages 'misogynists'.[23] Since Nietzsche, conceiving man and
woman as natural enemies, gives a positive value to that relationship, we should distinguish it from a kind of hatred for women that
he does denounce:

> Misogynists – 'Woman is our enemy' – out of the man who says
> that to other men there speaks an immoderate drive which hates
> not only itself but its means of satisfaction as well.
>
> (Nietzsche 1982: 165)

What distinguishes the Nietzschean and 'misogynist' versions of
'enemy relations' between the sexes is activity as opposed to reactivity. For Nietzsche asserts that where the misogynist takes women
as his enemy, he expresses instincts of self-hatred, indeed those
same instincts which Rousseau is said to express in his lofty idealism
and thus in his elevating women to a lofty ideal.

Rather than Nietzsche's ideal man abasing himself before woman
in love, he is said to be rendered 'richer in "himself"' ' (Nietzsche

1974b: 319), and his forces increase when woman gives herself to him in an unreserved and unrestrained gift. So, Nietzsche's account would need to be assessed in terms of whether or not the protagonists' forces increase through their encounter – Nietzsche certainly considers that those of men would, in ideal relations between the sexes. But this will occur only if woman is the worthy, strong opponent, so that while man *covets* her as a servile object, she must *resist* that man, or that version of herself. When she does give herself over to man, this must not be in the spirit of surrender in so far as this implies a weakening of forces, but in a complete, affirmative gift of herself.

So we might well ask about woman's forces, which Nietzsche does not mention often. There are times when Nietzsche does not restrict the growth of forces that is produced by sexual antagonism to men alone, when he speaks generally of 'the increase of forces, for example, in the dance between the sexes'[24] (Nietzsche 1972: 328) and elsewhere again he speaks specifically of woman's forces which increase from the dance between the sexes, in the 'drunkenness called love' (Nietzsche 1968b: 425). Since Zarathustra tells women that their greatest hope should be to bear the overman (Nietzsche 1969: 92), Nietzsche is sometimes taken to exclude the concept of the noble woman. Yet there is an account in *Daybreak* of ideal relations between 'complete men' and 'complete women' which suggests otherwise:

> *Different kinds of pride* – Women grow pale at the thought that their beloved may not be worthy of them, men pale at the idea that they may not be worthy of their beloved. I am speaking of whole women, whole men.
>
> (Nietzsche 1982: 174)

Here, Nietzsche goes on to explain that, 'Such men, as men who are *customarily* confident and full of the feeling of power, acquire in a state of passion a sense of shame and doubt', and the women, who, says Nietzsche, 'normally feel themselves the weak and *surrendering* sex' (trans. modified, my emphasis: '*solche Frauen aber fühlen sich sonst immer als die Schwachen, zur Hingebung Bereiten*')[25] now, in a Nietzschean ideal of relations between the sexes:

> acquire in the exceptional state of passion their pride and their feeling of power – which asks: who is worthy of me?

So we could read Nietzsche's account of the 'perfect' woman (*ein vollkommeneres Weib*) in *The Gay Science* who devotes herself entirely to man so that his own forces grow (Nietzsche 1974b: 319), *with* the account of the 'whole' woman (*von ganzen Frauen*) in *Daybreak* whose forces grow such that they proudly ask who merit them. The repetition between these passages of the idea of 'wholeness' or 'perfection' as opposed to the idea of 'surrender' is important here. First, although the 'devoted' woman in *The Gay Science* is described as thereby becoming what Nietzsche terms 'perfect', this seems less like the rhetoric for the perfect housewife (the complete, devoted woman) given that Nietzsche *also* describes the 'proud' woman who goes *beyond surrender and docility* as a 'complete' woman. Second, the 'devoted' woman of *The Gay Science* is like the 'proud woman' in that she is defined *against* (in opposition to) a weak and *'surrendering'* woman [*vollkommene Hingabe (nicht nur Hingebung)*] – in both cases, there is a going-beyond of a certain kind of women's surrender to man. Although the version of the 'proud' woman emphasizes more strongly an increase in women's forces than does the account of the 'devoted' woman, I think that in both cases the point may be the kind of women both proud and devoted women are set against – weak, or restrained women of surrender.

Certainly, in both cases, the point is the 'why' – *why* does Nietzsche emphasize a notion of a 'complete' woman? In both cases, antagonistic sexual relations are conceived entirely in terms of producing an increase in the forces of the protagonists. The point, even of the 'devoted' woman, is that she does not give herself half-heartedly, but unreservedly, affirmatively. Perhaps Nietzsche's immoderate devoted woman is a re-evaluation of the traditional ideal of the devoted woman, who like Rousseau's Sophie, resists man modestly and temporarily, and subdues her own passions so as to manipulate those of Emile.

Nietzsche's account of the devoted woman does focus on the maximization of *men's* forces, but it is not that the non-maximization of women's forces is the necessary condition of the maximization of men's forces. This is the importance of the opposition to 'women of surrender'. The woman's unrestrained gift of herself is, in Nietzsche's view, affirmative – but so is the woman of pride who asks who is worthy of her – and so is the woman who is dangerous, who is to be feared, resisting man's ideals of woman, in the most obvious account of the resistance between the sexes.

In resisting Emile, it is important that Sophie is deliberately complicit with Emile's 'version' of her, as elevated, superior object towards whom he must strain, and that the tutor indirectly advises

Sophie that her role must be to sustain this version of woman. In comparison, we must ask if Nietzsche requires of women that they cut the cloth of themselves according to the image demanded of them. Certainly, he acknowledges that woman often does form herself such that she is complicit with a masculine version of herself (Nietzsche 1974b: 126). But he also presents an ideal of woman as a dangerous opponent who resists rather than abets man's version of her, and must in fact do so if the kind of sexual antagonism which might sharpen the wits and forces of each is to be sustained. We might add that it is perhaps congruent with such an account that such a woman may sometimes give herself over in a passionate, perfect gift.[26]

Nietzsche's critique is not aimed at the fact that there will always be a masculine investment in the production of certain interpretations of women. He seems to suggest that this is inevitable, just as it is inevitable that he has his own interpretations, his own truths of women (Nietzsche 1966: 162). Therefore, a Nietzschean critique of the Rousseauist conception of woman would not denounce this as being 'merely' Rousseau's conception of woman, for the status of this 'mere' is lost at the point of the exclusion of ultimate truths about women, Nietzsche's facetious comment about his own 'mere' truths about women notwithstanding. A Nietzschean critique of the Rousseauist conception of women would not be aimed at the fact that Rousseau's interpretation of woman was mediated by a certain desire to produce a certain interpretation of woman. The Nietzschean critique would not be directed at the terms and notions of woman deployed by Rousseau (difference, distance, no touching at the veil, abhorring the contra-nature) for these are terms deployed by Nietzsche himself. But a Nietzschean critique would nevertheless devastate the Rousseauist conception of woman, because of the instincts the Rousseauist conception of woman expresses. The Rousseauist fear of woman is not love of antagonism, but fear of contamination. The Rousseauist fear of contamination is not distancing from the weak, but a rendering weak of oneself. The Rousseauist idealization of woman is not a vision of a woman of maximized forces, but a lowering of forces in self-abasement. The Rousseauist notion of the contra-nature is not a 'contra', the stunting of our own forces, but an abasement before a transcendental directive. The question, for Nietzsche, is not whether man is 'overly' invested in producing 'his' woman, but rather, the nature of the instincts which are manifest in the interpretation.

ACKNOWLEDGEMENTS

This material formed part of a longer work submitted as a DEA in History of Philosophy, Université de Paris I, 1991. Sarah Kofman's 1990–91 *Ecce Homo* seminar was a constant influence. Thanks also to Jean-Philippe Mihière, Sarah Kofman, Richard Peres, Florence Laborir, Paul Patton and Paul Redding for critical comments and assistance with language difficulties.

NOTES

1 It so happens that each of these three is associated with deconstruction, and that each asserts a series of very surprising resemblances between Rousseau and Nietzsche in a string of footnotes and asides in their work. Paul de Man suggests similarities between their conceptions of a will to power or a 'power to will' (de Man 1979: 140), between their critiques of organized, politicized Christianity (de Man 1979: 223), between their conceptions of metaphor as the origin of 'literal' meaning (de Man 1979: 122–3, 154), between their conceptions of the specifically human mode of the promise (de Man 1979: 273), between their conceptions of physiological foundations to our notions of good and evil (de Man 1979: 244) and in the fact that they are both what he calls 'rhetorically self-conscious' philosophers (de Man 1979: 226). Sarah Kofman also argues that the Rousseauist and Nietzschean accounts of metaphor as the origin of 'literal' language are akin; however, she argues that both the early Nietzsche and Rousseau conserve a 'logocentric' hierarchy of original over tributary meaning (Kofman 1983: 18, 57, 153). Kofman also suggests that Rousseau's texts accord with the Nietzschean version of woman's modesty as her highest virtue (Kofman 1986: 246). This last is a point that I return to later in the chapter.

2 Here, I am thinking of Nietzsche's account of a 'healthy' instinct: 'My instinct for cleanliness is characterized by a perfectly uncanny sensitivity so that the proximity or – what am I saying? – the inmost parts, the "entrails" of every soul are physiologically perceived by me – smelled' (Nietzsche 1969a: 233).

3 The suggestion is that the account of Nietzsche's perspectivism in terms of artistic metaphors such that (as this is expressed by Nehamas), in any representation, certain elements are foregrounded at the expense of others and the subject matter thereby 'created' by the artist (Nehamas 1985: 55), applies here to Nietzsche's account of Rousseau and feminism. Here, Nietzsche's 'foregrounding' is an extreme 'foreshortening', in which it is the presence of *ressentiment*, idealism and egalitarianism only which are dramatically at the fore, and the precise detail and content of 'Rousseau' or 'feminism' dramatically obscure. This is a different account of Nietzsche's 'foreshortening' than that to be found in Kofman (1988: 186). Here, Kofman uses the term to describe Nietzsche's account of the flattening, 'frog perspective' in which the weak defer before and interpret the world in terms of elevated 'high' concepts (God, truth, reality) such that their perspective of evaluation is 'bottom' to 'top'.

4 '*Dem ganzen europäischen Femininismus (oder Idealismus, wenn man's lieber hört)*'.

5 It seems '*Weib an sich*' is not so much 'woman *as such*' as translated by R. J. Hollingdale but 'woman in herself' as Kaufmann does here (though not consistently) translate it. This strengthens the suggestion that in these passages Nietzsche attacks feminists not for their contravention of the eternal feminine, but for their deployment of a notion of the eternal feminine, a conception that he rejects. Or, we might say that any notion of the eternal feminine that Nietzsche does invoke to denounce the idealist notion of an eternal feminine is a re-valued 'eternal feminine' and not the 'same', idealist eternal feminine he denounces. Thus, an alternative to seeing Nietzsche as *ambivalent* on this point would be the idea of the 're-evaluation of old nouns'. Kofman insists on the constant reading of Nietzsche in these terms (Kofman 1988: 178) – here, the 'eternal feminine' would be the re-valued 'old noun'.

6 (*Das Weib, das ewig Weibliche: ein bloß imaginärer Werth, an den allein des Mann glaubt.*) Here, Nietzsche tells us that only men believe in the 'entirely imaginary' values, 'woman' and the 'eternal feminine'. Elsewhere, as we see, he tells us of the propensity of certain women to believe in these 'imaginary values', also the emancipists, for example.

7 '*Die absolute Hingebung (in der Religion) als Reflex der sklavischen Hingebung oder der weiblichen (– das Ewig-Weibliche ist der idealisirte Sklavensinn)*'.

8 One could pursue Diprose's question of whether Nietzsche does invoke the notion of the eternal feminine that he denounces (Diprose 1989: 32). For one thing, the phrasing of 'the emancipated are anarchists in the world of the eternally feminine' is ambiguous (*Im Grunde sind die Emancipirten die Anarchisten in der Welt des 'Ewig-Weiblichen'*). Is Nietzsche attacking emancipists because they undermine the eternal feminine, or because they invoke it? There is an element of mockery in the phrase '*der Welt des "Ewig-Weiblichen"*' which suggests the latter. For another thing, the preceding passage: 'Perhaps I am the first psychologist of the eternal feminine. They all love me', etc., seems rather tongue-in-cheek given that it immediately precedes Nietzsche's mockery of such a notion. Even if Nietzsche does deploy an 'eternal feminine', this must certainly be read *with* his own sarcasm about such a conception, and can't be simply seen as 'self-contradiction' without raising the question of how to read Nietzsche's constant 'self-contradictions' – sometimes as his masks, sometimes as his re-valuation of old terms and so on. Diprose does not assert that Nietzsche has simply contradicted himself. For, on her reading, the 'essential self' that Nietzsche rejects is not *the same* as the eternal feminine that she considers he does insist on. The difference, she says, is that Nietzsche admits that he is interpreting an image of himself when he acknowledges his dependence on the 'eternal feminine'. We could add – the emancipist who believes in the eternal feminine would be like Rousseau, and unlike Nietzsche, in believing in the 'truth of woman'.

9 Its aim is to generate or reinforce a version of the self: it is not aimed at, or open to the other. Thus it is an expression of the will to power masquerading as a superior moral virtue.

10 For his employment of this term, see also Nietzsche (1974b: 176).

11 It should be noted that apart from other scathing accounts of the psychology of pity which Nietzsche gives, he also sometimes refers to his own 'pity' for humanity. Here, pity has taken on a re-valued sense for Nietzsche, so that this is not, of course, incoherent with his denunciation of pity. See, for example, Nietzsche's description of what he calls 'my kind of pity' (Nietzsche 1968b: 198).

12 Derrida has pointed out (Derrida 1976: 173) that Rousseau particularly uses mothers and their maternal love for their child in his examples of the expression of pity for the weak. There is also the fact that Julie finally capitulates to Saint-Preux and to her own desire because of her pity for him, and Rousseau's references to slaves and women being the only people 'weak' (susceptible) enough to try to prevent brawlers about to tear each other's throats out (Rousseau 1987a: 55).

13 It seems to me that this interpretation can be sustained despite the occurrence of an association by Nietzsche of strength and active forces with 'virility', see for example the use of the term 'emasculation' to describe the weak rendering the strong weak (Nietzsche 1969a: 124). Although this might seem to reinforce the notion of 'surprising similarities' between Rousseau and Nietzsche, the distinction between these two accounts of the fragility of 'virility' would still have to be traced in terms of the difference between their accounts of the fragility of the strong, as suggested above.

14 Of course, we have to tread a little carefully with this qualification, for Nietzsche does not mean that these are only 'his' truths as opposed to some truths that might be the eternal and final truths. Given that he rejects the possibility of the latter, the status of the 'qualification' *only* becomes ambiguous and interesting.

15 However, it is important that this would not be the mask of Nietzsche's 'anti-feminism'. Nietzsche's 'anti-feminism' entirely expresses his notion of a 'healthy' distance from the reactive. He does not consider the weak the 'worthy enemy' but rather the threat to pure air. He does consider that the strong may be repelled by and desire distance from the weak without this being the equivalent of their own weakness or *ressentiment*. Strangely, it is not Nietzsche's denunciation of women but rather a certain mode of his *elevation* of women that we might identify as reactive, in so far as it is a conversion into a lofty vision of women of what is in fact a fear of the abyss. Here, interpretations of women as castrating might be reactive – while the affirmation of the abyss would be active.

16 Draft for *The Birth of Tragedy*, Notebook fragment, 1870–71 cross-referenced by Colli and Montinari for section no. 1, *The Birth of Tragedy* (Roughly: 'The fact that nature tied the birth of tragedy to these two fundamental instincts, the Apollonian and the Dionysian might appear as much of a fissure of reason as an arrangement by that same nature which tied the propagation of the species to the duality of the sexes, something which grand Kant always found surprising. For the common secret is the fact that from two enemy principles something new can be born such that these two divided instincts appear to be a unity: in this sense, reproduction is just like a work of tragic art in that

its worth can be like the pledge of the rebirth of Dionysus, like a beam of hope on the eternally mourning aspect of Demeter.') The themes raised by Ainley (1988) about procreation, generation and childbirth as affirmative in Nietzschean terms and as giving Nietzsche a metaphor for an affirmative, creative principle are interesting here. Kofman has also pointed out that where childbirth and woman give rise to a general, Nietzschean metaphor, that Nietzsche has already mediated that exploitation of the metaphor of woman as a generating, life-giving force with his interpretation of woman as affirmative in these terms.

17 These comments give another complexion to the passage in *Zarathustra*: 'Woman is not yet capable of friendship' [which is to say enemy relations, since the best friend is, of course, the best enemy]. In any case, Nietzsche immediately continues there: 'But tell me, you men, who among you is capable of friendship?' (Nietzsche 1978: 57). Nietzsche, while sometimes dubious about woman's capacity for enemy relations with man, seems to consider at least that this is their ideal relationship, and is dubious that men are ready for such relations. In *Zarathustra*, we are told that woman is *not yet* capable of being man's friend – and this is the same passage in which we are told that the best friend is the best enemy, in which enemy relations and the notion of the 'worthy' enemy are affirmed. Thus, 'You should honour even the enemy in your friend. . . . In your friend you should possess your best enemy. Your heart should feel closest to him when you oppose him.' And, 'Are you a tyrant? If so, you cannot be a friend. Are you a slave? If so, you cannot have friends. In woman, a slave and a tyrant have all too long been concealed. For that reason, woman is not yet capable of friendship: she knows only love' (Nietzsche 1969b: 83).

18 This ideal relation needs to be distinguished from Nietzsche's account of all-too-human women, 'typed' as weak, reactive, rancorous, prone to 'the cult of pity' (1968b: 460) for whom Nietzsche bears an antipathy which is not the ideal antagonism he speaks of – although there is often blurring between these accounts. This point about needing to distinguish different conceptions that are nevertheless blurred in Nietzsche is tangly. It might involve distinguishing on the one hand his contempt for the [weak, reactive] woman 'mastering' man (Nietzsche 1968b: 460) from a 'fear' of women expressed in an affirmative 'antagonism between the sexes'.

In general, obviously Nietzsche's antipathy for the weak needs to be distinguished from the kind of antagonism that is valorized in ideal enemy relations. In one kind of antagonism, Nietzsche recommends distance *from* the weak (distancing the strong from the weak), in another kind of antagonism, he considers that [antagonistic] enemy relations imply a *respect* and acknowledgement of the enemy. While Nietzsche values an engagement with the enemy, this does not preclude his also valuing distance between enemies, certainly in so far as one should not attempt to know the enemy 'too well', and in so far as one does not learn the 'truth' of the enemy through engaging with her/him. Perhaps this is best articulated as the difference between distancing oneself *from* [the weak], and the distance *between* [the strong and the strong].

19 *'Wohlwollens'* is the term employed both in *Ecce Homo* (Nietzsche 1969b: 232) and *Beyond Good and Evil* (Nietzsche 1966: 167), although the repetition is less evident where the latter has been translated as benevolence, but the former has been translated as 'goodwill'.

20 Again, here there has to be a distinction between the notion of equality as loss of individualism, or inability to encounter the individual, and here, a re-valued notion of equality – finding the worthy equal – a worthy enemy: 'Equality before the enemy: the first presupposition of an honest duel' (Nietzsche 1969a: 232).

21 'Man, when he loves a woman, wants precisely this love from her' (Nietzsche 1974b: 319).

22 This resistance is woman's strategem since, as Emile's tutor instructs Sophie, it allows her to govern her husband. Woman's modesty is also nature's strategem, since the modesty with which woman is endowed restrains both women and men from the excess of sexual relations which would lead to their own destruction.

23 Colli and Montinari suggest that Nietzsche's reference here is to Schopenhauer (Nietzsche 1970: 317), which is particularly interesting in the light of Nietzsche's comments in *On the Genealogy of Morals* about Schopenhauer's *need* for enemies, including women (Nietzsche 1969b: 106). At one point then, Nietzsche would seem to read Schopenhauer's misogyny as reactive, at another as active.

24 *'Das Mehr von Kraft z.B. beim Tanz der Geschlechter'*.

25 In a footnote to his translation of *The Gay Science*, p. 363 (Nietzsche 1974b: 319), Kaufmann emphasizes his translation of *'nicht nur Hingebung'* as 'not mere surrender' rather than 'not mere devotion'. However, in *Daybreak*, the fact that 'complete women' again are said to go beyond their 'usual' state of weakness and surrender is obscured by the fact that the repetition of 'Hingebung' is suppressed, here by Hollingdale. In my text, however, I do want to focus on the repetition of the idea of 'surrender' as that which women go beyond either in 'pride' or in the 'complete gift'.

26 In the French translations of Nietzsche established by Colli and Montinari, the 'total abandon' and not 'mere surrender' that woman is said to understand by 'love' is translated as a 'perfect gift', thus: *'Ce que la femme entend par amour est assez clair: parfait don (non pas seulement abandon) du corps et de l'âme sans restriction et sans réserve'* (Nietzsche 1989: 270).

   If 'perfect gift' is appropriate in this context, might we suspect here after all a fantasy of an 'unveiled', 'authentic woman' – finally a woman who would *not* be 'giving herself' (acting, holding in reserve) even as she 'gave herself'? (In that case, would Nietzsche's mask here be other than that whereby he affirms woman as dissimulation, who might thereby be considered an 'imperfect' gift in the fantasy of the total presence of woman?)

BIBLIOGRAPHY

Ainley, A. (1988) ' "Ideal selfishness" – Nietzsche's metaphor of maternity', in D. F. Krell and D. Wood (eds) *Exceedingly Nietzsche*, London: Routledge.

de Man, P. (1979) *Allegories of Reading*, New Haven, Conn. and London: Yale University Press.

Derrida, J. (1976) *Of Grammatology*, trans. G. C. Spivak, Baltimore, Md.: Johns Hopkins University Press.

—— (1979) *Spurs/Eperons*, trans. B. Harlow, Chicago and London: University of Chicago Press.

Diprose, R. (1989) 'Nietzsche, ethics and sexual difference', *Radical Philosophy* 52: 27–33.

Kofman, S. (1982) *Le Respect des femmes*, Paris: Editions Galilée.

—— (1983) *Nietzsche et la métaphore*, Paris: Editions Galilée.

—— (1986) *Nietzsche et la scène philosophique*, Paris: Editions Galilée.

—— (1988) 'Baubô: theological perversion and fetishism',* trans. T. Strong, in M. A. Gillespie and T. B. Strong (eds) *Nietzsche's New Seas*, Chicago and London: University of Chicago Press (*translation of excerpt from S. Kofman, *Nietzsche et la scène philosophique*).

Nehamas, A. (1985) *Nietzsche – Life as Literature*, Cambridge, Mass. and London: Harvard University Press.

Nietzsche, F. (1966) *Beyond Good and Evil*, trans. W. Kaufmann, New York: Vintage.

—— (1967) *The Birth of Tragedy and The Case of Wagner*, trans. W. Kaufmann, New York: Vintage.

—— (1968a) *Twilight of the Idols*, trans. R. J. Hollingdale, Harmondsworth: Penguin.

—— (1968b) *The Will to Power*, trans. R. J. Hollingdale and W. Kaufmann, New York: Vintage.

—— (1969a) *On the Genealogy of Morals and Ecce Homo*, trans. W. Kaufmann, New York: Vintage.

—— (1969b) *Thus Spoke Zarathustra*, trans. R. J. Hollingdale, Harmondsworth: Penguin.

—— (1970) *Aurore*, trans. J. Hervier, Paris: Gallimard (Folio).

—— (1972) *Nachgelassene Fragmente, Anfang 1888 bis Anfang Januar 1889*, Berlin and New York: Walter de Gruyter.

—— (1974a) *Nachgelassene Fragmente Herbst 1885 bis Herbst 1887*, Berlin and New York: Walter de Gruyter.

—— (1974b) *The Gay Science*, trans. W. Kaufmann, New York: Vintage.

—— (1978) *Nachgelassene Fragmente Herbst 1869 bis Herbst 1872*, Berlin and New York: Walter de Gruyter.

—— (1982) *Daybreak*, trans. R. J. Hollingdale, Harmondsworth: Penguin.

—— (1989) *Le Gai savoir*, trans. P. Klossowski, Paris: Gallimard (Folio).

Rousseau, J. J. (1960) 'Letter to M. D'Alembert on the theatre', in *Politics and the Arts*, trans. A. Bloom, Glencoe, Ill.: Free Press of Glencoe.

—— (1966) 'Essay on the origin of languages', in J. J. Rousseau and H. Herder, *Two Essays on the Origin of Languages*, trans. J. H. Moran and A. Gode, Chicago and London: University of Chicago Press.

—— (1969) 'Lettre à M. Franquières', in *Oeuvres Complètes*, tome IV, Paris: Bibliothèque de la Pléiade, Editions Gallimard.

—— (1987a) 'Discourse on the origin of inequality', in *The Basic Political Writings*, trans. D. A. Cress, Indianapolis, Ind. and Cambridge: Hackett.

—— (1987b) 'Discourse on the sciences and the arts', in *The Basic Political Writings*, trans. D. A. Cress, Indianapolis, Ind. and Cambridge: Hackett.

—— (1991) *Emile*, trans. A. Bloom, Harmondsworth: Penguin.

10 The return of Nietzsche and Marx

Howard Caygill

The probity of a contemporary intellectual, especially a contemporary philosopher, can be measured by their attitude toward Nietzsche and Marx.

(Max Weber)

When Nietzsche observed that some are born posthumously, he might have added that some meet their significant contemporaries only after their deaths. He and Marx, for instance, were largely unaware of each other's existence, yet both were called back in the twentieth century to engage in a dialogue *d'outre-tombe*. Their debate has been one of the most consequential intellectual confrontations of twentieth-century thought, provoking some of its highest as well as its lowest moments. The names 'Marx' and 'Nietzsche' have come to carry an ideological and political charge which, when combined, has the power either to open or close debate. For the energy that motivates the profound reflections upon the question of the relation between Nietzsche *and* Marx is the same that drives it into the impasse of the choice between Marx *or* Nietzsche.

The history of the twentieth-century confrontation between Nietzsche and Marx moves between the two questions, with the either/or on the whole prevailing. The grotesque use of Nietzsche against Marx by the National Socialists in the 1930s is but an exceptionally grisly moment in a consistent history of pitting the two thinkers against each other. Other unedifying episodes include the image of Nietzsche propagated by the *nouveaux philosophes* of the 1970s and the imagined Nietzsche whose works now fill the spaces in east European bookshops previously reserved for the 'classics' of Marxism–Leninism. In both cases Nietzsche is cast as an alternative to Marxism, the thinker whose work would exclude and supersede that of Marx.[1]

The inverse holds for the Nietzsche of Lukács' *The Destruction of Reason* (1980: esp. ch. 3) and other Marxist readings who is

cast as a bourgeois intellectual who prefigured and contributed to the rise of fascism. In the words of one of the last books
to be published by the philosophical section of the late East
German Academy – *Moderne-Nietzsche-Postmoderne* (Buhr 1990)
Nietzsche's philosophy is but 'an anticipation of the bourgeois
imperialist barbarism of our century'.[2] This philosophy is naturally
contrasted with Marx's anticipation of twentieth-century socialist
internationalist civilization. Both the Nietzschean anti-Marxists and
the Marxist anti-Nietzscheans are clear that a choice has to be made
between either one or the other; the main point, however, is to
read neither. For the choice of either Nietzsche or Marx is largely
the reflex of an opposition between Marxists and Nietzscheans, one
which has very little to do with the differences between two bodies
of work produced in relative isolation during the second half of the
nineteenth century.

The most interesting and important reflections upon Nietzsche
and Marx have been beyond good and evil, beyond the manichean
opposition of saint and satan. They have not necessarily been written by those who attempted a 'synthesis' – such as the 'left-
Nietzscheans' of the early twentieth century – but rather by those
who reflected upon what is implied in the 'and' of Marx and
Nietzsche. Their attitude is exemplified by Max Weber in a comment made towards the end of his life in 1920:

> Whoever claims that they could have accomplished the most
> important parts of their own work without the work done by
> both [Marx and Nietzsche] deceives themselves and others. The
> world in which spiritually and intellectually we live today is a
> world bearing the imprint of Marx and Nietzsche.[3]

For Weber, the character of the imprint left by Nietzsche and Marx
combined the features of an insight into power and its inversions
and the materialist conception of history. Later in the 1930s Walter
Benjamin and Georges Bataille regarded Marx and Nietzsche as
the pre-eminent thinkers of revolutionary excess and 'active nihilism';[4] while for other readers, particularly those critically engaging
with the thought of Heidegger, such as Levinas and Irigaray, they
are the last metaphysicians whose thought ultimately cannot contain
ethical exteriority.[5]

Two shared themes emerge from the reading of Nietzsche *and*
Marx: both are taken to analyse the nihilistic condition of modern
subjectivity, and both explore the possibility of an excessive return
or 'revolution'. They are both thinkers of crisis, but crisis thought

not only in the pathological sense of the critical moment in the progress of a disease, but also in the sense of a moment of judgement or decision. The texts of both Marx and Nietzsche are informed by an often unbearable tension between crisis as condition and crisis as decision, or in other words, the diagnosis of the critical condition of nihilistic subjectivity and the prescription of its decisive over-turn.[6]

The crisis they explore is that of the Kantian autonomous, legislative subject of modernity. This is the subject which would give itself its own laws, the subject for whom the claims of traditional values have been stripped of their legitimacy by the 'critical tribunal', who is free but nevertheless subjected, one who is dissatisfied and locked into oppressive and exploitative relations of its own making.[7] It is the crisis of this subject – for whom 'all that is solid melts into air,' and for whom 'God is dead' – that is the object of Marx and Nietzsche's analysis; they analyse both the aetiology of the crisis and the conditions under which the subject may return to itself.

Central to both Nietzsche and Marx's analysis of crisis is the concept of return. Indeed, it is this concept which, in various guises, has informed the entire twentieth-century reception of their thought. 'Return' is the site of the 'and' which cleaves the thought of Marx and Nietzsche. The affinities and differences between their analyses of return can already be detected in the word they choose for the concept: Marx, in the *Grundrisse* and *Capital*, uses *Wiederholen*, while Nietzsche, in *The Gay Science* and *Thus Spoke Zarathustra* uses *Wiederkehren*. Both words signify return, and both are used reflexively of a subject (*sich wiederkehren, sich wiederholen*), but with a subtle difference of emphasis in each case. *Wiederholen* implies repetition, going over the same old thing, fetching back again and again in the manner of Freud's repetitive *Fort/Da*; while *Wiederkehren* implies return as a turning back. Yet in spite of these slight differences, the deployment of the notion of return by the two thinkers is strikingly similar. For both Nietzsche and Marx, 'return' signifies not only a crisis in the subject, but also an excessive or 'revolutionary' 'return' or 'conversion' which transforms the subject.

The problem of return has implicitly determined both the depths and the heights of the twentieth-century understanding of Nietzsche and/or Marx. Even the lower reaches of the either Marx or Nietzsche 'debate' is informed by the distinction between the 'revolutionary' and 'reactionary' character of the preferred thinker, overlooking that both terms are compounds of the Latin equivalent of *wieder*, namely *re* – re-action, re-volution.

The more profound reflections on the 'and' of Nietzsche and Marx are almost without exception conducted in terms of an analysis of their concepts of return. For Benjamin and Bataille the return of both thinkers is excessive: 'revolution' or 'eternal return' is open and cannot be contained within restricted economies of circulation. Conversely, for Levinas and Irigaray, Marx and Nietzsche's return is ultimately closed – there is no exteriority or excess, only what is given can return. For these readers, Nietzsche and Marx's notions of return can give rise only to closed, unethical matricidal regimes.

Both Marx and Nietzsche depict the crisis of modern subjectivity in terms of the experience of time, and the locus of this crisis is the uncanny experience of return. But by taking as their theme the tension between analysing and provoking a crisis (crisis as diagnosis and decision), between return within a closed and restricted economy and return as open and excessive, Nietzsche and Marx encountered great difficulties in realising their texts. The most striking of these is their oft remarked inability to complete: neither was able to finish his main work.[8]

Marx could complete only the first volume of *Capital*. We have re-constructions from his notes of volumes two and three by Engels: the planned volumes on legislation and the state were never realized. The reason for this inability to complete was not simply Marx's growing ill-health (which in his and Nietzsche's case may be seen more as a symptom than a cause), but rather the impossibility of completing a text which would both analyse and evoke a crisis of return. This will be illustrated through the analysis of some crucial passages from the *Grundrisse*, a text which comes closest to an overall conspectus of Marx's project. The situation is similar with *Thus Spoke Zarathustra*, which also remained incomplete because uncompletable.

Zarathustra begins with the protagonist's descent from the mountains to the cities in order to teach the eternal return of the same. Most of this and the second book of *Thus Spoke Zarathustra* traces the systematic misunderstanding of this philosophy by Zarathustra's contemporaries and disciples. The third book ends with Zarathustra acknowledging the defeat of his address and retreating to the mountains where, in an *opera buffa* sequel, he is visited in the fourth book by the 'higher men'. Nietzsche envisaged continuing to address them as contemporaries, in a way they would understand. But it was impossible to write this conclusion, since the doctrine of eternal return was both a diagnosis of the nihilistic culture of the 'last man' and an attempt to evoke a decision. The evocation of this crisis was the task [*Aufgabe*] of the 'fish hook' texts of Nietzsche's last four years of sanity.[9] Zarathustra itself remains incomplete – we are left not knowing how he would have spoken – thus or thus.

Neither Marx nor Nietzsche could finish: their main texts remained open, and remain so in spite of the efforts of some Marxists and Nietzscheans to close them. And significantly, both texts are interrupted at the same moment, at the cross between crisis as diagnosis and prescription, between the analysis of a condition and the provocation of a decision. Both texts founder at the moment of legislation, the moment of giving a law which is also the subject's 'autonomous' taking on of law. And the paradoxes of this moment – aptly described by Irigaray as the 'attempt to square the circle' (Irigaray 1985: 212) – emerge in the difficulty of thinking return, a difficulty framed in terms of time and subjectivity. What is at stake in this difficulty may be exemplified by briefly considering Kant's analysis of the return of the law and its relation to time.

Time for Kant is neither the frame within which events occur, nor the relation between events. We can best understand his position if we look at his early text from 1763 *The Only Possible Proof for the Existence of God*.[10] Here Kant makes the celebrated claim that being is not a predicate, but the position of predicates. He uses the term *Setzen* for position, which should be read actively as the act of putting, positioning or placing. This term is significantly the one Marx uses to name the operation of that particular relation between being and time that he calls 'capital'.[11]

Kant distinguishes between relative and absolute *Setzung*: relative *Setzung* is the ascription of a predicate to a subject, but such ascription can be accomplished only if both subject and predicate have *already been* posited absolutely.[12] We are able to predicate being of an object only if we have already 'posited the relation' which makes such predication possible. Kant designates this positing of the relation as time, and gives it certain formal properties. Time cannot be derived from the relation between events or appearances, nor may it be regarded as their frame, receptacle or horizon; it is an event of absolute position which is the 'condition' of the events and appearances of relative position (judgement).

Kant further defines this absolute event in terms of *schema*. In an earlier text, the *New Exposition of the First Principles of Metaphysical Knowledge* (1755), Kant introduced the term – crucial to the later *Critique of Pure Reason* – as the continuous activity of divine intelligence, 'the origin of all existents' and their mutual relations. Although the divine subject of the schema has been effaced, become an 'unknowable' by the time of the first Critique,[13] the character of its activity remains constant – it both *realizes* and *restricts*. Time allows events and appearances to be realized, but restricts the way in which they may occur and appear. Kant went on in the third Critique to develop the movement of 'realization and restriction' into a theory of culture in which communities are the agents of realization and restriction, thus anticipating the union of philosophy and social theory which was axiomatic for Marx and Nietzsche.

According to Kant we are victims of a transcendental illusion or paralogism around time; from the appearance of objects and the occurrence of events *in time* we infer that time may be thought and measured in terms of 'appearances' and 'events'. Against this Kant suggests that we should think of events and appearances as posited through and not *in* time; in this way we become aware of time as a schema, as an absolute position which determines the relations between events and appearances. If we persist in reducing absolute position to the terms of relation, we shall be led into the kinds of antinomy and paralogism diagnosed by Kant in the 'Dialectic' of the first Critique.

For Kant time is originary (*ursprunglich*): it does not appear or occur in time but is a schema of the event of absolute position which allows appearances and events to take their place in the temporal order. Yet with the notable exception of the third Critique, the subject of the act of *Setzung* is usually disavowed by Kant. The schematizing God of the *New Exposition of the First Principles of Metaphysical Knowledge* is transformed into the 'mysterious art' whose works and ways are closed to us. This is entirely consistent, for Kant argues that it is impossible to think the foundation of thought without falling prey to dialectical inferences. Whether this dialectic can be mobilized to think, the absolute is the Hegelian wager whose implications have still yet to be fully grasped and worked through. But according to the Kantian account 'we' are not in a position to accept responsibility for the absolute positing of time: we may become aware of it in the progressive development of culture and the 'signs of history' but *qua* absolute it cannot be said to be in our power.

Both Nietzsche and Marx are heirs to Fichte and Hegel's challenge to this disowning of time. Indeed this challenge continues to haunt post-Kantian philosophy in the guise of thinking the difficult relation of being, time and subjectivity. Nietzsche and Marx take their place within this heritage: both develop the distinction between the absolute and the relative aspects of the position of time and its relation to being and subjectivity. This heritage forms the condition of the 'and' of Marx and Nietzsche, and it is analysed in terms of the concept of 'return'.

Nietzsche's question of eternal return in *The Gay Science*, provoked by the demon's words 'life as you now live it and have lived it, you will have to live once more and innumerable times more' (Nietzsche 1974: 273) can be answered in relative or absolute terms. It is this which makes the answer a judgement on the answerer, as is spelt out in *The Gay Science*:

> If this thought gained possession of you, it would change you as you are or perhaps crush you. The question in each and everything 'Do you desire this once more and innumerable times more?' would lie on your actions as the greatest weight. Or how well disposed would you have to become to yourself and to life to crave nothing more than this ultimate eternal confirmation and seal.
>
> (Nietzsche 1974: 273)

In Kantian terms, the question of eternal return reveals the work of the schematism of time by driving it to its limit where it yields to paradox (eternal return). Faced with these limits the questioner may either become stiflingly aware of its restriction and be paralysed by the 'greatest weight' – or become realized and return to themselves in an 'eternal confirmation' that accepts responsibility for giving the time within which things and events return anew.[14]

The question of eternal return challenges Kant's disowning of time – it proposes that we take absolute responsibility for time – that we cease to accept time as given but instead repeat the event of the giving of time, its absolute position. We must return the gift of time, find time to give it back. The implications of this return for subjectivity are developed through the imagined *übermensch* who in refusing the gift accepts responsibility for the giving of time. The *übermensch* do not act as if they have time, are in time or are measured by time, but posit time through every act, and by so doing change themselves and their experience of events and objects. They are no longer restricted to 'taking place' in time, but realize themselves in an originary positing of time.

As Nietzsche acknowledges, such a view of time and experience is nightmarish, but he nevertheless insists on posing the stark alternatives: either we own the foundation of time, or are owned by time. If we are owned by time, then our actions and our possessions are not ours, the meaning they seem to have and which we seem to bestow on them is illusory. Nietzsche is not proposing in place of this experience of the crisis of meaning a 'modern' full, authentic possession of the meaning of our actions and things, nor a 'postmodern' embrace of their meaningless; rather he is calling the subjectivity that finds itself in this condition to judge itself and come to a decision, one whose outcome he leaves open. There arises a 'struggle for time' which Nietzsche casts in terms of a nihilistic subjectivity being crushed by meaninglessness and seeking revenge on time, and one that is transformed by accepting responsibility for its time. The former are the modern and postmodern subjectivities who oscillate between the desire to possess meaning and the vengeful celebration of its absence, while the latter are the *übermenschen*, those beyond measure who accept the responsibility for the giving of measure: they are those who have become what they are – 'the unique, the incomparable, the self-legislating, the self-creating' (Nietzsche 1974: 266 – extraneous 'human beings' deleted from Kaufmann's translation).

Nietzsche saw socialism as the epitome of the vengeful subject, the one taking revenge on the order of time within which it is restricted.[15] However, if we return to Marx with the question of time and return, we shall find an analysis of time and subjectivity which in crucial ways both questions and supplements the one provided by Nietzsche.

In the later sections of the *Grundrisse* Marx makes some fascinating comments about time and capital. In them capital is presented as doing the work of the Kantian schematism. He writes that capital 'posits' not only the commodities which are produced and circulated (relative position), but also the time within which their circulation takes place (absolute position). Furthermore, the time of production and circulation is posited 'restrictively', as repetition in an already given time through which capital realizes itself. The time of capital may be thought relatively, in terms of motion/process/turnover, or absolutely, as their position:

> On the one side labour time, on the other circulation time. And the whole of the movement appears as unity of labour time and circulation time, of production and circulation. This unity itself is motion, process. Capital appears as this unity-in-process of production and circulation, a unity which can be regarded both

as the totality of the process of its production, as well as the specific completion of *one* turnover of the capital, *one* movement returning into itself.

(Marx 1977a: 620)

Capital then both founds the time of the unity of production and circulation (the 'totality of the process') and yet eternally returns to itself as a 'specific turnover' in this time. Capital performs the Kantian paralogism: it is driven to overcome its disowned absolute position of time by repeating the act of relative position, increasing the speed of turnover within the time posited by capital, an enterprise which is prone to self-destructive crisis. In this condition of crisis there is no decision regarding the absolute position of time, only an adaptation to the relative position of things and events as commodities.

Marx outlines how capital strives to overcome the interval between absolute and relative position of time by nihilistically accelerating its returns, in relative time:

the sum of values which can be created in a given period of time depends on the number of repetitions of the production process within this period. The repetition of the production process, however, is determined by circulation time. . . . The more rapid the circulation, the shorter the circulation time, the more often can the same capital repeat the production process.

(Marx 1977a: 627)

The acceleration of the turnovers of capital in relative time leads to the 'abolition of time' – a form of eternal return which evokes all the paradoxes of the thought: '*Circulation without circulation time* – i.e. the transition of capital from one phase to the next at the speed of thought – would be the maximum, i.e. the identity of the renewal of the production process with its termination' (Marx 1977a: 631, see also 671). This abolition of difference, in which production, circulation and consumption approach the limit of simultaneity, recalls Nietzsche's nightmare of eternal return thought restrictively as a return *in* time rather than *of* time. This is a closed temporal economy, a regime of the identical in which time and difference are dissolved in simultaneity, a moment at which time collapses upon itself.[16]

Implied in both Nietzsche and Marx's thoughts on time and subjectivity is the Kantian distinction of relative and absolute positing of the events and appearances in time. In the words of Marx,

capital does not posit the time of 'merely *one turnover*, one circulation; but rather the positing of turnovers; positing of the whole
process [*Es ist nicht mehr nur Ein Umschlag, eine Zirkulation;
sondern Setzen von Umschlägen, Setzen des ganzen Verlaufs*]' (Marx
1974: 532; Marx 1977a: 639). The various turnovers of capital are
really eternal returns of the same, since for capital everything is
Gleichzeitig, at the same time; the nihilistic truth of capital is its
abolition of difference at the limit. Yet capital does not ask itself
the question of eternal return, does not assume responsibility for
its time, but nihilistically strives to abolish time and difference
within the limits of a disowned event of time.[17]

The absolute time of capital is a condition for the appearance of
objects and events – capital is their schema which realizes and
restricts them – but it is a disowned founding of time. Capital, says
Marx, posits itself as its own measure, and breaks down other
measures of time such as the seasons, day and night, the 'working
day'. Yet it does not behave responsibly toward this founding of
time, but instead tries to overcome itself in terms of the events and
appearances which it realizes and restricts. In the face of this crisis
Marx analyses the emergence of a different subjectivity which resists
capital's measures of time. One of the uncanny features of the
Grundrisse is Marx's dual diagnosis of the crisis of capital: he takes
the abolition of time under capital to mean either the destructive
end of human life or the possibility of a decision to re-constitute
the conditions of subjectivity.[18] In the terms of Nietzsche's question
of eternal return, capital may be the 'greatest weight' that crushes
the subject, or the chance for the subject to transform itself into
an *übermensch* capable of giving itself time.

As with Nietzsche, Marx puts the struggle for time at the centre
of his work. It is a struggle which may be confined to the time of
capital, as with the struggle over the length of the working day
described in *Capital*, or it may involve the question of capital's
positing of time as such. Both mark the struggles of a subjectivity
striving to constitute itself through taking responsibility for its constitution of time – initially in the vengeance of sabotage and resistance, but increasingly in terms of autonomous organizations such
as trade unions and political parties.[19] Yet Marx's inability to complete the sections of *Capital* concerned with legislation suggest that
he was well aware of the difficulties in constituting a political subjectivity free of a vengeful relation to the time of capital. The passage
from the proletariat as constituted by capital in opposition to the
bourgeoisie to the proletariat as constituting a new time, a new

relation to subjectivity, and a new relation to being became literally unthinkable once Marx abandoned the early humanist logic of a return to a human 'species being'. As with Nietzsche's *übermensch*, this 'new' or 'original' subjectivity cannot be described in terms of existing categories, nor may it be presented as a return to something that has been alienated or lost. The 'return' is intended to provoke a crisis and a decision of subjectivity: it does not prescribe or give a utopian image of a future subjectivity.

Both Nietzsche and Marx sought to provoke the emergence of a subjectivity responsible for its constitution of time, the one by posing the question of eternal return to the nihilistic time of modernity, the other by evoking a subjectivity that would challenge the repetitions of capital with another founding of time. Both thinkers reject a return to full possession or self-presence, but this leaves them with the difficulty of a return which is original, one which involves the return *of* time rather than return *in* time. Both see intimations of a new subjectivity inhabiting its own time, the one in the 'free spirit', the other in the nascent forms of proletarian political organization, but neither of them prescribed the forms which this return to time would take.

Both Marx and Nietzsche were unable to complete their work, but this should not be regarded as their failure. Their texts remain open and in question, partaking of the crisis of subjectivity which is their theme. The inability to end, or worse, the sense of never having begun that haunted both authors, evokes the experience of a subjectivity that is not responsible for its own time, and can find no meaning in the things and events that it encounters in time.

Their response to this condition was to recommend neither a return to the possession of time, self and meaning, nor an apocalyptic celebration of its loss, but instead to return constantly to the difficult question of what it means for a subject to assume responsibility for time. It is this return to the difficulty of modern subjectivity and its experience of time that characterizes the 'and' of Marx and Nietzsche.

NOTES

1 A particularly clear example is supplied by *The Times*, which drew an extravagant connection between the 1989 Revolutions and the foundation of the Nietzsche Society of Great Britain: 'Recent events may not have treated Karl Marx very kindly, but the formation of the new Nietzsche society reflects the upturn in the reputation and fashionability of another 19th century German philosopher, Friedrich Nietzsche'.

2 Robert Steigerwald, 'Die Wahrheitskonzeption im Werk von Friedrich Nietzsche' (Buhr 1990: 46).
3 Uttered to students on the Ludwigstrasse in Munich following a depressing evening's debate with Spengler, cited in Baumgarten (1964: 554–5). For a recent discussion of Nietzsche and Weber see 'The traces of Nietzsche in the works of Max Weber' (Hennis 1988).
4 See especially G. Bataille, 'Nietzsche and the Fascists' (Bataille 1985) and W. Benjamin, 'Theologico-political fragment' and 'The destructive character' (Benjamin 1979) and 'The work of art in an age of mechanical reproduction' (Benjamin 1977).
5 For programmatic statements see Levinas's 'Ideology and idealism' (Levinas 1989: 236–48) and Irigaray's 'The poverty of psychoanalysis' (Irigaray 1991a: 79–104). Their fundamental positions are worked through in Levinas (1961) and Irigaray (1991b).
6 The two-sided character of crisis is explicated in Heidegger's reading of Nietzsche's sentence 'The doctrine of eternal return; as fulfilment of it [i.e. nihilism] as *crisis*' (Heidegger 1991: 159): 'Seen from this vantage point, the thinking of the thought of eternal recurrence, as a questioning that perpetually calls for decision, is the fulfilment of nihilism. . . . The doctrine of eternal return is therefore the 'critical point', the watershed of an epoch become weightless and seaching for a new centre of gravity. It is the crisis proper.'
7 For a detailed exposition of this reading of Kantian subjectivity see my *Art of Judgement* (Caygill 1989: chs 4 and 5).
8 The temptation to read this failure superficially is too often indulged. One exception is Irigaray, whose analysis of the sufferings of the philosopher legislator is never superficial, but overemphasizes the 'greatest weight' of the eternal return, its interiority, over its exteriority: 'But now everything has moved inside the house the subject has made, or is. And whether the scene seems set inside, or outside, whether in his room or in his study, sometimes enjoying a fire fancied to be burning in baroque coils of smoke or else gazing out through the/his window at the still in(de)finite space of the universe, the action is always inside his house, his mind. And what or who can now put it outside? Only a messenger of revolution perhaps? Or else the fact that this hearth is made of glass and that those glasses – rather tarnished by age, their brilliance dimmed, having always in fact been unsilvered or blackened by smoke – mirror so deadly a boredom that, whatever one's firm intent, one might finish by wishing to die – to die of love, were that still possible – rather than have things just go on. Forever' (Irigaray 1985: 212).
9 The fish hook texts, for which there no fish, were dedicated to 'conjuring up a day of decision' (Nietzsche 1969: 22).
10 See my discussion in *Art of Judgement* (Caygill 1989: 220–2).
11 The concept of *Setzen* became one of the central concepts of post-Kantian idealism, and was especially prominent in Fichte's *Doctrine of Science*. Marx's usage in the *Grundrisse* follows Hegel's exposition of it in the *Science of Logic*. For a sustained critique of the implications of this concept for Hegel and subsequent social and political theory see Gillian Rose (1981).

12 See Kant (1979: 58–9).

13 In the *New Exposition* (1755) Kant describes 'the schema of divine intelligence, the origin of all existents' as God's 'constant activity' (Kant 1986: 110); in the *Critique of Pure Reason* schematism is described as 'an art concealed in the depths of the human soul, whose real modes of activity nature is hardly likely to allow us to discover, and have open to our gaze' (1929 A141/B181).

14 In this reading the eternal return is neither a cosmological thesis of the return of all events and appearances that have ever taken place in the universe, nor a version of the categorical imperative 'will so that your actions will return eternally'. Rather it is intended as a call to responsibility for the subject's positing of the time in which it acts and experiences, a time which appears to it as if it were distinct. In this way it may be contrasted with the cosmological and psychological readings of Löwith and Klossowski.

15 In a fragment from the *Nachlass* Nietzsche explicitly contrasts the socialism of the nihilistic 'last man' with the eternal return of the *übermensch*: it is available in 'Translations from Nietzsche's *Nachlass* 1881–1884', trans. K. Ansell-Pearson and R. J. Hollingdale (1991) *Journal of Nietzsche Studies* 1 (Spring): 6.

16 Marx offers some fascinating insights into how the moment of crisis may be deferred by the institutions of credit, but adds presciently that these institutions will themselves eventually exacerbate the crisis. On the first point: 'The necessary tendency of capital is therefore circulation without circulation time, and this tendency is the fundamental determinant of credit and of the capitalist's credit contrivances' (Marx 1977a: 659). For a philosophical reading of Marx sensitive to the importance of time and credit see Lyotard (1988: 171–9); for an apocalyptic interpretation of the acceleration of turnover, see Virilio (1986).

17 This emerges in a compulsion to accelerate circulation, a movement Marx consistently describes 'as a spiral, as an expanding circle' (Marx 1977a: 620) but one which can preserve itself only by constantly increasing its speed of circulation until it reaches a self-destructive point of collapse in crisis.

18 Marx develops a double reading of this crisis: on the one hand, 'The violent destruction of capital not by relations external to it, but rather as a condition of its self-preservation, is the most striking form in which advice is given to it to be gone and to give room to a higher state of social production' and on the other – in contrast to its internal violence of devaluation of commodities and the suspension of labour power – a 'violent overthrow' which would lead to the development of a subjectivity able to 'grasp its own history as *process*, and to recognise nature (equally present as practical power over nature) as its actual body' (Marx 1977a: 749–50).

19 The most sustained Marxist analysis of the organizational conditions for the formation of a new subjectivity was conducted by Lukács in the early 1920s. He gives Lenin's distinction of trade union and political 'consciousness' from *What is to be Done* a Nietzschean twist, seeing in the former a vengeful subjectivity, in the latter a new subjectivity

embarking upon a re-founding of time and space. See 'Towards a methodology of the problem of organisation' (Lukács 1971).

BIBLIOGRAPHY

Bataille, G. (1985) *Visions of Excess: Selected Writings 1927–1939*, ed. A. Stockl, Minneapolis, Minn.: University of Minnesota Press.

Baumgarten, E. (1964) *Max Weber – Werk und Person*, Tübingen: J. C. B. Mohr (Paul Siebeck).

Benjamin, W. (1977) *Illuminations*, trans. H. Zohn, London: Fontana.

—— (1979) *One Way Street and Other Writings*, trans. E. Jephcott and K. Shorter, London: Verso.

Buhr, M. (ed.) (1990) *Moderne-Nietzsche-Postmoderne*, Berlin: Akademie-Verlag.

Caygill, H. (1989) *Art of Judgement*, Oxford: Basil Blackwell.

Heidegger, M. (1991) *Nietzsche*, 4 vols, trans. D. F. Krell, San Francisco, Calif.: Harper & Row.

Hennis, W. (1988) *Max Weber: Essays in Reconstruction*, trans. K. Tribe, London: Allen & Unwin.

Irigaray, L. (1985) *Speculum of the Other Woman*, trans. G. C. Gill, Ithaca, NY: Cornell University Press.

—— (1991a) *The Irigaray Reader*, ed. M. Whitford, Oxford: Basil Blackwell.

—— (1991b) *Marine Lover of Friedrich Nietzsche*, trans. G. C. Gill, New York: Columbia University Press.

Kant, I. (1929) *Critique of Pure Reason*, trans. N. Kemp Smith, London: Macmillan.

—— (1952) *Critique of Judgement*, trans. J. C. Meredith, Oxford: Clarendon Press.

—— (1979) *The One Possible Proof for the Existence of God*, trans. G. Treach, New York: Abaris Books.

—— (1986) *Kant's Latin Writings*, ed. L. W. Beck, New York: Peter Lang.

Levinas, E. (1961) *Totality and Infinity – An Essay on Exteriority*, trans. A. Lingis, Pittsburgh, Penn: Duquesne University Press.

—— (1989) *The Levinas Reader*, ed. S. Hand, Oxford: Basil Blackwell.

Lukács, G. (1971) *History and Class Consciousness*, trans. R. Livingstone, London: Merlin.

—— (1980) *The Destruction of Reason*, trans. P. Palmer, London: Merlin.

Lyotard, J.-F. (1988) *The Differend – Phrases in Dispute*, trans. G. van den Abbeele, Manchester: Manchester University Press.

Marx, K. (1974) *Grundrisse der Kritik der Politische Okonomie*, Berlin: Dietz Verlag.

—— (1977a) *Grundrisse*, trans. M. Nicolaus, Harmondsworth: Penguin.

—— (1977b) *Capital – A Critique of Political Economy Volume One*, trans. S. Moore and E. Aveling, London: Lawrence & Wishart.

Nietzsche, F. (1969) *Ecce Homo*, trans. W. Kaufmann, New York: Vintage.

—— (1974) *The Gay Science*, trans. W. Kaufmann, New York: Vintage.

—— (1975) *Thus Spoke Zarathustra*, trans. R. J. Hollingdale, Harmond-sworth: Penguin.
Rose, G. (1981) *Hegel Contra Sociology*, London: Athlone Press.
Virilio, P. (1986) *Speed and Politics*, trans. M. Polizotti, New York: Semiotexte/Autonomedia.

11 Child of the English Genealogists
Nietzsche's affiliation with the critical historical mode of the Enlightenment

Paul Redding

INTRODUCTION: NIETZSCHE AND THE ENLIGHTENMENT

In an early essay, 'On the uses and disadvantages of history for life', Nietzsche described the sense of oppression with which a person may experience the past as something which 'pushes him down or bends him sideways, . . . encumbers his steps as a dark, invisible burden which he would like to disown' (Nietzsche 1983: 61). One way in which modern Europeans have attempted to free themselves from their past is by subjecting traditional beliefs, values, practices and institutions to critical interrogation and transformation. Indeed, where a thinker stands on this question has typically been taken as central in determining their position on the political spectrum.

It is difficult to think of a philosopher who has been assigned to a greater number of places on this spectrum than Nietzsche himself. Among recent interpretations, that of Jürgen Habermas for example, has construed Nietzsche as a definite *enemy* of the philosophical and political project of the Enlightenment. For Habermas, Enlightenment culture is such that it can find a place within itself for its own 'immanent' self-critique. Hegel's critique of modernity, for example, had this characteristic and thus worked within the Enlightenment's own 'dialectic'. Nietzsche's, however, did not. It was a totalizing critique and set itself 'outside the horizon of reason' (Habermas 1987: 96). In keeping with this, Nietzsche is seen as advocating the abandonment of the politically emancipatory thrust of modernity. For Habermas, Nietzsche does not advocate the liberation *of* the individual as much as a liberation from individuation itself in a type of aesthetically generated ecstatic self-abandonment: 'A "break up of the principle of individuation" becomes the escape route from modernity' (Habermas 1987: 94).

In contrast, Michel Foucault saw Nietzsche as belonging to a form of philosophical life characteristic of philosophical modernity or 'Enlightenment'. This philosophical orientation commenced with Kant and is marked more by the existence of a critical relation or 'ethos' adopted towards the philosopher's own present than any common doctrine (Foucault 1984: 32–50).[1] Here Nietzsche's close probing of the infrastructure of our epistemic and evaluative claims is seen as a development of Kant's transcendental reflection, despite Nietzsche's abandonment of the ahistorical and universalistic claims of the original Kantian critical project.

One reason for such diverging interpretations would seem to be due to the apparent radical moves in relation to Enlightenment critique that Nietzsche himself makes between different periods of his writings. In order to focus on Nietzsche's relation to the project of Enlightenment, this chapter explores the relation between Nietzsche's mature 'genealogical' method and the historical and critical reflection on society and culture more characteristic of progressive Enlightenment thought, a project of critical history he came to refer to as the 'English Genealogy'. Between his early and middle writings Nietzsche had swung sharply between seemingly antithetical relations to Enlightenment culture and in his later work interpreted himself as standing in a quite complex relation to it. Attempting to unravel some of the complexities of this relationship might help to better understand Nietzsche's project by locating him within this framework even if, once we have understood him, we might look back and understand the Enlightenment and its values in a new way.

NIETZSCHE'S *VOLTE-FACE*

Much of Nietzsche's early essay on history is given over to a polemic against the ascendancy of science, in particular, historical science, within German culture. Its basic motto is that while knowledge should serve life, scientific culture has put life in the service of knowledge. Nietzsche's overall resistance to scientific culture here is strongly suggestive of the German romantic reaction against eighteenth-century Enlightenment rationalism. In keeping with this there is more than a hint of a conservative historicist critique of rationalism. This critique is based on two related central ideas: an insight into the nihilistic and denormativizing effects of the scientific interrogation of tradition and the historicist understanding of a person or a culture as a product and inheritor of its own past.

Historical investigation undermines things of value because it always 'brings to light so much that is false, cruel, inhuman, absurd, violent that the mood of pious illusion in which alone anything that wants to live can live necessarily crumbles away' (Nietzsche 1983: 95). This idea that life needs such a 'mood of pious illusion' in order to exist reflects the somewhat 'life-philosophical' epistemology that Nietzsche sketches in this work. A living culture must draw around itself a horizon and so place limits on its experience, knowledge and memory, in order to produce the ambience in which it can thrive. While a healthy culture can indeed push back the borders of this horizon, assimilating the new and unfamiliar, this process has real limits. But as science tries to push these horizons to infinity, it disregards these limits and starts to work against rather than for the life of that culture.

For Nietzsche, the historical turn within Christianity exemplifies the devaluation attendant upon historical investigation: 'A religion . . . which is intended to be understood through and through as an object of science and learning, will when this process is at an end also be found to have been destroyed' (Nietzsche 1983: 95). This principle operates despite the intention on the part of those who wish to use the apparatus of historical inquiry and explanation for religious purposes: 'Recent theology especially seems to have entered into partnership with history out of pure innocence, and even now it almost refuses to see that, probably much against its will, it has thereby placed itself in the service of the Voltairean *écrasez*' (Nietzsche 1983: 96). Later, and in a different mood, he was to describe this type of historical explanation of religion as providing its 'definitive' refutation:

> In former times, one sought to prove that there is no God –
> today one indicates how the belief that there is a God could
> *arise* and how this belief acquired its weight and importance: a
> counter-proof that there is no God thereby becomes
> superfluous . . . in former times . . . atheists did not know how
> to make a clean sweep.
>
> (Nietzsche 1982: 54)

The Enlightenment rationalists might indeed have wanted to make a clean sweep of all that had been transmitted from the past, a total *écrasez* of the ubiqitous *infâme* historical inquiry had revealed. But for the historicist this can spell nothing but total annihilation because of the role played by tradition in constituting the very identity of the critic:

since we are the outcome of earlier generations, we are also the outcome of their aberrations, passions and errors, and indeed of their crimes; it is not possible wholly to free oneself from this chain. If we condemn these aberrations and regard ourselves as free of them, this does not alter the fact that we originate in them.

(Nietzsche 1983: 76)

And yet five years after the publication of the essay on history Nietzsche was to dedicate a work, *Human, All Too Human*, to the high priest of the enlightened, rationalist *'écrasez'*: Voltaire. In this work the change in attitude towards the Enlightenment and its critical historiography could not have been more striking. Here, and in those following works which together with it constitute Nietzsche's 'middle period', one finds both an espousal of science as well as recurrent denunciations of those in need of those 'pious illusions' earlier deemed as necessary for life. While the problem of the Enlightenment scientific outlook is still acknowledged, it is by now by no means that intractable problem of before. Rather than putting limits on Enlightenment cultural investigation and critique, what is needed is simply a correction: 'only after we have corrected in such an essential point the historical way of thinking that the Enlightenment brought with it, may we once again carry onward the banner of Enlightenment. . . . Out of reaction we have taken a step forward' (Nietzsche 1984: 32).

In *Human, All Too Human* Nietzsche's identification with the scientific investigation of culture is particularly revealed in his announcement of an 'enormous task of the great minds of the next century', the creation of scientific knowledge of the 'conditions of culture, a knowledge surpassing all previous knowledge, as a scientific standard for ecumenical goals' (Nietzsche 1984: 31) – a project which will essentially develop into Nietzsche's own later 'genealogy'.

Nietzsche's role as standard bearer of the Enlightenment was not to persist; nevertheless, he was not to revert back to his earlier Romantic position. Rather he was to struggle to define for himself a critical and yet affirmative relation to Enlightenment thought and, in particular, to its critical historiography, a relation exemplified in that between his own genealogical project and what he refers to as 'English Genealogy' – essentially the scientifically conceived rationalistic investigation into the historical origins of cultural phenomena that he had warned against in *On the Uses and Disadvantages of History for Life*.

THE RIDDLE OF THE ENGLISH GENEALOGISTS: SWAMP DWELLERS, TUNNELLERS AND MOLES

In *On the Genealogy of Morals* (published in 1887) Nietzsche resumed the project of the investigation of the historical grounds of culture started nine years earlier. In the preface he notes that the earlier impulse to publish his hypotheses on the origins of morality was the appearance of Paul Rée's *The Origin of the Moral Sensations*, an 'upside down and perverse species of genealogical hypothesis, the genuinely *English* type, that attracted me – with the power of attraction which everything contrary, everything antipodal possesses' (Nietzsche 1968a: 453).

Throughout this work Nietzsche has a number of things to say about this inverted, perverted 'English' version of his own project. It is never clear exactly which Englishmen Nietzsche has in mind here; although a number of actual English writers are mentioned in the text – Darwin, the social Darwinists Spencer and Huxley, the positivist historian Buckle – the only explicitly identified 'English' Genealogist is his friend Rée, a German Jew![2] However, it is not at all crucial to search for names in order to get a general idea of what the English style of genealogy comprises. Nietzsche commonly uses a type of national stereotyping of intellectual and cultural attitudes (Germans, for example, are typically romantic and anti-scientific, pessimistic and prone to fanaticism), and from what he says about the English Genealogists, as well as what he says elsewhere about the English in general, a clear enough picture of the English Genealogists emerges.

Simplifying, we might describe the English species of genealogy of morals as a form of historical investigation of morality which looks to its historical *origins* in an attempt to understand it and yet which is marked by an unquestioning *commitment* to 'morality' itself, that is to that form of morality that has come to characterize modern Europe.

Nietzsche describes these 'English psychologists' (or genealogists or historians) as always grubbing around in the murk of human existence, looking for the lowly and the base lying beneath or behind the sort of behaviour we normally esteem as virtuous:

> One always discovers them voluntarily or involuntarily at the same task, namely at dragging the *partie honteuse* of our inner world into the foreground and seeking the truly effective and directing agent, that which has been decisive in its evolution, in just that place where the intellectual pride of man would least

desire to find it (in the *vis inertiae* of habit, for example, or in forgetfulness, or in a blind and chance mechanistic hooking-together of ideas, or in something purely passive, automatic, reflexive, molecular, and thoroughly stupid).

(Nietzsche 1968a: 460)

And yet they are 'no easy riddle' because, despite this, *morality itself* has not become lowly and base for them. In Book 5 of *The Gay Science*, added to its second edition and published in the same year as *On the Genealogy of Morals*, Nietzsche tells us that the English Genealogists are usually themselves 'still quite unsuspectingly obedient to one particular morality and, without knowing it, [its] shield-bearers and followers' (Nietzsche 1974: 284).

The riddle of these thinkers lies in this apparent contradiction between the way they understand values from a theoretical point of view on the one hand and the way they adhere to them from a practical point of view on the other. While theoretically they have looked for the 'essence' of values in their historical origins, practically they seem to have located this essence at the assumed *telos* of their developmental history:

> Their usual mistaken premise is that they affirm some consensus of the nations, at least of tame nations, concerning certain principles of morals, and then they infer from this that these principles must be unconditionally binding also for you and me.
>
> (Nietzsche 1974: 284–5)

Beside his earlier warnings against scientific history, Nietzsche had suggested this relation between the genetic analysis of moral motivation and moral scepticism in *Human, All Too Human* by linking Rée's work to the sceptical moral observations of that master of 'soul searching', Duc François de la Rochefoucauld. He too had offended the intellectual pride of man by practising an art 'which seems to implant in the souls of men a predilection of belittling and doubt' – an art which 'the spectator who is guided not by the scientific spirit, but by the humane spirit, will eventually curse' (Nietzsche 1984: 41).[3]

The fact that the English Genealogists root around in the swamp of our base motivations looking for the internal workings of our moral lives has led to their disparagement as 'old, cold, and tedious frogs'. But, paradoxically, it would appear that for Nietzsche this is precisely the environment in which one would find *noble* thinkers.

In Book 5 of *Daybreak* he proclaims the following 'order of rank' of thinkers:

> There are, first of all, superficial thinkers; secondly, deep think-
> ers – those who go down into the depths of a thing; thirdly,
> thorough thinkers, who thoroughly explore the grounds of a
> thing – which is worth very much more than merely going down
> into its depths! – finally, those who stick their heads into the
> swamp: which ought not to be a sign either of depth or of
> thoroughness! They are the dear departed underground.
>
> (Nietzsche 1982: 188)

That such a thinker is a 'dear departed underground' presumably
puts them in the category of 'the thinkers and the workers in science
[who] have dug away quietly under their mole-hills' (Nietzsche
1982: 28). It also puts the swamp dweller in the same category as
Nietzsche himself. The first paragraph of the preface to *Daybreak*
tells us:

> In this book you will discover a 'subterranean man' at work, one
> who tunnels and mines and undermines. You will see him –
> presupposing you have eyes capable of seeing this work in the
> depths – going forward slowly, cautiously, gently inexorable,
> without betraying very much of the distress which any protracted
> deprivation of light and air must entail.
>
> (Nietzsche 1982: 1)

This paragraph ends with a description of himself as a 'solitary
mole'.[4]

In works like *Daybreak* and the earlier *Human, All Too Human*
Nietzsche had recurrently reworked the seams of close and detailed
empirical moral psychology in the tradition of La Rochefoucauld's
Maxims, even to the extent of following his aphoristic form, constantly looking for the origins of our 'higher' actions in the lowly
motives characteristic of our 'all too human' selves. Translated on
an individual level we might think of this project of the descent
into the stuff of the self as psychology, on a collective level, as
history. But as for Nietzsche 'we are the outcome of earlier generations', the projects of psychology and history cannot be kept simply
apart: the unravelling of the make-up of the self – one's beliefs,
feelings, desires, evaluations and so on – will necessarily lead
beyond one's own individual limits to that mass of inherited *contingent* ways of interpreting, dealing with and feeling about the world.
This science of 'psychology' or 'history' or 'genealogy' is fundamen-

tally a descent *into* this mass in order to trace the seams of these ways of acting, thinking, feeling that have been laid down, organized and reorganized over generations of human social existence.[5]

There is another aspect of this science of the self which makes the 'mole' analogy particularly relevant for Nietzsche. In the works of the middle period Nietzsche's admiration of science seems to be particularly bound up with its limiting itself to empirical evidence in the development of its account of the world: 'Even great spirits have only their five-fingers' breadth of *experience* – just beyond it their thinking ceases and their endless empty space and stupidity begins' (Nietzsche 1982: 226). Such modest empiricism which avoids flights into abstraction is yet another English trait according to Nietzsche's national typology and he links its emergence with a complex change in the *meaning* that knowledge has for its bearers once the world becomes interpreted in secular ways.

Thus it is pointed out in *Daybreak* that 'in the past the salvation of "the eternal soul" depended on knowledge acquired during a brief lifetime, men had to *come to a decision* overnight – "knowledge" possessed a frightful importance' (Nietzsche 1982: 204). This thought is resumed a few pages later:

> The march of science is now no longer crossed by the accidental fact that men live for about seventy years, as was for all too long the case. Formerly, a man wanted to reach the far end of knowledge during this period of time and the methods of acquiring knowledge were evaluated in accordance with this universal longing . . . . the knowability of things was . . . accommodated to a human time-span.
>
> (Nietzsche 1982: 219)

What the collapse of the religious interpretation of the significance of knowledge has now allowed is that now the thinker can pursue those 'small single questions and experiments' which the older culture had 'counted contemptible' (Nietzsche 1982: 219), those 'little, humble truths . . . discovered by a strict method, rather than the gladdening and dazzling errors that originate in metaphysical and artistic ages and men' (Nietzsche 1984: 15).

NIETZSCHE'S CRITICAL RELATION TO THE ENGLISH GENEALOGY

In his preface to *On the Genealogy of Morals* Nietzsche reflects back upon the development of his own project in the middle period and on its relation to the English Genealogy. In *Human, All Too Human* he had 'advanced for the first time those genealogical hypotheses to which this treatise is devoted – ineptly . . . still constrained, still lacking my own language for my own things and with much backsliding and vacillation' (Nietzsche 1968a: 454). We might take the English Genealogy as that project which although approximating his own, represented a constant danger for it: it was that into which Nietzsche's project was in danger of 'sliding back'. But, I believe, Nietzsche's own genealogy is commonly taken in a way which makes these two projects roughly equivalent. Understanding the English Genealogy and what, from a Nietzschean perspective, constitutes its shortcomings, helps us to clarify Nietzsche's own project.

Enlightenment history or 'English Genealogy', by the close scrutiny of the motivations behind moral actions, attempted to reveal what their 'essence' or meaning consisted in and as such was continuous with that deflating tradition of the critique of morality found, for example, in Plato's Thrasymachus in antiquity, or in Hobbes, Mandeville or, of course, La Rochefoucauld in early modernity. The basic premiss of the critique here is that what appears as moral or selfless is, upon close empirical examination, egoistic and hence amoral. All morality is therefore dissimulation.

This is the basic thought behind that form of moral scepticism Nietzsche attributes to La Rochefoucauld. In his form of scepticism it is denied that 'the moral motives which men claim have inspired their actions really have done so – it is thus the assertion that morality consists of words and is among the coarser or more subtle deceptions (especially self-deceptions) which men practise' (Nietzsche 1982: 60).

It is obvious how the presupposed epistemology of La Rochefoucauld's approach is out of step with what is now understood as Nietzsche's own 'perspectival' epistemological position. *Qua* perspectivist Nietzsche is understood as articulating a type of post-Kantian view of knowledge somewhat like that put forward by current 'antirealists' inspired by the later Wittgenstein.[6] Knowledge must be understood as always formed from within particular conditioning circumstances such that its object cannot be conceived as the 'thing in itself', independent of its relations to the knowing subject. This latter conception seems to presuppose the idea of the knower as freed from any conditioning factors, as grasping the object from the 'God's-eye view'; and so to avoid what is at base a theological conception of the nature of knowing subjectivity, the perspectivist or antirealist renounces the idea of *the* definitive view, *the* complete and comprehensive account. Just as all perception is perspectival, so is all *con*ception.

La Rochefoucauld in his stark contrast between the deception of the would-be moral agent's claims concerning their actions and the underlying reality of their actual motives seems clearly to be a realist. In *Daybreak*, Nietzsche differentiates his denial of morality from that of La Rochefoucauld in a way which seems to move away from the latter's implicit realism. For example, by wanting to give a place for the non-deceiving and non-self-deceiving moral agent, Nietzsche no longer makes the actor's intentions the touchstone of the action's meaning (Nietzsche 1982: 60).[7] And yet, despite this difference, Nietzsche seems to agree on the fact that morality involves, at some stage of its genesis, an *illusory appearance* which is cast over and which idealizes an underlying reality.[8]

In *Human, All Too Human* the following analogy is suggested for this process of idealization:

> One principle means to ease life is to idealize all its processes; but from painting one should be well aware what identification means. The painter requires that the viewer not look too hard or too close; he forces him back to a certain distance to view from there. . . . So anyone who wants to idealize his life must not desire to see it too closely, and must keep his sight back a certain distance.
>
> (Nietzsche 1984: 169)

The model here suggests that while viewing from a certain distance and in a certain way the viewer will see the painting in terms of what is represented in it, but that on moving closer or viewing with a different attitude, importantly, in the attitude *of* a painter interested in the technique of its creation, the representation might dissolve into the play of brush-strokes from which it is constructed. The idealizations making up moral phenomena therefore must be like artistic representations, only in *their* case one normally mistakenly believes that one is looking at the real thing. This suggests what the psychological investigation of moral phenomena might look like: the psychologist will presumably view the actions of the person not in terms of what they represent but, with an eye like that of the painter, according to what has gone into making them up. In *Daybreak* we find this idea made explicit:

> How much an actor sees and divines when he watches another

act! He knows when a muscle employed in some gesture fails in its duty; he segregates those little, artificial things which have been practised one by one cold-bloodedly before the mirror and then refuse to integrate themselves into the whole . . . – If only we possessed the eye of this actor . . . for the domain of human souls!

(Nietzsche 1982: 211)

Idealization and illusion result from not looking too closely, from looking at the thing (the painting, the acting of the actor and of the moral agent) in terms of what it attempts to represent rather than what makes it up. But just as the close inspection of the painting will reveal it to be actually paint, and as close inspection of the actor's performance will reveal *it* to be a construction made out of artificial, practised gestures, so too will close psychological examination of moral behaviour reveal it to be something quite other than moral behaviour.[9]

The idea that when something is viewed from a distance it will appear differently than when viewed from close range might seem to suggest a perspectivist epistemology; on reflection, however, this is not the case. Rather, the idea of the moral psychologist as the close observer of moral action who can perceive in ostensively moral behaviour that which goes into it in a way analogous to the painter's perception of a painting or the actor's perception of another actor's performance, seems to beg a realist view.

As representational the painting and the performance are, in some sense, illusions: to understand them in terms of that which they are representing involves participation in this illusion, the 'suspension of disbelief'. There is no equivalent sense, however, that what is seen when one moves in for the 'close view' is an illusion: the paint is real in a sense in which the apples in the still life are not, and the actor's practised gestures are real in a way in which the character's actions are not. The most obvious way to think of moral behaviour on these analogies is that of a cloak of illusionary interpretation draped over a different underlying amoral reality. But if this is so then, as we have seen, it is not consistent with perspectivism.[10]

However, from the standpoint of Nietzsche's mature genealogical method to see all this predominantly in terms of the epistemological 'errors' of the English Genealogy is surely mistaken. In his mature genealogy, Nietzsche is not interested in the origins of cultural phenomena like morality *per se*; rather his focus is the practical transformation of culture – knowledge here is in the service of a re-valuation of existing values. Thus, from his later stance, Nietzsche reinterprets 'what was at stake' in his own earlier project. The project there was not, after all, that which it had taken itself to be – the activity of a pure scientific spirit. Rather his concern there was really 'something much more important than hypothesis mongering, whether my own or other peoples' on the origin of morality. . . . What was at stake was the value of morality' (Nietzsche 1968a: 455).[11]

In fact what seems to reappear in the *Genealogy* with its shift in emphasis from the conditions of morality to its value is a type of 'life-philosophical' framework something like that of the early history essay. What is now criticizable about moral motives such as pity has nothing to do with the 'errors' of the judgments they are based upon; rather, it has to do with the fact that such motives manifest an unhealthy, degenerating form of life, in the terminology of the late Nietzsche, a reactive will to power. They manifest 'the will turning against life, the tender and sorrowful signs of the ultimate illness' (Nietzsche 1968a: 455).

We can now see how the English Genealogy is an inverted/perverted version of Nietzsche's own. *It* was primarily interested in the scientific question of origins of certain values and as a result of this activity was from there led into the 'problem' of those values. In contrast, Nietzsche's primary concern *is* with the value of certain values and he tries to articulate this value in terms of a story of their development, a story which gives expression to the baseness which he sees as characterizing the values themselves. We might say that, paradoxically, Nietzsche is critical of 'morality' not from an epistemic point of view but rather, from something more approximating a moral one.

Thus in the 1886 preface to *Daybreak*, Nietzsche points out that in this work 'faith in morality is withdrawn – but why? *Out of morality!*' (Nietzsche 1982: 4). That is, the sort of moral scepticism found in this book results from the paradoxical fact that here a moral 'thou shalt' still continues to speak: 'that we too still obey a stern law set over us – and this is the last moral law which can make itself audible even to us'. It is from moral reasons that, in the spirit of science, he in that text abandons belief in all those things which are demonstrated as 'unworthy of belief'. The moral system had interpreted moral actions as self-less and it has been precisely the adoption of a scientific approach to moral motivation which has shown such an interpretation *as* unworthy of belief. To be true to the type of morality constitutive of the scientific spirit, one must then surely abandon such beliefs. This refusal of the moral system on moral grounds is an example of the 'self-sublimation of morality' (Nietzsche 1982: 5).[12]

NIETZSCHE'S REINTERPRETATIVE REDEMPTION OF THE ENLIGHTENMENT

In his early writings, Nietzsche had wavered radically in his attitude towards the Enlightenment and its rigorously historical approach to the beliefs and values making up the fabric of society and the self. In the history essay he perceived the nihilistic threat accompanying this type of generalization of historical accounting while in *Human, All Too Human* he embraced just this project. And yet that the threat of a disastrous collapse of societal values remained at the centre of his concerns is apparent in his later attempt to put himself at a critical distance from the 'English' version of the genealogical project. The unintended effect of the English Genealogy, or of the Enlightenment cultural project more generally, would be the nihilistic collapse of values. In contrast, Nietzsche's intentional project is to bring about, not the simple collapse, but the radical transformation or 're-valuation' of values. The two projects are similar in appearance and easily confused: both involve the profound problematization of all that is held to be valuable by revealing its lowly, contingent history. But the outcomes of these projects are as poles apart as are death and (re)birth.

It is clear that Nietzsche is keenly aware of the proximity and yet radical opposition between these two projects and accordingly he perceives his relation to the English Genealogy (and hence the Enlightenment in general) as deeply complex. There can be no question of being simply 'for' or 'against' the Enlightenment because Nietzsche stands to it as both critic and offspring. As instanciated in Rée's work, the English Genealogy forms part of the conditions of the genesis of Nietzsche's own work: it therefore must occupy a place within the 'genealogy' of Nietzsche's own genealogy. That is Nietzsche's work itself must be counted among the outcomes of this form of cultural reflection, and as such must inherit its 'aberrations, passions, errors and crimes'. Nietzsche's mere condemnation of those aberrations will not be enough to free himself from their effects: such a move 'would not alter the fact that [he] originate[d] in them' (Nietzsche 1983: 76). But then how can these errors be corrected?

We get some hint of how Nietzsche conceives of success here from one of the central conceptions of his mature thought, the doctrine of the 'Eternal Recurrence'. Whatever the full meaning of this doctrine, one thing is clear: rather than expressing any denial of the past, or any attempt to negate or break with it, it is meant to express its most profound acknowledgement and affirmation. To embrace the thought of the eternal recurrence is to say 'yes' to all that is past – to will it.

A simple argumentative critique of English Genealogy would involve an implicit denial of filiation, a denial that one shares in the aberrations, passions and errors of the parent method. From the perspective of the Eternal Recurrence however, filiation must be affirmed and redeemed. In *Twilight of the Idols*, when discussing the assessment of whether an individual represents ascending or descending lines of life Nietzsche reminds the reader that the individual is no atomistic 'link in the chain', but rather 'the whole single line of humanity up to himself' (Nietzsche 1968b: 534). One cannot break away from one's inheritance, intellectual or otherwise. One can only redeem it, somehow retroactively restore it to the status of an ascending rather than descending movement and one can only do this through the success of one's own acts. In *Thus Spoke Zarathustra*, Zarathustra, the teacher of the eternal recurrence, declares 'In my children I want to make up for being the child of my fathers' (Nietzsche 1968b: 233) and 'In your children you shall make up for being the child of your fathers: thus shall you redeem all that is past' (Nietzsche 1968b: 318).[13]

That Nietzsche's attitude towards English Genealogy is not so much 'critique' as 'redemption' is manifest in his odd and apparently contradictory statements about it. The English Genealogy with its presupposed English morality must, from Nietzsche's point of view, be a manifestation of a degenerating form of life, a sign of a reactive will to power. So it would then seem that it would have to be condemned as such. And there is much within Nietzsche's text which testifies to this sort of evaluation: 'And at this point we return to the genealogists of morals. To say it again – or haven't I said it yet? – they are worthless' (Nietzsche 1968a: 498). And yet while some, finding these genealogists in the 'swamp', will condemn them as 'frogs':

> I rebel at that idea; more, I do not believe it; and if one may
> be allowed to hope where one does not know, then I hope from
> my heart that they may be the reverse of this – that these

investigators and microscopists of the soul may be fundamentally brave, proud, and magnanimous animals, who know how to keep their hearts as well as their sufferings in bounds and have trained themselves to sacrifice all desirability to truth, *every* truth, even plain, harsh, ugly, repellent, unchristian, immoral truth. – For such truths do exist.

(Nietzsche 1968a: 461)

In *Daybreak* Nietzsche had registered that a renunciation of the past was simply the habitual outlook of the modern 'herd', in a sense, equivalent to an earlier reflex adoption of tradition. There is certainly nothing heroic in such a disavowal:

Why does one nowadays endure the truth about even the most recent past? Because there is always a generation which feels itself to be in opposition to this past and in criticizing it enjoys the first fruits of the feeling of power. Formerly the new generation wanted, on the contrary, to *found* itself on the older, and it began to *feel* secure in itself when it did not merely adopt the view of its fathers but where possible took them more *strictly*. Criticism of the fathers was then considered wicked: nowadays our younger idealists *begin* with it.

(Nietzsche 1982: 106–7)

In Book 1 of *On the Genealogy of Morals* we find a further analysis of this reflexive critique of the past in terms of the sort of will to power underlying the 'reactive', habitual 'nay' sayer. Any straightforward negation of some existing practice and its claims is like the slave's negation of the master's 'evil' life and perspective. Because the slave's negative evaluations are simply reversals of an existing set of affirmations – those of the master, they are unable to create anything new in its place and simply repeat the old structure in a hidden form. And so it would seem that adopting a critical, adversarial stance towards one's past, the stance typical of the Enlightenment for example, could provide only an illusory sense of actually being liberated from it.[14]

We can appreciate the paradoxical character of the problem that Nietzsche is faced with here. Conservative historicists typically urge the inheritance of a culture that has stood the test of time: where else is one to find one's values? Enlightenment rationalists want to disinherit themselves from all that has merely persisted: why should one regard as normative that which is merely factual? Nietzsche has the problem of wanting to inherit the progressivists' capacity to disinherit themselves. Thus Nietzschean genealogy's relationships with a practice like English moral history must be paradoxical and contradictory. From the point of view of Nietzsche's genealogy, the English practice must be revealed as expressing a declining or reactive will to power. Genealogy *must* occupy an antipodal position. However, in its attempt to establish itself as reflecting an ascending, active will to power, Genealogy must interpret itself as belonging to an ascending line, showing its filiation with English Genealogy which is redeemed and brought back from the antipodes in the process.

In *On the Genealogy of Morals* Nietzsche had to reinterpret his own earlier project of *Human, All Too Human*, but because he is 'the whole single line of humanity up to himself' this reinterpretation must be able to be extended back further to the conditions from which his own project emerged and applied to the English Genealogy itself. It too can presumably be interpreted as investigating the worthiness of certain values but 'ineptly . . . still constrained, still lacking *its* own language for *its* own things and with much backsliding and vacillation' (Nietzsche 1968a: 454). And so, while interpreted one way, as a purely reactive turning against the existing Christian culture, Enlightenment thought will be diagnosed as expressing that same degenerating form of life, that reactive will to power characterizing the slave revolt which gave birth to Christianity, interpreted in another, it will be seen as a culture that takes its values so seriously that, concerned that it may be esteeming that which is unworthy, it brings into question the value of its own values.

Interpreted in the former way, the Enlightenment faces an immanent collapse of its values because it had never really taken them seriously. Reactive cultures really have no values of their own, they just have disguised and inverted versions of those values that belong to the culture they reacted against.[15] Interpreted in the latter, the crisis of values brought on by the Enlightenment is the trauma associated with the emergence of new values in the process of replacing the old, just as its new knowledge is replacing older forms. From Nietzsche's genealogical outlook we must evaluate the Enlightenment in terms of the nature of the will to power that it expresses, but there seems to be two equivalent and opposed readings of this. The English Genealogists seem to be both worthless frogs and noble souls.

From Nietzsche's perspectivist epistemology one should not, of course, be surprised at this situation. The two perspectives on to the English Genealogists coincide with characteristics of the type of life that informs them. (There is no English Genealogy 'in itself' with some particular determinate quality.) To interpret them as reactive frogs is exactly what we would expect *of* a reactive frog – that is of one who wishes to simply negate them in the way that they are understood as having negated their past. To interpret them as noble souls is exactly what we would expect of a noble soul, of one who generously affirms their great achievements and ignores their shortcomings. As Nietzsche puts it in *Beyond Good and Evil*: 'Anyone who does not *want* to see what is lofty in a man looks that much more keenly for what is low in him and mere foreground – and thus betrays himself' (Nietzsche 1968a: 413). Of course, Nietzsche's interpretation *must* be the noble one, in both senses. Like Luther, he can do no other.

The idea of redeeming the past by reinterpreting it can sound as if a mad magical power is being attributed to words and ideas. But just as Kant is misunderstood as 'Idealist' in the traditional 'metaphysical' sense of the word, so too is Nietzsche misunderstood if interpreted in this way. For the perspectivist, a thing *is* the sum of its effects (Nehamas 1985: ch. 3). But, as existing in time, chains of effects radiate into an open future. Among some of the effects of Enlightenment culture is Nietzsche himself, and so the effects that Nietzsche propagates into his future will themselves be among the more distant effects of that culture. If the Enlightenment looks like it is leading to disaster and, on the basis of a certain 'redeeming' interpretation the course of its subsequent history is effected for the better, this has not been on account of magical powers of that interpretation. It will simply indicate that it was all along healthy enough to transform itself in this way.

Nietzsche is nothing if not extreme and his vision of the nature of modernity is terrifying in the extreme. One must throw one's lot in with modernity, with its Enlightenment and its nihilism which are the two sides of the same coin. And with this one might thereby be participating in the bringing about of a terrible catastrophe: the total collapse of the fabric of its values. There is something more terrifying in such a vision, it seems to me, than in the traditional pessimist's vision of modernity as hurtling towards disaster. There, one can at least dig in one's heels. Even if this has absolutely no effect there is the consolation that one did not participate in nor affirm this catastrophe. But for Nietzsche, the only hope for avoiding the catastrophe, for turning its reactive collapse into an active re-valuation, is to will it.

ACKNOWLEDGEMENT

I would like to thank Paul Patton for many helpful comments on an earlier version of this chapter.

NOTES

1 For example, in 'What is Enlightenment?' (Foucault 1984: 32–50).
2 Alexander Nehamas has suggested (at a conference in Sydney in 1989) that Nietzsche was referring ironically to *his own work* in *Human, All Too Human* with the term 'English Genealogists'. This is, I think, half right. As I shall argue, Nietzsche's relation to the 'English Genealogists' includes both the identification of belonging to the same line *and* a critical distance.
3 For Nietzsche the moral maxims of La Rochefoucauld exemplify how a science can owe its origin to a form of culture which is quite other than scientific. 'It is true that countless individual remarks about things human and all too human were first detected and stated in those social circles which would make every sort of sacrifice not for scientific knowledge, but for a witty coquetry'. However, the origin of this science in non-science should not deter the scientist from taking it seriously as 'already it is becoming clear that the most serious results grow up from the ground of psychological observation' (Nietzsche 1984: 41–2).
4 Similar imagery is found again at the start of *Thus Spoke Zarathustra* in Zarathustra's Prologue. Here the intention to undertake a similar journey is announced as Zarathustra tells the sun: 'I must descend to the depths, as you do in the evening. . . . Like you I must *go under* – go down, as is said by man, to whom I want to descend' (Nietzsche 1968b: 121).
5 The image of the genealogist as tunneller or miner also reveals something more about its own genealogy. If the English Genealogy had a French forebear in the witty coquetry of La Rochefoucauld, it also appears to have had some German ancestry as well for in *Daybreak* Nietzsche tells us how *Luther* was a *miner*'s son who 'for lack of other depths and "mine shafts", descended into himself and bored out terrible dark galleries' (Nietzsche 1982: 51). It was in these galleries that he discovered that he was not fit for a saintly contemplative life and consequently denied the reality of such a life. That is, Luther's mining *undermined* the existing religious culture, transforming Catholic Christianity into something different – Protestantism. Indeed the image of mining and a boring out of the ground of one's culture suggests that this must also be an undermining of what sits on top of this ground. What does sit on the top of this ground is precisely all of those 'higher' edifices of human life – its forms of knowledge, rationality, virtue and so on – all that which belongs to that realm of life to which the activity of scientific burrowing itself belongs!
6 See Nehamas' account (Nehamas 1985: ch. 2).
7 Nietzsche can give up the appearance/reality dichotomy at the level of the motivations of the individual agent precisely because he has abandoned the implicit individualism of the French moralist's framework.

Psychology and history are no longer distinct. Thus in *Daybreak* he is interested in the way the feelings and the interpretations accompanying actions are differentially transmitted over generations. A feeling which was associated with a particular judgement about the world can be inherited but reinterpreted. For example, although Nietzsche sees certain moral actions as arising from cruel motives, this need not necessarily be so on an individual level (Nietzsche 1982: 60).

8 The moral motives he unmasks are seen as themselves formed on the basis of an underlying erroneous judgment about the world: 'it is *errors* which, as the basis of all moral judgment, impel men to their moral actions' (Nietzsche 1982: 60).

Given the transitional position of these middle works, this 'realism' is perhaps not so surprising. In *The Birth of Tragedy*, Nietzsche had depicted the human condition as only tolerable given the casting of a fabric of illusion over life's chaotic and ugly truth. It is now not uncommonly argued that much of this early work is contradicted by rather than consistent with his later perspectivism. The schema in which illusions are seen as cast over a chaotic flux to protect the knower from the world's ugly truth presupposes that there is such a definitive ugly truth. For the antirealist or perspectivist, however, what characterizes the realist position has really nothing to do with the character of that which is taken to be the ultimate underlying nature or 'truth' of things. Rather it has all to do with the idea that there is such an underlying ultimate nature of things to which our accounts may or may not correspond. Thus the traditional idealist is a 'realist' by these standards because the idealist is basically claiming that the underlying ultimate nature of things is 'mind-like'. And if this is realism, then so must the position expressed in *The Birth of Tragedy* for it seems to be saying something along the lines that the underlying ultimate nature of things is 'chaos'.

9 This is clearly expressed in the first of La Rochefoucauld's maxims: 'What we take for virtues are often merely a collection of different acts and personal interests pieced together by chance or our own ingenuity' (La Rochefoucauld 1959: 37).

10 Perhaps the conventionality of Nietzsche's epistemological assumptions in *Human, All Too Human* come out in his Laplacian considerations of omniscience and determinism in § 106:

> if one were omniscient, one would be able to calculate each individual action in advance, each step in the progress of knowledge, each error, each act of malice. . . . if the wheel of the world were to stand still for a moment and an omniscient, calculating mind were there to take advantage of this interruption, he would be able to tell into the furthest future of each being and describe every rut that wheel will roll upon.
>
> (Nietzsche 1984: 74)

Omniscience is thus intelligible and thinkable, in a way that it should not be for a perspectivist. (The perspectivist is not simply sceptical about our ability to achieve the god's eye view, she wants to abandon it as an intelligible conception of the nature of knowledge.) And again in this paragraph we get the dichotomous contrast between reality and illusion. The acting man is not omniscient but 'caught in his illusion of volition'. Such a 'delusion about himself, his assumption that free will exists, is also part of the calculable mechanism' (Nietzsche 1984: 74).

11 What Nietzsche has to say about the English Genealogists in Book 5 of *The Gay Science* (added in 1887) must surely apply to his own position in the middle period:

> The mistake made by the more refined among them is that they uncover and criticize the perhaps foolish opinions of a people about their morality, or of humanity about all human morality – opinions about its origin, religious sanction, the superstition of free will, and things of that sort – and then suppose that they have criticized morality itself.
>
> (Nietzsche 1974: 285)

12 This suggests that the problem of the English lies in their having been insufficiently moral to abandon morality. Indeed, in *Twilight of the Idols* Nietzsche does seem to paint the morality of English secular moralists such as George Eliot as the expression of a type of moral failure: 'They are rid of the Christian God and now believe all the more firmly that they must cling to Christian morality. That is an English consistency'. That is the English have not yet achieved that degree of morality which forces its abandonment for moral reasons. But it would seem to be part of the logic of 'morality' that it will eventually turn upon itself: 'For the English, morality is not *yet* a problem' (Nietzsche 1968b: 515–16, emphasis added).

13 This formula has a telling history in Nietzsche's writings. In the early history essay he speaks of the necessity to 'give oneself, as it were *a posteriori*, a past in which one would like to originate in opposition to that in which one did originate' (Nietzsche 1983: 76). But such an attempt to deny one's past by the project of implanting through 'stern discipline' a 'new habit, a new instinct, a second nature' sounds very much like that futile revenge *against* the past – the simple *denial* of it – that Nietzsche was later to diagnose as the clearest expresssion of the reactive will to power.

This theme of a type of autochthonous self-creation was continued in *Human, All Too Human*: 'If someone does not have a good father, he should acquire one' (Nietzsche 1984: 194). This is not out of keeping with the generally scientific and Enlightenment spirit of that work. Science seems to progress by constantly bringing into question and attempting to transcend existing opinion, that is by criticizing and breaking with its past. There is, however, a significant shift in the idea in a passage in Zarathustra where the idea of replacing one's father/past is transformed into the idea of redeeming it or making up for it.

14 On the logic of the reactive inversion of values see Redding (1990).

15 The prototype is the slave's inversion of the master's valued 'good' life into the negatively valued 'evil' one. What the slave values as good is then just the negation of evil. Whereas the master has an applicable concept of a valued, worthy form of life, the slave has only a negative concept of a worthy life – a life which abstains from determinate *evils*.

See *On the Genealogy of Morals*, Essay 1 Paragraphs 10 and 11 (Nietzsche 1968a).

BIBLIOGRAPHY

Foucault, M. (1984) 'What is Enlightenment?', trans. C. Porter, in P. Rabinow (ed.) *The Foucault Reader*, New York: Pantheon.

Habermas, J. (1987) *The Philosophical Discourse of Modernity: Twelve Lectures*, trans. F. Lawrence, Cambridge, Mass.: MIT Press.

La Rochefoucauld, F. de (1959) *Maxims*, trans. L. Tancock, Harmondsworth: Penguin.

Nehamas, A. (1985) *Nietzsche: Life as Literature*, Cambridge, Mass.: Harvard University Press.

Nietzsche, F. (1968a) *Basic Writings of Nietzsche*, trans. W. Kaufmann, New York: Random House.

—— (1968b) *The Portable Nietzsche*, trans. W. Kaufmann, New York: Viking.

—— (1974) *The Gay Science, with a Prelude of Rhymes and an Appendix of Songs*, trans. W. Kaufmann, New York: Random House.

—— (1982) *Daybreak: Thoughts on the Prejudices of Morality*, trans. R. J. Hollingdale, Cambridge: Cambridge University Press.

—— (1983) *On the Uses and Disadvantages of History for Life*, in *Untimely Meditations*, trans. R. J. Hollingdale, Cambridge: Cambridge University Press.

—— (1984) *Human, All Too Human: A Book for Free Spirits*, trans. M. Faber with S. Lehmann, Lincoln, Nebr.: University of Nebraska Press.

Redding, P. (1990) 'Nietzschean perspectivism and the logic of practical reason', *Philosophical Forum* 22(1): 72–88.

12 The postmodernist politicization of Nietzsche

Ted Sadler

> There is perhaps nothing about the so-called cultured, the believers in 'modern ideas', that arouses so much disgust as their lack of shame, the self-satisfied insolence of eye and hand with which they touch, lick and fumble with everything; and it is possible that more relative nobility of taste and reverential tact is to be discovered today among the people, among the lower orders and especially among peasants, than among the newspaper-reading demi-monde of the spirit, the cultured.
>
> (*Beyond Good and Evil*, no. 263)

INTRODUCTION

According to tradition (Diogenes Laertius, IX, 3) the Pre-Socratic philosopher Heraclitus of Ephesus was once found playing 'dice' with children in the Temple of Artemis. Upon being called to account, he is said to have replied that children's games were better than 'playing politics' with the rest of the Ephesian citizenry. Heraclitus was well known in antiquity for his solitude and disdain for the 'herd', attitudes fully shared by his nineteenth-century disciple Friedrich Nietzsche. For Nietzsche as for Heraclitus, politics is one of the most overestimated things in the world, mainly because it caters for the instincts of the common, unphilosophical natures who are always in the majority. Politics stands in opposition to the radically individualizing character of philosophy as expressed in Heraclitus' statement (Diels-Kranz: Fragment 246) 'I searched out myself'. Of course, the philosopher does not want anything so nonsensical as the abolition of politics: what he wants is to stand aside from this sphere. As Nietzsche puts it in Aphorism 438 of *Human, All Too Human*:

> If the purpose of all politics really is to make life endurable for as many as possible, then these as-many-as-possible are entitled to determine what they understand by an endurable life . . . there is little to be objected to, always presupposing that this

narrow-mindedness does not go so far as to demand that *every-thing* should become politics in this sense, that everyone should live and work according to such a standard. For a few must first of all be allowed, now more than ever, to refrain from politics and step a little aside: they too are prompted to this by pleasure in self-determination; and there may also be a degree of pride attached to staying silent when too many, or even just many, are speaking. Then these few must be forgiven if they fail to take the happiness of the many, whether by the many one understands nations or social classes, so very seriously and are now and then guilty of an ironic posture; for their seriousness lies elsewhere, their happiness is something quite different.

(Nietzsche 1986: 161)

The kind of 'self-determination' sought in the political realm is rejected by Nietzsche as *philosophically* irrelevant because it is oriented to herd-autonomy, the autonomy of the herd-self. To this he opposes, in typical Heraclitean spirit, the autonomy of the solitary philosopher whose 'seriousness is located elsewhere'. Nietzsche maintains this attitude with complete consistency to the end of his career. In *Daybreak*, he speaks of the 'indecency' of politics (Nietzsche 1982: 120), while in *The Gay Science* he brands it as 'prostitution of the spirit' (Nietzsche 1974: 103). Again, in the 'Foreword' to *The Antichrist*, one of Nietzsche's last works, he counts, as one of the prime conditions for understanding him, that 'one must be accustomed to living on mountains – to seeing the wretched ephemeral chatter of politics and national egoism *beneath* one' (Nietzsche 1968: 114).

Such statements of Nietzsche do not by themselves preclude a political interpretation of his philosophy. It is possible to argue that Nietzsche really rejects only a certain kind of politics, or that there are 'political implications' of his thought which Nietzsche himself does not pursue. During the Third Reich in Germany, Nietzsche was used to support an authoritarian ideology of strength, a strategy which, at least superficially, by no means lacked textual support. From the opposite political pole, Georg Lukács, writing after the Second World War, attacked Nietzsche as an 'imperialist' and 'bourgeois' thinker (Lukács 1980: 309–99). For all their differences, Lukács and the Nazis concur in drawing authoritarian political consequences out of such prominent Nietzschean motifs as the 'will-to-power' and the '*übermensch*'. More recently, however, an altogether different image of Nietzsche's 'politics' has emerged.

Originating among French intellectuals who since the 1960s have been seeking an anti-authoritarian response to conventional politics (including Marxism), the 'postmodernist' tendency of Nietzsche-interpretation finds quasi-anarchistic and pluralist values in his writings. Key figures from this school include Jacques Derrida, Michel Foucault and Gilles Deleuze, but its influence now extends far beyond France, having attained what is probably a dominant position in English-speaking countries. Typical of this tendency is Mark Warren's recent book *Nietzsche and Political Thought*, which sets out to show the relevance of Nietzsche for 'postmodern politics'. According to Warren, when appropriately purged of subjective 'political views', Nietzsche's philosophy implies 'a pluralistic society in which egalitarianism underwrites individuality' (Warren 1988: 157).

The aim of the following discussion is to refute the postmodernist attempt to install political values at the centre of Nietzsche's thought. Obviously, the whole range of postmodernist literature on Nietzsche cannot be reviewed here. By reference to just a few representative texts, I shall be content to indicate the essentials of the postmodernist position, particularly its emphasis on Nietzsche's 'perspectivism' and the pluralism which purportedly follows from this. I shall then indicate the counter-principle to the postmodernists' favoured motif of perspectivism: the principle of rank-order, which, it will be shown, presupposes the 'supra-perspectival' truth which the postmodernists deny. The position thus arrived at will then be further illustrated by a brief discussion of Nietzsche's views on freedom, obedience and the self. The outcome of the study will be a verification of the attitude expressed by Nietzsche in the quotations given at the outset, i.e. that philosophy and politics are worlds apart. It has always been tempting to find one's direction in philosophy by 'getting political', thinking that one is thereby becoming 'relevant'. For Nietzsche, this attitude is not at all the solution, but a large part of the problem.[1]

PERSPECTIVISM AND PLURALISM

No other aspect of Nietzsche's thought has received so much attention from his postmodernist commentators than has his so-called 'perspectivism'. The reason for this is easily understood. What the postmodernists want above all is a critique of authority, including a critique of dogmatic and politico-ideologically interested discourses. The collapse of any metaphysically guaranteed source of authority, which is what Nietzsche's perspectivism supposedly implies, is seen as holding out the promise of liberation from repressive 'closures' in discourse and practice. Thus Bergoffen describes Nietzsche's thought as 'inaugurating a higher history of humanity by constructing a philosophy of perspectivism where the concept of the interpretative centre replaces the convention of absolute centredness' (Bergoffen 1990: 68). Babich says that 'Nietzsche's multivalently heterogeneous perspectivalism anticipates the inherent ambivalence of the postmodern challenge to hierarchized discourse, specifically to the question of the authorial or traditional authority and the presumption of a final word' (Babich 1990: 259). Nehamas refers to Nietzsche's perspectivism as 'a refusal to grade people and views along a single scale' (Nehamas 1985: 68). For the postmodernists in general, liberation from 'singular' definitions of truth and 'the presumption of a final word' is not just an intellectual, but a politico-ideological accomplishment. Thus Warren can say that, although Nietzsche himself did not appreciate the 'progress-ive' implications of his fundamental perspectivist standpoint, and remained captive to a reactionary political ideology, this aspect can be deleted from his genuine philosophy, which will then stand forth as an 'implicit critique of domination' (Warren 1988: 11).

In its essentials, perspectivism is not a difficult idea to grasp. It is even, nowadays in western democratic societies and increasingly in the former territories of communism, very much a popular idea. The idea that everyone is entitled to their own 'point of view' and that there should be 'equal rights to all perspectives' is basic to modern political culture. A 'pluralist society' is seen as a natural development of ever-deepening democratization: in 'more advanced' countries the values of pluralism are expressed in law. Naturally there are many (the 'vanguard' of pluralism) who think that this process has not gone far enough and is not proceeding fast enough. But the general direction away from dogmatism towards an open political culture in incontrovertible and irreversible. The micro-structure of social life is just as important in this as are the over-arching political institutions. Definitions of social roles and value choices are more fluid than ever before: experimentation in life-style and morality have almost become the norm, while toler-ation of social deviance is at an all-time high. All this, considered as a world-historical development, is perspectivism in action, and certainly cannot be attributed to the writings of Friedrich Nietzsche. The importance of Nietzsche, as the postmodernists see him, lies in his philosophical legitimation of this development, and in his demand for its further radicalization. In the words of Warren, 'Nietzsche considers the dissolution of the Christian-moral [read 'dogmatic'] world-view through recognition of the claims of experience to be the genuinely progressive aspect of European nihilism, opening the possibility of a practice-oriented culture' (Warren 1988: 42).

Pluralism at the level of culture and politics depends on pluralism at the level of truth. The deeper meaning of 'perspectivism' is that there is no such thing as One Truth but rather a multiplicity of mutually inconsistent 'truths' dependent on the particular conditions constituting different kinds of discourse. Metaphysics had assumed the possibility of a final, certain, and authoritative theory of ultimate reality. It is this assumption, so the postmodernists insist, that Nietzsche rejects by affirming the unavoidably anthropomorphic character of all knowledge. Kant had already recognized the subject-dependency of knowledge in the *Critique of Pure Reason*, but in Nietzsche's opinion Kant went astray in postulating universal structures of subjectivity, and thus re-installed a form of dogmatism at the level of phenomena. Nietzsche's perspectivism, Warren and other postmodernists say, is a 'radicalization' of the Kantian critique of knowledge (Warren 1988: 122f). If there are unlimited possibilities for human subjectivity there are also unlimited perspectives on the world. These perspectives cannot be judged in terms of a fanciful adequacy relation to ultimate reality, for this would presuppose a non-anthropomorphic form of knowledge. All that can be said is that the various perspectives are useful or not useful in varying degrees for the purposes they serve, purposes which are themselves contextual and historically relative. Some perspectives, of course, have become hardened and fixed in the course of time, giving the impression that they are true in some absolute sense. However, what Nietzsche calls the 'genealogical' method will always reveal ('unmask') the hidden forces which underlie fictitious claims to universality. So, the postmodernists conclude, perspectivism is an invitation to experimentalism and pluralism in theory and practice.

The postmodernists see the 'political implications' of perspectivism as grounded in the connection between perspectives and 'interests': to adopt a particular perspective is the same as becoming involved in a certain constellation of interests. As Warren puts it, 'these involve interests in the material, social and cultural worlds as means to and conditions of power organized as subjectivity. Knowledge cannot be extricated from the interest the self has in increasing its "feeling of power" ' (Warren 1988: 90). If there are to be 'equal rights to all perspectives' there must also be 'equal rights to all interest-constellations', which is exactly what political pluralism is all about. Just as there is no metaphysically guaranteed theory of the world, so there is also no metaphysical or supra-perspectival source of authority for any particular structure of power or form of social existence. The struggle between perspectives is at bottom a struggle between opposed political forces, between the different interests of different social actors. This means, however, that the expression 'philosophy of perspectivism' is a misnomer. If no overarching standpoint is possible, whether in theory or in life, the concept of philosophy becomes obsolete. The philosopher gives way to the 'intellectual' or 'writer' who promotes a particular perspective and particular interests, conscious all the while that it is not an imaginary Truth he is serving but just himself and his own herd. In this sense perspectivism seems, at first sight paradoxically, to provide the intellectual with the good conscience for his own partisanship, for his own 'higher' dogmatism. Or is it the case, as suggested by Spivak, that 'if one is always bound by one's perspective, one can at least deliberately reverse perspectives as often as possible?' (Spivak 1974: 19). The purpose of wandering in and out of various perspectives is not entirely clear. It cannot be to get a better view of the 'whole', since every perspective itself defines the whole. And who is to say that any nebulous 'enrichment' of life thus attained is of greater value than a dogged uni-perspectival existence? In any case, whether one frequently 'reverses' perspectives or not, the main point of postmodernist perspectivism is that there is no absolute standard to which one is beholden. There is self-interest and there is group-interest, but the idea of a 'universal' interest goes the same way as the 'presumption of a final word'.

It is natural to ask how the perspectivists are aware of the existence of different perspectives. Does this knowledge originate from within a perspective, or is it supra-perspectival? If the former, then how does perspectivism differ from any other piece of advocacy? If the latter, is not perspectivism self-refuting? These are ticklish questions, which postmodernist perspectivism in general prefers to avoid. In fact, it avoids them in precisely the same way that our 'pluralist' society prefers to leave the meaning of 'pluralism' in decent obscurity, in order to handle practical difficulties 'as the occasion arises'. However, the problem of the One and the many, even when not explicitly posed, makes itself felt, and cannot be wished away by antipathy to a One which is taken as synonymous with terrible dogmatism. The difference between Nietzsche and the postmodernists emerges at precisely this point. *Nietzsche does not doubt the necessity of the One*, that is of truth in a philosophical sense. Contrary to the postmodernists, perspectivism is for Nietzsche a second-order and not a first-order principle: it is subordinate to a concept of philosophical truth which implies, not pluralism, but an *order of rank*.

RANK-ORDER AND SUPRA-PERSPECTIVAL TRUTH

Nietzsche writes in the 1886 'Preface' to *Human, All Too Human* that 'it is *the problem of the order of rank* of which we may say it is *our* problem, we free spirits' (Nietzsche 1986: 10). In *On the Genealogy of Morals* (1887) it is likewise stated that 'all the sciences have from now on to prepare the way for the future task of the philosophers: this task understood as the *problem of value*, the determination of the *order of rank among values*' (Nietzsche 1967a: 56). The task of clearly marking off what is 'aristocratic' from what is 'plebian' in the realm of the spirit first emerges in Nietzsche's writing when in *Human, All Too Human* (1878) he includes a section entitled 'Tokens of Higher and Lower Culture'. It remains an abiding concern thereafter. Of course, Nietzsche understands that talk of 'rank-order' is unwelcome in a democratic and egalitarian age. He realizes that there will be an almost irresistible tendency among 'men of modern ideas' to suppress this fundamental theme from his philosophy and thus to distort the real meaning of 'free-spirit':

> In all the countries of Europe and likewise in America there exists at present something that misuses this name, a very narrow, enclosed, chained up species of spirits who desire practically the opposite of that which informs our aims and instincts. . . . They belong, in short and regrettably, among the *levellers*, these falsely named 'free-spirits' – eloquent and tirelessly scribbling slaves of the democratic taste and its 'modern ideas', men without solitude one and all, without their own solitude, good clumsy fellows who, while they cannot be denied courage and moral respectability, are unfree and ludicrously superficial, above all in their fundamental inclination to see in the forms of existing society the cause of practically *all* human failure and misery: which is to stand the truth happily on its head . . . their two most oft-recited doctrines and ditties are 'equality of rights' and 'sympathy for all that suffers'.
>
> (Nietzsche 1973: 53–4)

Contemporary postmodernist commentators cannot be unaware that rank-order is a prominent motif in Nietzsche's writings. However, because it is somewhat of an embarrassment for the all-important message of pluralism, they adopt one or other of two strategies (or a combination thereof) to deal with it. Either, like Warren, they consign it to Nietzsche's allegedly reactionary 'political views' and deny any organic connection with his basic philosophical standpoint. Or, like Nehamas, they try to subordinate the principle of rank-order to perspectivism, whereupon it becomes legitimate to speak of 'noble' and 'plebian' perspectives. Nietzsche obviously does not speak in a very pluralist spirit when comparing his own philosophy with other outlooks, but this, according to Nehamas, only reflects his right to a forthright and creative defence of his own perspective (Nehamas 1985: 59). While Warren sees rank-order as a foreign body in Nietzsche's thought, Nehamas reduces it in glib fashion to an ordering of subjective preferences. Both strategies are artificial and untrue to Nietzsche, because, as will now be shown, rank-order is a fundamental principle of Nietzsche's thought without which his perspectivism cannot be comprehended at all.

In the statement from *On the Genealogy of Morals* quoted at the beginning of this section Nietzsche speaks of the 'order of rank among values'. Two questions immediately arise. First, what are 'values'? Second, in respect of what are values to be ranked? For Nietzsche, values do not exist just as abstract ideals but as concrete practices, specific modes of living and acting. Throughout his works, Nietzsche ranks in the sense that he 'evaluates' values, for example the values of religion, politics, money-making, family life, honour-seeking, sensual pleasure, scholarship, science, and so on. One does not need to read very far in Nietzsche to realize that all these latter are accorded a low, or at least relatively low, rank. As to what is ranked highly, Nietzsche praises such virtues of the 'aristocracy' as strength, courage, trust, gratitude, lack of sentimentality, capacity for solitude, etc. What *measure* of rank, then, yields a rank-*order* of this kind? To understand Nietzsche's answer one must keep firmly in mind his basic opposition between the 'herd' and the 'individual': 'First question concerning order of rank: how solitary or how herd-bound (*herdenhaft*) one is' (Nietzsche 1967a: 472). All values which are rooted in the herd-nature of man are ranked low, while values are ranked high in the degree to which they express real independence from the herd. Now it may appear at first sight that this approach to ranking affirms a kind of pluralism and individualism not unwelcome to Nietzsche's postmodernist interpreters.

Nothing, however, could be more wrong. For the kinds of individu-alism and independence so extolled by Nietzsche are attainable only through a relation to something universal. This universal value, this ultimate principle of rank-order, is truth.[2]

If this latter claim is correct, there must be a meaning to 'truth' in Nietzsche which is different from 'perspectival truth'. It has long been recognized that Nietzsche does indeed (and very regularly) use the word 'truth' (*Wahrheit*) and its cognates in ways which suggest a non-perspectival meaning. It has long been acknowledged that Nietzsche's philosophy as a whole strongly suggests the need for a conception of *absolute* non-perspectival truth.[3] But certain prejudices of the western metaphysical tradition have impeded the understanding of what Nietzsche thereby intends. The most import-ant of these prejudices is the assumption that 'truth' can refer only to something doctrinal-theoretical, or at least to something linguis-tic. Once this assumption is made, one immediately runs up against Nietzsche's insistence on the perspectival character of all theory and all language, so that his apparently non-perspectival use of 'truth' has to be explained away as ironic. However, Nietzsche breaks with the said assumption. He breaks from the idea that truth is something which is stated, that truth consists in acts of signifi-cation. Although truth in the supra-perspectival sense is indeed inseparable from thought, Nietzsche denies that thought is insepar-able from language.

Since the thesis that I have just stated runs contrary to accepted (particularly postmodernist) opinion on Nietzsche, let me quote a pertinent passage from *The Gay Science*:

> This is the essence of phenomenalism and perspectivism as *I* understand them: owing to the nature of *animal consciousness*, the world of which we become conscious is only a surface-and-sign-world, a world that is made commoner and meaner; what-ever becomes conscious *becomes* by the same token shallow, thin, relatively stupid, general, sign, herd-signal; all becoming conscious involves a great and thorough corruption, falsification, reduction to superficialities, and generalization.
>
> (Nietzsche 1974: 299–300)

The difficulty of reconciling this passage with a postmodernist understanding of perspectivism is at once apparent, because how could one thereby explain the pejorative tones in which the 'surface-and-sign-world' (the world of perspectives) is described? It seems that perspective-creating consciousness produces some kind of 'corruption' and 'falsification', but what exactly is corrupted and falsified here? A clue is given in a passage a little earlier in the same aphorism:

> My idea is, as you see, that consciousness does not really belong to man's individual existence but rather to his social or herd nature; that, as follows from this, it has developed subtlety only insofar as this is required by social or herd-utility. . . . Our thoughts themselves are continually governed by the character of consciousness – by the genius of the species that commands it – and translated back into the perspective of the herd. Fundamentally, all our actions are altogether incomparable, personal, unique, and infinitely individual; there is no doubt of that. But as soon as we translate them into consciousness *they no longer seem to be.*

The herd nature of man: every reader of Nietzsche knows that he detests nothing more than this. If thoughts are translated by consciousness into herd-perspectives, then a great deal, on Nietzsche's reckoning, must be 'lost in translation'.

Is it possible to 'think' without having one's 'thoughts' translated by 'consciousness' into 'herd perspectives'? Can the animal nature of man be overcome to this extent? For Nietzsche, the answer in both cases is yes. To begin with, some familiarity with what is prior to consciousness must be presupposed if Nietzsche is to speak of a process of 'falsification' and 'corruption'. And more generally, Nietzsche's whole concern to break from the 'herd' and affirm 'individual existence' would otherwise be senseless. To be sure, Nietzsche realizes that every time he opens his mouth to speak or puts pen to paper, he becomes enmeshed in some perspective or other. On the other hand, he is also quite emphatic that the significance of his own utterances is not given along with the publicly available words or signs in which he expresses himself. This is the reason that Nietzsche knows he will not be understood by those (the vast majority) who do not share his basic experiences. The average human being, and therefore Nietzsche's average reader, is inattentive and unalert to what is prior to consciousness, is fundamentally dominated by his herd nature and the perspectives which go along with it, by words, concepts and conventions. And as long as one tries to understand Nietzsche merely through his words or his 'perspective' one is doomed to failure:

> We no longer have a sufficiently high estimate of ourselves when

we communicate. Our true experiences are not garrulous. They could not communicate themselves if they wanted to: they lack words. We have already grown beyond whatever we have words for. In all talking there lies a grain of contempt. Speech, it seems, was devised only for the average, medium, communicable. The speaker has already *vulgarized* himself by speaking.

(Nietzsche 1968: 82–3)[4]

Those whose existence is not bound to words and perspectives are called by Nietzsche 'philosophers' and 'free-spirits'. This is not to deny that philosophers too employ speech and find herd-perspectives indispensable for life. But it is to affirm that philosophers are able in some degree to transcend their animal natures, to look beyond the sphere of utility and herd-interests to experience the ground, or perhaps the abyss, of Being itself. Not, to repeat, in order to 'know' anything or to construct a 'theory' about anything, but simply to be who they are, humans and not just animals;

We must be raised up – and who are they, who raise us up? They are those true *human beings, those who are no longer animal, the philosophers, artists, and saints.*

(Nietzsche 1983: 159)

'Rank-order', therefore, does not refer at all to a hierarchy of perspectives but to the degree in which perspectival existence and perspectival thinking is overcome. The reason that perspectivism is none the less important for Nietzsche is that he wishes to deny the equation of 'truth' in the philosophical sense with any kind of doctrine or theory of the world: just on account of the perspectival (relative) character of all doctrines and theories, philosophical (absolute) truth cannot be theoretical-doctrinal. Despite the 'radical' posturing of Nietzsche's postmodernist commentators, they do not understand the genuine radicalism of his thought. Obsessed by the bogey of a 'singular truth', they wish to free up theory, doctrine, knowledge, 'writing', etc. from the normative constraint of a 'final perspective'. They take perspectivism to be Nietzsche's conclusion whereas in reality it is only a premise. They fail to see that Nietzsche is not just a critic of some narrow concept of rationality which would subject discourse to an authoritarian 'closure', but goes beyond this to reject the assimilation of discourse and truth. Nietzsche of course does not oppose a pluralism of discourses and perspectives: he regards this as desirable in so far as the relative character of these latter are thereby exposed. But pluralism is not an end in itself. On the contrary, those who remain within the sphere of pluralism and perspectivism are for Nietzsche precisely the non-philosophers, precisely those who live outside the truth, and who pursue, just like animals do, their perspectivally conditioned 'interests'.

Writers like Nehamas, who see Nietzsche's perspectivism as primary, very naturally conclude that Nietzsche refuses 'to grade people and views along a single scale'. But the opposite is true. Nietzsche takes the utterly uncompromising attitude that there is only one standard which counts: the degree to which a given individual is a philosopher. Everything else is secondary, relevant only to the second-order realm of perspectival living:

> The great majority of people does not consider it contemptible to believe this or that and to live accordingly, without first having given themselves an account of the final and most certain reasons pro and con, and without even troubling themselves about such reasons afterward: the most gifted men and the noblest women still belong to this 'great majority'. But what is goodheartedness, refinement, or genius to me, when the person who has these virtues tolerates slack feelings in his faith and judgements and when he does not account the desire for certainty as his inmost craving and deepest distress – as that which separates the higher human beings from the lower.
>
> (Nietzsche 1974: 76)

It does not follow, just because philosophy is an *absolute* value, that everything else is to be denigrated and declared as worthless. Other values have their place, but they are *relative*. For Nietzsche, what is perverse and 'contemptible' among human beings is the adherence to relative values as if they were absolute, something which is ultimately identical with the denial of absolute value as such and the celebration of complete relativity. There is no essential difference, in Nietzsche's view, between the person whose 'absolute' value is something like 'family life' or 'the nation', and the person who, like the 'last men' portrayed in *Thus Spoke Zarathustra*, confesses himself a nihilist. The point is that relative values retain their integrity only to the extent that they exist in a proper relation to an absolute value. Herein is the key to Nietzsche's attitude to politics. What Nietzsche objects to in politics is its absolutization as a value, to the lack of appreciation of the relativity of all political values *vis-à-vis* philosophy and truth. This tendency to an absolutization of politics, he considers, is particularly strong in democratic –socialistic movements, because driven by a moral faith in the absolute value of 'equal rights'. But although historical circumstances dictate that Nietzsche gives a particularly sustained critique of democratic egalitarianism, it is clear that any other political value (e.g. the nation-state) is equally objectionable to him if it is absolutized.

FREEDOM, OBEDIENCE AND THE SELF

The advocates of politics and pluralism have the word 'freedom' constantly on their lips. Nietzsche would have little argument with the proposition that to be genuinely human is the same thing as to be 'free'. However, what Nietzsche understands by 'freedom', and what the pluralists, perspectivists and postmodernists understand by this, are very different things. The essence of this difference is that, for Nietzsche, freedom is attainable exclusively through philosophy, that is exclusively through overcoming all perspectival orientations to the world. Like Kant, Nietzsche believes that freedom is possible only through *obedience* to a universal value, but for him it is the intellectual conscience which binds one to the supreme value of truth.[5] The vulgar conception of freedom, which is the one held by Nietzsche's postmodernist critics, is not positive but negative: it is freedom *from* authority and *from* obedience of every kind. Once again, Mark Warren provides an exemplary illustration of the postmodernist approach. According to Warren,

> Nietzsche's philosophy is in many ways an extended answer to a pivotal question: How can humans be subjects of actions, historically effective and free individuals, in a world in which subjectivity is unsupported by transcendent phenomena or metaphysical essences?
>
> (Warren 1988: 7)

Warren believes that Nietzsche's thought is directed to a 'crisis of human agency' and tells 'a political story about the relation between oppression, culture, and the constitution of subjects' (Warren 1988: 17–18). The question of *for what* human beings should be 'historically effective' and 'free' admits of no general answer on this account, because it depends in every case on perspectivally constituted interests. Gilles Deleuze takes a similar view in a chapter entitled 'Nomad thought', where he suggests that Nietzsche 'announces the advent of a new kind of politics', the politics of the 'nomad' who wants to 'evade the codes of settled people', particularly the codes of 'the despotic and bureaucratic organization of the party or state apparatus' (Deleuze 1977: 149). Especially through the influence of Foucault and Derrida, Nietzsche's 'genealogical' method is seen by postmodernists as a tool of 'deconstruction', able to unmask hidden 'strategies of power' which 'repress subjectivity'.

These views have very little to do with Nietzsche's thought. In reality, Nietzsche has no interest whatsoever in the quasi-anarchistic autonomy intended by the postmodernists because this latter is based on a negative conception of freedom characteristic of 'slave morality':

> the longing for freedom, the instinct for the happiness and the refinements of the feeling of freedom, belong just as necessarily to slave morality and morals as the art of reverence and devotion and the enthusiasm for them are the regular symptom of an aristocractic mode of thinking and valuating.
>
> (Nietzsche 1973: 178)

The vulgar idea of freedom is negative because it is reactive. It proceeds from experienced repression, exclusion, or wounded dignity, and turns on the sources of these, wanting 'liberation'. It is accompanied by the mistrust also characteristic of the slave, the mistrust which always suspects ulterior motives where 'values' are spoken of or commands issued.[6] If it wants anything in particular (which it often does not) this will be something thoroughly perspectival, variable, changing from one moment to the next. The postmodernists, with their anarchistic proclivities, pride themselves on an ideal of freedom which goes beyond the rather staid ambitions of law-abiding democrats and socialists. For Nietzsche, however, anarchism is just a more hysterical manifestation of the *ressentiment* mentality which governs all those who believe in a political idea of (negative) freedom:

> they (the anarchists) are in fact at one with them all in their total and instinctive hostility towards every form of society other than that of the *autonomous* herd (to the point of repudiating even the concepts 'master' and 'servant'); at one in their tenacious opposition to every special claim, every special right and privilege, at one in their mistrust of punitive justice.
>
> (Nietzsche 1973: 107)

On Nietzsche's thinking, liberation into herd-autonomy does not amount to any kind of liberation worth mentioning. This does not make him a political 'reactionary', as Warren concludes. It indicates only that his 'seriousness lies elsewhere'. The democrats and anarchists can be left to themselves in the political arena, and need be opposed only when their pseudo-ideals threaten to usurp the authority of philosophy. It is not the case, as the postmodernists believe, that Nietzsche is especially relevant to the marginalized or disfranchised elements of society, whose interests are legitimized by the slogan 'equal rights to all perspectives'. His thought is relevant to everyone, provided only that it is responded to in a philosophical manner. A response of this kind, however, is impossible on the basis of a reactive conception of freedom.

Nietzsche's own philosophical conception of freedom is non-reactive and positive. It is non-reactive because philosophers simply do not feel repressed, excluded, or wounded in their dignity, even in the most unfortunate circumstances. This is what Nietzsche expresses with his idea of the 'eternal return': the philosopher 'affirms life' to the ultimate degree, to the point of wanting the repetition of his own life, right down to the most minute details, an infinite number of times (Nietzsche 1974: 273–4). The philosopher can do this only to the extent that he has detached himself from all perspectives and their attendant interests, for after all, who cannot imagine their interests accommodated more happily, if only to the slightest degree, by a different course of events to the one actually lived through? Furthermore, the freedom of the philosopher is positive because, in his orientation to supra-perspectival and disinterested truth, he is responding to a positive command:

> But there is no doubt that a 'thou shalt' still speaks to us too, that we too still obey a stern law set over us – and this is the last moral law which can make itself audible even to us, which even we know how to *live*, in this if in anything we too are *men of conscience* . . . it is only as men of *this* conscience that we still feel ourselves related to the German integrity and piety of millenia, even if as its most questionable and final descendants, we immoralists, we godless men of today, indeed in a certain sense as its heirs, as the executors of its innermost will.
>
> (Nietzsche 1982: 4)

Nothing is more antithetical to postmodernist sentiment than the idea of obedience, because it is automatically associated with 'repression' and runs counter to the negative, reactive conception of freedom. However, everything depends on what is obeyed. There is a species of obedience based on fear and weakness, where one obeys because of one's real or imagined perspectival interest. Although political radicals ostensibly revolt against obedience of this kind, they frequently fall into it themselves, through the conformism euphemistically called 'solidarity': the trendiness and jargon-ridden nature of postmodernist writing is a case in point. But philosophical obedience, as Nietzsche knew, is based on, and at the same time engenders, strength and self-command. This is what Nietzsche means by self-overcoming: command over one's herd-self, obedience to the absolute command to become who one authentically is.[7]

The postmodernists believe that for Nietzsche there is no such thing as the 'self', more precisely that he sees the 'self' as constituted through variable perspectives and not as a stable entity. What they thereby fail to notice is the difference between the 'herd-self', which is indeed perspectivally constituted, and the supra-perspectival 'philosophical-self', which is always oriented to one thing alone, to truth. Nietzsche is well known for his 'fundamental hostility and irony for selflessness': for him, the self should want above all itself (Nietzsche 1973: 177). This 'itself', however, is not a herd-self, but something universal, something which is attainable only *in* truth and *as* truth. Thus Nietzsche can comment, in the 'Preface' to the seond edition of *Human, All Too Human*:

> Shall my experience – the history of an illness and recovery was what eventuated – have been my personal experience alone? And only *my* 'human, all too human'? Today, I would like to believe the reverse; again and again I feel sure my travel books were not written solely for myself, as sometimes seems to be the case.
>
> (Nietzsche 1986: 213)

In other words, Nietzsche's books were not written for his own 'perspectival-self', for the perspectivally constituted 'empirical' self. They were written for the self which exists deep down, underneath all social determinations, for the self which is attainable only to the 'subterranean man' who tunnels and burrows beneath all perspectival reality (Nietzsche 1982: 1). The postmodernists are blind to this latter self, which explains why they are also blind to the very prominent motif of solitude in Nietzsche. As observed above, Nietzsche sees the 'falsely-named free spirits' of his own time as 'men without solitude one and all, without their own solitude'. Our contemporary postmodernists are no different. In their desire to politicize everything in sight, in their garrulousness and exaltation of 'writing', in their preference for idolatry and hero-worship over reverence, they betray a fear of solitude and lack of self-confidence which is the hallmark of what Nietzsche calls *ressentiment*. Again in Nietzsche's words, they 'are unfree and ludicrously superficial, above all in their fundamental inclination to see in the forms of existing society the cause of practically *all* human failure and misery, which is to stand the truth happily on its head'. The real cause of human failure, as Nietzsche recognized, is not 'society', but the underlying perversity of human nature, the perversity through which demands of the true self are sacrificed for the ephemeral interests of the herd-self. In truth, the overcoming of human failure begins with the examination of oneself, something which cannot be undertaken within the raucous arena of 'postmodernist ideas'.

NOTES

1 A good start in the critique of the 'postmodernist Nietzsche' has been made by Robert Solomon in his article 'Nietzsche, postmodernism, and resentment: a genealogical hypothesis', in Koelb (1990: 267–93). The present chapter fully concurs with Solomon's views that 'perspectivism was never itself the key to Nietzsche's outlook or method' (270) and that postmodernism has its origins in resentment, as 'an expression of disappointment, a retreat, a purely negative thesis' (282). However, Solomon's study fails to situate Nietzsche's perspectivism with respect to his notion of supra-perspectival truth, and thus does not provide a real alternative to the postmodernist position. Correspondingly, he fails to give sufficient attention to Nietzsche's crucial opposition between the 'individual' and the 'herd'.

2 To be noted is the statement from *Ecce Homo*, that 'Zarathustra is more truthful (*wahrhaftiger*) than any other thinker. His doctrine, and his alone, posits truthfulness (*Wahrhaftigkeit*) as the highest virtue' (Nietzsche 1967a: 328).

3 See e.g. the section 'Nietzsche's passionate longing for unlimited Truth' in Jaspers (1965). Other major studies which do not fall into 'perspectivist' errors are those of Heidegger (1979–87), Löwith (1987) and Fink (1960).

4 Note the statement from *On the Genealogy of Morals*: 'Whoever thinks in *words* thinks as an orator and not as a thinker' (Nietzsche 1967a: 110).

5 The fact that Nietzsche, after his early period, maintains an almost exclusively hostile attitude to Kant, should not obscure their common commitment to absolute value and indeed to 'duty' (see the quotation from *Daybreak* in the text below). An illuminating recent discussion of the relation between the two philosophers is Simon (1989).

6 Postmodernism, particularly in connection with its campaigns of deconstruction, fosters an attitude of mistrust and suspicion towards all established values and theories. Nietzsche himself says that the philosopher

'has today a duty to be mistrustful, to squint wickedly up out of every abyss of suspicion' (Nietzsche 1973: 47), but on the other hand, he also regards mistrust as a basic feature of 'slave morality' (e.g. Nietzsche 1973: 176). The difference lies in the *motives* of mistrustfulness: the slave or 'common' type is anxious lest his practical herd-interest is adversely effected; the philosopher's 'interest', however, is 'incomprehensible and impractical' (Nietzsche 1974: 78). Postmodernism's neglect of this distinction is conspicuous.

7 Aphorism 270 of *The Gay Science* consists of the single question and answer '*What does your conscience say?* – "You shall become who you are" ' (Nietzsche 1974: 219).

BIBLIOGRAPHY

Allison, D. B. (ed.) (1977) *The New Nietzsche*, Cambridge, Mass.: MIT Press.

Babich, B. E. (1990) 'Post-Nietzschean postmodernism', in C. Koelb (ed.) *Nietzsche as Postmodernist*, Albany, NY: State University of New York Press.

Bergoffen, D. B. (1990) 'Perspectivism without nihilism', in C. Koelb (ed.) *Nietzsche as Postmodernist*, Albany, NY: State University of New York Press.

Deleuze, G. (1977) 'Nomad thought', in D. B. Allison (ed.) *The New Nietzsche*, Cambridge, Mass.: MIT Press.

Fink, E. (1960) *Nietzsches Philosophie*, Stuttgart: Kohlhammer.

Heidegger, M. (1979–87) *Nietzsche* (4 vols), trans. D. F. Krell, J. Stambaugh and F. Capuzzi, New York: Harper & Row.

Jaspers, K. (1965) *Nietzsche: An Introduction to the Understanding of his Philosophical Activity*, trans. C. F. Wallraff and F. J. Schmitz, South Bend, Ind.: Gateway.

Koelb, C. (ed.) (1990) *Nietzsche as Postmodernist*, Albany, NY: State University of New York Press.

Löwith, K. (1987) *Nietzsches Philosophie der ewigen Wiederkehr des Gleichen*, in K. Löwith, *Sämtliche Schriften* 6, Stuttgart: J. B. Metzlersche Verlag.

Lukács, G. (1980) *The Destruction of Reason*, London: Merlin.

Nehamas, A. (1985) *Nietzsche: Life as Literature*, Cambridge, Mass.: Harvard University Press.

Nietzsche, F. (1967a) *On the Genealogy of Morals and Ecce Homo*, trans. W. Kaufmann and R. J. Hollingdale, New York: Vintage.

—— (1967b) *The Will to Power*, trans. W. Kaufmann, New York: Vintage.

—— (1968) *Twilight of the Idols and The Anti-Christ*, trans. R. J. Hollingdale, Harmondsworth: Penguin.

—— (1973) *Beyond Good and Evil*, trans. R. J. Hollingdale, Harmondsworth: Penguin.

—— (1974) *The Gay Science*, trans. W. Kaufmann, New York: Vintage.

—— (1982) *Daybreak*, trans. R. J. Hollingdale, Cambridge: Cambridge University Press.

—— (1983) *Untimely Meditations*, trans. R. J. Hollingdale, Cambridge: Cambridge University Press.

—— (1986) *Human, All Too Human*, trans. R. J. Hollingdale, Cambridge: Cambridge University Press.

Simon, J. (1989) 'Die Krise des Wahrheitsbegriffs als Krise der Metaphysik', *Nietzsche-Studien* 18.

Spivak, G. C. (1974) 'Translator's preface', to J. Derrida, *Of Grammatology*, Baltimore, Md. and London: Johns Hopkins University Press.

Warren, M. (1988) *Nietzsche and Political Thought*, Cambridge, Mass.: MIT Press.

Index